More Praise for

MEMOIR OF A DEBULKED WOMAN

"Even the most skeptical and finicky reader—even the healthy reader, even the healthy male reader—will not put this book down. Some of its appeal comes from Ms. Gubar's skill with textual analysis, and some from various appealing verbal shenanigans. . . . Ms. Gubar deserves the highest admiration for her bravery and honesty as she bangs down yet one more door in her career—even if, sadly, it belongs to a place she had not wanted or intended to enter."

—*New York Times Science Times*

"Brave, honest . . . intimate, unsentimental, and darkly funny."

—*Boston Globe*

"Here [Gubar] chronicles, with a sense of genuine bafflement, how an early acceptance of her 'death sentence' gave way to . . . debulking. . . . Despite her suffering she infuses her book with profound gratitude for family, friends, and colleagues."   —*The New Yorker*

"Gubar pulls no punches. . . . This raw narrative is as close to therapy and is written as close to the bone as one is likely to find among cancer memoirs. Even so, there is a certain beauty that only someone of Gubar's prodigious abilities can impart to such a painful experience."

—*Booklist*, boxed and starred review

"Gubar masters the honest, from-the-gut sharing that is the basis of any good memoir. Equal parts emotional examination and graphic descriptions of medical procedures, Gubar's account will leave readers wondering whether the surgery she underwent is worth it. . . . Beautifully written. . . . A must-read." —*Library Journal*, starred review

"Brutally honest. . . . Not just a grueling memoir of facing a deadly disease but a powerful exposé of the failure of medical science to find better ways to detect and treat it." —*Kirkus Reviews*

"Gubar's passionate and brave polemic is critical reading for anyone concerned with the state of women's health care in America." —*Publishers Weekly*

"The prose is as stark and steely-eyed as the title. . . . A no-holds-barred account." —*Chronicle of Higher Education*

"*Memoir of a Debulked Woman* is an extraordinary testament to the human spirit—at least, to Susan Gubar's indomitable spirit—a rare mixture of honesty, eloquence, humor, and passionate curiosity about the truth, as it pertains to her condition as an ovarian cancer patient who is both poised to fight her cancer and, when it's time, to accept her mortality. The 'voice' is so utterly intimate, the reader will find herself, or himself, drawn into sharing the author's deepest thoughts, fears, and wishes. The memoir is a treasure-chest of wonderful, uncommon cultural allusions and lines of poetry; the reader feels honored to be in the presence of a first-rate, restless mind, being taken to a place of devastating clarity. There is pathos

here, but not self-pity; amid the tragic and sorrowful, sudden flashes of wit, as when Susan Gubar quotes her husband Don, quoting 'an old Billy Wilder movie: the situation is hopeless but not serious.' "
—Joyce Carol Oates

"Susan Gubar combines a scholar's breadth of reflection with the fearlessness of someone committed to telling the whole, intimate truth about having cancer. *Memoir of a Debulked Woman* offers ill people the healing gift of seeing in print the truths already experienced on their bodies."
—Arthur W. Frank, author of
At the Will of the Body and
The Wounded Storyteller: Body, Illness, and Ethics

"An unflinching account of one woman's arduous journey from the shock of diagnosis to the hard-won acceptance of cancer's terrible temporality. Susan Gubar shows, in sometimes harrowing detail, how difficult it is live with extreme pain and also demonstrates, with poignant intensity, how salutary it is to share her experience in writing."
—Nancy K. Miller, author of
What They Saved: Pieces of a Jewish Past

"Surfacing from the elective hell of invasive cancer treatment, Susan Gubar's fiercely candid pages master without palliating—through her vitalizing wit and eloquence, and no little black comedy—an ordeal in which, while 'living with cancer,' she becomes not only the despondent 'protagonist' of her own dying but its true heroine and finally its redemptive coauthor. An overwhelming achievement—of prose and of human spirit."
—Garrett Stewart,
James O. Freedman Professor of Letters, University of Iowa

"*Memoir of a Debulked Woman* provides a clear-eyed and moving autobiographical account of current medical approaches to ovarian cancer. Living with cancer, as Susan Gubar shows, may require us to live a life defined by love and culture, rather than by cancer and its treatments." —Sander L. Gilman, Distinguished Professor of the Liberal Arts and Sciences, Emory University

MEMOIR
OF A
DEBULKED
WOMAN

ALSO BY SUSAN GUBAR

The Madwoman in the Attic (with Sandra M. Gilbert)

Shakespeare's Sisters (with Sandra M. Gilbert)

The Norton Anthology of Literature by Women
(with Sandra M. Gilbert)

No Man's Land (with Sandra M. Gilbert)

For Adult Users Only (with Joan Hoff)

English Inside and Out (with Jonathan Kamholtz)

MotherSongs (with Sandra M. Gilbert and Diana O'Hehir)

Masterpiece Theater: An Academic Melodrama
(with Sandra M. Gilbert)

Racechanges: White Skin, Black Face in American Culture

Critical Condition: Feminism at the Turn of the Century

Poetry After Auschwitz

Rooms of Our Own

Feminist Literary Theory and Criticism
(with Sandra M. Gilbert)

Lo largo y lo corto del verso Holocausto

Judas: A Biography

True Confessions: Feminist Professors Tell Stories Out of School

MEMOIR
OF A
DEBULKED
WOMAN

· Enduring Ovarian Cancer ·

SUSAN GUBAR

W. W. NORTON & COMPANY

NEW YORK · LONDON

For information about permission to reproduce selections from this book,
write to Permissions, W. W. Norton & Company, Inc.,
500 Fifth Avenue, New York, NY 10110

For information about special discounts for bulk purchases, please contact
W. W. Norton Special Sales at specialsales@wwnorton.com or 800-233-4830

Manufacturing by RR Donnelley, Harrisonburg, VA
Book design by Ellen Cipriano
Production manager: Julia Druskin

Library of Congress Cataloging-in-Publication Data

Gubar, Susan 1944–
Memoir of a debulked woman : enduring ovarian cancer / Susan Gubar. — 1st ed.
p. cm.
Includes bibliographical references.
ISBN 978-0-393-07325-6 (hardcover)
1. Gubar, Susan 1944– —Health. 2. Ovaries—Cancer—Patients—United States—
Biography. 3. Cancer—Psychological aspects. I. Title.
RC280.O8G83 2012
616.99'465—dc23
2011053073

ISBN 978-0-393-34589-6 pbk.

W. W. Norton & Company, Inc.
500 Fifth Avenue, New York, N.Y. 10110
www.wwnorton.com

W. W. Norton & Company Ltd.
Castle House, 75/76 Wells Street, London W1T 3QT

1 2 3 4 5 6 7 8 9 0

FOR DON

CONTENTS

FOREWORD

I GO ON THE Web, click "Favorites," and scroll down to a site with hundreds of testimonials from grandmothers, mothers, daughters, sisters, husbands, sons, aunts, and nieces. Each recounts her own or a relative's medical history, often concluding with advice:

> "Please don't give up and stay strong because miracles happen."
> "I want to tell people that you can deal with anything that life throws at you."
> "I just want to say to everyone who is dealing with this or any type of cancer, KEEP THE FAITH AND KEEP GOD FIRST BECAUSE GOD HAS THE LAST WORD."
> "If you are fighting this fight, keep a smile on your face and think good thoughts."

On bookshelves too, there are many urgent instructions from brave people trying to triumph over or grapple with sickness. Quite a few of their maxims seek to sustain hope in patients and caretakers struggling with disabling and frightful circumstances. My story, lacking directives, will not help them, a fact that fills me with consternation. It is not comforting. I often wanted to give up coping with experiences that made me miserable with my existence. How can I justify a disquieting account that may only heighten anxieties in such an understandably distraught population?

In no way do I mean doubtfulness about my personal fate to infect the spirit of others in need of resilience and grit. Being true to what I have undergone hardly excuses hardheartedness or cynicism. For those who have reason to believe or need to believe that their cancer is curable, please remember that this book is not about you. Imagine instead that it comes from someone in your local support group or someone posting letters on your listserv message board, the sort of site that contains questions, requests, reactions from individual patients in the midst of treatment. Her experiences—my experiences—need not be yours, for yours will and should be exceptional, uniquely your own. You are sharing her (or my) concerns, but not her (or my) conditions. I did not write this book in order to disabuse the hopeful of their hopefulness or to promote pessimism. Who would want to be such a spoiler?

Rubbing a reader's nose in repugnant body disorders strikes me as a revolting and perverse act. The thought of people I know and people I don't know acquiring intimate information about the most private aspects of my being twists me into knots. I worry, will these people, the known and the unknown, be embarrassed of or for me since at many moments I am ashamed of myself? Yet a compulsion to relate my encounter with disease and its treatments drove me in part because I suspected (and continue to suspect) that my story could not be quite as anomalous as it appears to be. Beyond a potentially misguided effort to relate my physical, mental, and emotional states to those of others who have described their acquaintance with disease and its treatments, my central motive consists of a fierce belief that something must be done to rectify the miserable inadequacies of current medical responses to ovarian cancer.

The composition of this narrative kept me sane during a hard time. It let me come to terms with my attitudes toward death, with my ideas about the resonant role played by the arts as we live with awareness of death, and also with my family history and the loves of my life. Only while in the midst of the writing and treatment processes did I fully realize that my personal travails, like those of many, are grounded in widely sanctioned health-care protocols. At least at times, therefore, I take an activist's stance. Go little book, I want to say, do some good work in the world. "Like throwing stones in a lake, Mom," one of my daughters ruefully cautions. Still, I pray that its polemic will rapidly sound outdated and unneeded, that it will become an anachronism or historical curiosity quite soon, as soon as possible, sooner than possible.

MEMOIR
OF A
DEBULKED
WOMAN

· 1 ·

DIAGNOSIS

WHEN I HEARD the diagnosis of ovarian cancer on November 5, 2008, I assumed it was a death sentence. Lying on a gurney in a hospital hallway, I concentrated on accepting my impending mortality with equanimity. Scientific advances have not yet made a significant impact on detection or treatment and ovarian cancer remains largely incurable.

The January 2010 Mayo Clinic website contests my judgment by suggesting that medical science has progressed far enough for us to jettison depressing assumptions. "Until recently," MayoClinic.com states, "ovarian cancer was known as a 'silent killer' because it usually wasn't found until it had spread to other areas of your body. But new evidence shows that most women may have symptoms even in the early stages, and awareness of symptoms may hopefully lead to earlier detection." Upbeat as these sentences sound, note the hedges and qualifiers: "*most* women *may* have symptoms" and "awareness of symptoms *may hopefully lead* to *earlier* detection." A standard guide to ovarian cancer, produced by Johns Hopkins University

Hospital, opens with related but different assurances, namely that the informed patient–reader "will be quite comfortable with the language of the disease as well as the treatment philosophies." In various venues, courageous women speak poignantly about ovarian cancer as a chronic and treatable illness with which they continue to live. Statistics, however, tell another, more pessimistic tale. "Long-term survival rates have hardly improved since the 1970s" because "more than 70% of women present with disease spread beyond the ovaries." Even with sophisticated medical care, most of these patients suffer terminal recurrences a few years after diagnosis. "People with ovarian cancer die of ovarian cancer," a blunt doctor explains in a novel by Richard Powers.

What do women experience between diagnosis and death or, within a narrower framework, during initial and successive treatments? There were 21,550 new cases of ovarian cancer that occurred in the United States in 2009, and an additional 14,600 women died from it. It used to be estimated that one out of seventy American women will get the disease, the deadliest of all gynecological cancers, though recently the number sometimes cited is one in fifty-five. There are very few published personal accounts for them to consult since for decades, indeed for centuries, women have generally maintained silence about the silent killer. Possibly theirs were not stories about being "quite comfortable" with their physicians' language or treatments. Possibly the disintegration of the body stalled the composing of narratives or despondency attendant upon the disintegration of the body took its toll. Soon after the diagnosis, I realized that my quirky responses and encounters could not possibly convey the tribulations of all the variously situated women who struggle to endure between diagnosis and death, but certain factors in my background and situation would make it possible for me to find the few accounts that do exist and to record what has thus far gone unrecorded. I have frequently in the past set out to investigate matters that I wanted to write about. So I began to inquire into the disease and to write about it and its medical treatment. Even at the moment of diagnosis, my age, family history, and scholarly habits helped me to accept the disease and then to describe subsequent medical responses.

But I was not prepared for the horrific ordeals many ovarian cancer patients undergo. Acquiescence upon hearing the diagnosis would not sustain me or could not be sustained during the six months that followed. Resolute acceptance tangled with dismay, snarled with depression as I descended into deeper circles of an inferno in which I suffered less from the disease, more from grotesque surgeries and procedures performed by the most enlightened and proficient practitioners of contemporary medicine. "My treatment imperils my health," the main character in Margaret Edson's play *Wit* exclaims about protocols that damage the patient's capacity to confront mortal illness with equanimity. As imaginative (rather than medical) authors insist, current remedies do not cure the disease. Instead, they debilitate the person dealing with it until she barely recognizes her mind, spirit, or body as her own. Enduring ovarian cancer mires patients in treatments more patently hideous than the symptoms originally produced by the disease, while ovarian cancer itself endures as it has for centuries, unchecked in any significant way by the new findings of contemporary science. Surely at this point I should have been ready to relinquish the proactive advice of physicians, bow to the consequences of the incurable nature of the disease, and embrace my imminent fate.

Yet weirdly, unpredictably, even after those horrific six months, I continued to seek out medical interventions. If I started out skeptical about the current treatments of ovarian cancer and soon grew convinced of their barbarism, why then did I—a woman persuaded that I had been granted a richly rewarding existence, a person for some time committed to hospice and to the acknowledgment of my own mortality—continue to pursue subsequent protocols that prolonged or escalated my misery? Under what circumstances and why do the incurably ill delay the decision to relinquish expensive and debilitating treatments that cannot cure our diseases? These questions, and their provisional answers, proliferate on the slippery slope leading to the state called terminal.

At times it may be difficult to ascertain exactly where and when that slippery slope begins to exert its gravitational pull on the debulked woman. Debulking—the surgical removal of a part of a malignant growth that cannot be totally excised—remains the standard initial response to advanced ovarian cancer. Yet it is "used only in specific malignancies, as generally *partial removal of a tumor is not considered a worthwhile intervention*," according to the entry on Wikipedia (emphasis mine). Can it be possible that none of the medical responses to ovarian cancer should be judged worthwhile interventions? When my engagement with the disease began, such a frightful possibility did not enter my mind. Because I had previously enjoyed some sixty good years on earth as well as an appreciation of them, I had not yet comprehended the difficulty of weighing life-extending measures against their capacity to destroy the pleasures of existence.

At the close of the day on which Indiana turned a Democratic blue state for the first time in almost half a century, I watched that color cast a pall over the face of a young doctor interpreting a CT image in an emergency room. The hospitalist—what an odd name for a person with an important job—was clearly rattled. Neither acute pain nor a detected lump, only an odd feeling of satiety and digestive problems had brought me to the Bloomington Hospital for a scan on the afternoon of November 5. Though the scan could not be described as taxing, after dinner I felt uncomfortable and curious enough about the findings to make my way back to the hospital, where only the ER was open and staffed. There and then, a doctor hastily processed papers for admission to the hospital—presumably to get me more quickly to an oncologist. I remember a moment of extraordinary calm when left on a gurney with a whisper of the initial diagnosis of advanced ovarian cancer. The phrase "praying to accept" sounds patently inadequate to describe this experience, for it resonates with too many connotations of rigorous training in spiritual meditation, which I had never undertaken. Rather, left to my own devices in a generic hospital hall, relief was in some small measure part of what I felt descending, a spontaneous and weird sense of liberation, if not a sort of elation or euphoria. A pervasive sense of release or reprieve took hold, not unprompted but instead prompted by the worst possible news.

The preceding night, one of my dear British cousins had phoned me with high hopes for a Barack Obama landslide in the 2008 election, but I felt superstitious about predictions of victory being met with reprisals from the gods. Though for weeks I had been glued to CNN and the online *New York Times*, from the visit to the ER onward my window to the world began to be fogged or curtained so I could only intermittently peer through its gauzy veil as I emigrated from the world of the healthy to the domain of the ill, a habitat not nearly as monochromatic as it is often assumed to be. For at times fogs accentuate certain spectra, just as curtains filter

dusty shafts or glowing beams, calling forth uncanny new features
of lights and shadows. The external world of current events and
work-related matters may fade or flatten, but the internal realm
of the psyche tied to an ever modified and modifying body and to
intimate relationships with family and friends takes on nuanced
and absorbing patterns.

My composure contrasts sharply with the often expressed sentiment "why me?" that some cancer patients use as shorthand to
lament or protest the unfairness of their dreaded condition. But I
never believed that "people get what they deserve" or that "virtue
finds its rewards." Regardless of my efforts to live a responsible and
responsive life, it never entered my mind that I might be exempt
from the common lot. I have known many young and old people
with cancer, whose plight convinced me that it could strike anyone, anywhere, any time. Given the high incidence of cancer not in
my family or my family history but in my wider circle of acquaintances, "why *not* me?" might have been a more predictable question. Though the language designating persons with cancer remains
inadequate, many such victims, patients, and survivors know that
cancer just happens to happen, whether because of genetics, lifestyle,
diet, aging, or a radically compromised environment. I had always
agreed with many others who argue about illness that one should
never, or only under highly circumscribed conditions, blame the
victim; one should refrain from attributing the cause of disease to
the diseased.

Still, it is a far stretch from such righteous contentions about
proper public discourses, on the one hand, to a pervasive private
feeling of tranquility about the revelation of one's own cancer, on
the other. The author of a book entitled *Beating Ovarian Cancer*
emphatically opens one chapter with the assertion, "I don't care

what type of cancer you have; when you receive that diagnosis, it is devastating news." "A diagnosis of cancer is just about the worst thing that can happen to anyone," innumerable writers about breast cancer agree. How and why does my response fall outside this chorus of indignant distress and what does my curious sense of relief or release mean, given such a ruinous diagnosis?

For some time, maybe a decade or so, I had felt myself to be immobilized, even tormented, in a double bind. Watching the wretched aging process of my increasingly incapacitated ninety-three-year-old mother had filled me with revulsion at the physical humiliations and pettiness of old age. During the handful of years after I moved my mother to an assisted care facility in my hometown—first to an independent apartment, later to a room in the grotesquely named Health Pavilion—I was horrified by the narrowing parameters of her interests which (quite understandably) ricocheted back to the pains in her hands or her back, digestive and imbalance tribulations, tooth and bridge decay, hair and memory loss, the inability to open a jar, to use a key, to button a shirt, or to wipe herself. Though my mother displayed courage and fortitude, self-absorption threatened to become her default position. Yet were there any alternatives to the ferocious degradations of aging? As a fifteen-year-old adolescent, I had suffered acutely because of the decision of my fifty-six-year-old father to commit suicide, and resolved that I would never harm my children as I had been injured by a parent's decision to die.

There in that crevasse, between the steep tilt of debilitating old age (my ailing mother) and the blank rock face of self-destruction (my dead father), I had twisted for quite some time, bewildered by not knowing how to find a way out. In my sixties, as I approached retirement, I continually mulled over the fact that I didn't want to

grow increasingly decrepit and dependent, but I also did not want to
take my own life. Now, with the diagnosis of what I suspected to be
an unbeatable ovarian cancer, I apprehended that shades of the old-
age home need no longer close about me. And even if I eventually
resorted to some sort of pain management that hastened the dying
process, it would be interpreted not as a rejection of the husband and
daughters and friends I cherish but rather as a last-minute escape
from the unendurable suffering caused by a mortal disease.

Yet there were other elements to this free-floating sensation
of deliverance on the hospital gurney, one absent from the most
recent account I had happened to read about one of cancer's most
famous fatalities. Susan Sontag, according to her son's memoir of
her tenacious quest for cures, raged against the dying of the light
throughout her bouts with increasingly virulent forms of cancer.
For her, "extinction was unimaginable," given her "deep refusal of
death itself." An idol of mine—I especially profited from Sontag's
Illness as Metaphor—she apparently never expressed the sort of clarity and stillness that I felt myself inexplicably encountering here at
the start of a process in which I would inevitably have to follow her
footsteps through surgery, chemotherapy, weakness, nausea, and
all the rest. The unwilled surfacing of this moment of calm seemed
astonishingly unexpected, and, brief as it was, I wanted somehow
to bank on it, to find in it some resource to draw upon through all
the hardship to come.

If I was blessed, it was not through a conviction of personal
salvation, as in those accounts of people who credit God or Jesus
for pulling them through. Nor was my experience of equanimity an
instance of cheerful positive thinking about cancer as a grueling but
life-enhancing learning experience. First, I had no illusions about
being pulled through or back to life or health. I realized that there

is no cure for most cases of advanced ovarian cancer. Second, I had no conventional religious faith to speak of, though throughout my life I have clung to the paramount importance of everyday ethics that inspires many secular Jews and though in more recent years my academic engagement with the New Testament has taught me to cherish the sayings and deeds of Jesus along with those of his apostles. If not hope in physical recovery or spiritual rebirth, then, what were the origins of this curiously labile and lambent sense of composure?

We all live our lives intermittently wondering what will take us out, whether it will be sooner or later, what disease or accident, what natural or political catastrophe will carry us out of the existence we know without knowing where, when, how, and why it will end. All of us acknowledge that we will die, but we don't have a clue what we will die of. I still did not know the "when," but I now could intuit some of the "how," some of the "why," and some of the "where." Although unanticipated, the diagnosis clicked with the vague, if inconsequential, symptoms that had led to the CT scan. Knowledge clinched or confirmed always feels like a coin falling into the right slot, a ball landing in a basket, a peg knocked into its proper hole. I recognized, I believed, what would kill me. That there is pleasure even in such painful knowledge may seem perverse; however, the mind and spirit are subtle and mobile faculties.

Based not on my account of symptoms but on an image from a scan I would never see, the diagnosis of the disease as well as the impending mortality I attributed to it stunned me, but I believed that its progress would save my daughters and my husband from the trauma of my unexpected death, from the clinical depression of pathological bereavement. The shock of a sudden death, Joan Didion attests, is "obliterative, dislocating to both body and mind."

True, I had always hoped that I would be struck down instantaneously like a relative who was found dead in her seat after a performance of *Aida* by ushers cleaning up the Metropolitan Opera
House. But she, a widow with no children, was quite elderly. Should
I, in the first half of my sixties, have keeled over while teaching
or preparing supper or attending a concert, there is no doubt in
my mind that my daughters, and perhaps also my husband, would
have been plunged into that maelstrom of grief that has rendered
survivors guilt-ridden with the suspicion "*I did it, I am responsible,*"
or "prostrate, inconsolable, crazy with loss," unable to comprehend
fully the irreversibility of death.

Besides the welcome of sufficient warning time—I could draft
my own obituary, were I fatuous enough to want to—I gave thanks
for not leaving behind defenseless babies or children. I was old
enough at sixty-three to have acquired my share of wrinkles, gray
hair, and the comprehension that my case was not tragic, not the
tragedy, for instance, of a young woman robbed of her maturity.
Should my daughters be diagnosed with such a disease in their early
thirties: *that* would be devastating news, just about the worst thing
that could possibly happen. With my two girls healthy and grown
and most of my scholarly and pedagogic work done, I could hardly
rail against the injustice of my fate.

Of course, I understood even then that cancer metastasizes, but
at the moment following diagnosis ovarian cancer seemed like a
dying I could live with for a while without too much embarrassment about the body parts people would be envisioning when they
thought or spoke about me. Silly and wrongheaded as that notion
turned out to be, it played a part in my apprehension at the onset of
this disease, or at my belated awareness of its onset. I felt nothing
but admiration for the few women I knew (or knew of) who had

had to deal with the disease. How perverse or irrational to mull over role models at this moment on the gurney, but I assumed I had the most common form of ovarian cancer—what I now know as epithelial cancer, originating from the tissue covering or lining the ovary—and I did conjure up a cohort.

A dear friend of mine, Ilinca Zarifopol Johnston, died courageously seeking high and low for treatments of her ovarian cancer. Given her facility for languages (she spoke Romanian, French, Spanish, and English fluently) and her regal beauty (she looked a bit like Princess Diana), Ilinca felt like a comfort in my mind. There was Gillian Rose as well, a brilliant scholar of the Holocaust in whose philosophical works I had read widely; not to mention Gilda Radner, who at times had achieved the hilarious inanity of Lucille Ball. Wacko as it seems, at least I could imagine others in my situation, and I knew a little about my ovaries. I had spent my adult life studying women, specifically women's understanding of their bodies and how those understood bodies influenced the cultures they inhabited and created. Would I have wanted to die of diseases unfamiliar to me, say, Huntington's or Lou Gehrig's disease? Throughout my year or more with ovarian cancer, I would borrow from the library as many patient accounts and imaginative works as I could find, to twine my experiences with those of other women, fictional and real, from the past and the present.

Strange as it might seem, too, perhaps the descending peacefulness on the gurney related as well to my recent and disorienting inability to come up with a new book project. Had I perhaps completed at last the intellectual trajectory upon which I had energetically embarked so many decades ago? Was the beginning of my end arriving at a timely moment? My collaborative work on women's literature with Sandra Gilbert had dwindled into producing edited anthologies that were voluminous and useful but certainly not pioneering in the now established field of gender studies. The collaboration had been followed by a series of solo engagements with African American and Jewish studies and then, oddly, by a brand-new topic for me, the subject of Judas Iscariot, Jesus's twelfth apostle. With *Judas: A Biography* in page proofs by the fall of 2008, I had tinkered with fresh book ideas but without conviction. Here was a new topic arriving with a vengeance as well as an urgency, one that would teach me (I assumed) a great deal about women, about myself, about my family and friends, and about betrayal, but in a radically new and fearsome context.

Why betrayal? Like Judas, the unsuspected enemy within Jesus's band of followers, cancer—a malignant but undetected internal alien—had held a secret and destructive sway over me, despite my ignorance of it. Don't get me wrong, as God's people keep on saying in the Bible. I am not comparing myself to the son of man who, my most baffled students believe, bears the first name "Jesus," the surname "Christ." But because of the book I had just completed, my mind had been dwelling on an apostle generally allotted the role of traitor, one whose long evolution over twenty centuries turned him into the personification of humanity's capacity for error and misery. At the start of composing *Judas*, I had kept a single question in mind: how had one of (Jewish) Jesus's (Jewish) apostles become the embodiment of anti-Semitic traits? In the process of answering that question, it became clear that in all the gospels Judas finds himself ensnared within plots hostile to his well-being. Had he lived in more contemporary times, Judas would be a prime candidate for authoring what are derided as misery memoirs. He is the betrayer, but he also is betrayed and often in later depictions self-betrayed.

I felt that my body had been betrayed or had betrayed me, but I could not comprehend why or when or exactly how a malevolent presence had trespassed into the core of my being. "Ovarian cancer sneaks up on women," medical authorities agree. Its progress is often described as "insidious," a clinical term that means gradual, undetectable, harmful, but also an ethical term that means treacherous, lying in wait to ensnare, wily. "Like the kiss of Judas," Jackie Stacey explains about the malignant cancer cell, "its generosity masks a desire to destroy its keeper." Could I handle advanced and incurable ovarian cancer without being overpowered by anger and terror, without wreaking havoc on my husband's and children's lives? The oncologist in the Bloomington Hospital ascribed my spacey silence to shock at the diagnosis, and perhaps he was right. But I had been given an opportunity not available to the victims of fatal strokes or heart attacks or car crashes.

Absurd and ungrounded, the brief moment of tranquility in the hospital hall could become a tiny spool unwinding throughout the months to follow, or so I prayed. Hidden or lost and then found again, its thread, I hoped, would provide me a way to think about ovarian cancer, its treatments, its effects on my marriage and family, my friends and professional commitments, and ultimately my imminent dying. Because the diagnosis furnished an indeterminate time period denied those killed instantaneously by domestic violence or natural disasters or political repression, I could use the granted months or years to see if writing might sustain a degree of acceptance comparable to what meditation instills in others. During the duration of my treatment and the last year or years of my life, I would attempt to follow this string's sometimes tangled unraveling so I could address all those fears—of physical pain, of social isolation, of being a burden on caretakers, of relinquishing responsibility for the beloved people in my life, of the unknown, of the implacability of death—that arise when we are not cut down by an unforeseen cataclysm but are given the opportunity to reflect on our own mortality.

Now I know that the account you are reading is my attempt to discover if I could regain this sense of acceptance after the ferocious measures physicians take to deal with the ravages of advanced ovarian cancer. Alas, at times during the months to come, the thread of acquiescence would fray and break, leaving me anxious about whether I could somehow salvage it or splice it with another.

We have come a long way in the treatment of ovarian disease. Or have we? In 1998, one contributor to *Ovarian Cancer Journeys* recounted, she heard a doctor at a nationwide conference declare, "Few ovarian cancer activists existed, because women didn't live long enough to become activists." Over the next decade, there has been little improvement in survival rates. Put another way, unlike early detected breast or testicular, colon or prostate cancers, most ovarian cancer cases cannot be cured because they are not discovered before the disease has evolved into its third or fourth stages. Ovarian cancer "kills more women than all other gynecologic cancers combined." *A Gynecologist's Second Opinion*, published in 2003, opens its chapter on the disease with a sinister warning: "If *cancer* is one of the most dreaded words in the English language, then for most women, *ovarian* is the worst adjective to place before *cancer*. In all the bad news we sometimes deal with in gynecology, this is the most frightening." The research upon which I immediately embarked confirmed my hunch that my unexpected diagnosis was dire.

"Ovarian cancer is the most lethal of all the gynecological malignancies," doctors Mary L. Disis and Saul Rivkin state, "but little is known about the etiology, pathologic classification, or genetic progression of the disease." Writing in 2003, they explain that "Most patients diagnosed with more advanced stage disease go on to develop disease recurrence." Since the vast majority of women have their ovarian cancer diagnosed at stage III or IV, only a small percentage gain what is called a durable remission. The rest face recurrences. Here are statistics from a few years ago: "Of the 22,210 American women predicted to be affected in 2005, likely 75% will be diagnosed in advanced stages and mortality will exceed 16,000." When discerned in stages III and IV, "the overall median survival is 25 to 30 months," Chris Bledy states in a 2008 publication. A 2009 publication asserts that "the majority of epithelial ovarian cancer patients present with advanced (stage III/IV) high-grade disease; most of these patients therefore relapse after treatment and die." It is because warning signs and detection devices fail to reveal the early onset of most ovarian cancers that the diagnosis sounds like a death sentence.

The leading cause of American women's deaths from gynecologic cancers, ovarian cancer exhibits warning signs that are easily missed or dismissed. What woman, after all, does not experience and generally put up with one or several of its symptoms: bloating, fatigue, a feeling of satiety, indigestion, recurrent back or abdominal or pelvic pain, urinary frequency, flatulence, irregular periods, spotting, cramping, constipation, shortness of breath, pain during intercourse, or incontinence?

To be sure, on a literal level the Mayo Clinic website can

justifiably state that ovarian cancer is not always silent. Discussing frequent delays in diagnosis, an influential 2000 study concludes that "women with ovarian cancer do have symptoms in contrast to what is stated in most textbooks and taught in most medical schools." If women and their physicians were educated about early warning signs, they could assign them proper significance and receive more effective treatment: ovarian cancer can be cured when it presents in its early stages. One aim of the conclusion of the next chapter is to clarify to the common reader when and how to assign warning signs proper significance at earlier onset. However (and this is a big however), it is not easy to do so. There are good reasons why ovarian cancer has historically been labeled a silent killer, and for many women it remains a silent killer.

Subtle signs of the disease are often not registered or properly interpreted. The speech of ovarian cancer—*muted* because commonplace or *misunderstood* because it mimics that of other, more benign ailments—usually goes unheard and unheeded not only by physicians but by the sick person herself. One survivor explains about muting, "All the symptoms women with ovarian cancer experience are very likely, especially on a difficult day, to sound almost whiny or emotion-driven." Seemingly inconsequential, muted signs of the disease are easily blocked out, forgotten, or not experienced at all. The character in Powers's novel *Gain* (who is told by her physician that "People with ovarian cancer die of ovarian cancer") wonders, "No warning signs at all. *How could that be?*" The philosopher Gillian Rose, who had to cope with a chemo-resistant ovarian cancer, answers this question by explaining that her fitness led her initially to overlook nausea and untimely premenstrual tension: "I am so attuned to regular exercise of body and mind that I could easily take minor symptoms of ill-health in my stride."

While the antic comedienne who created the hilarious characters Roseanne Roseannadanna, Emily Litella, and Baba Wawa suffered fog-like fatigue, fever, stomach pains, pelvic cramping, aches in her legs, weight loss, and finally a swelling abdomen—"I looked like a malnourished African baby"—she consulted a host of specialists and received a succession of misdiagnoses from Epstein-Barr to "mittelschmertz" (cramping during the time of ovulation). Symptoms are often misunderstood because, as one gynecologic oncologist puts it, *"ovarian cancer is the great imposter—it masquerades as some of the most common symptoms in middle life."* At forty years of age, Gilda Radner was tested or treated with a barium enema, a sonogram, a pelvic exam, acupuncture, and a succession of protein supplements until a CT scan established the need for a quick operation and a long series of chemotherapies and radiations. "How could Gilda Radner, whose name was synonymous with comedy, now become synonymous with cancer," she wondered, as she judged cancer "the most unfunny thing in the world": it brings "life and death up close."

Doctors and nurse practitioners often attribute the muted or misunderstood signs of ovarian cancer to menopause, endometriosis, yeast infections, indigestion, aging with its aches and pains, gallbladder attacks, benign cysts, diverticulitis, irritable bowel syndrome, urinary tract infection, stress, depression, pulled muscles, ulcers, etc. Misdiagnosis can also result from the unreliability of the CA-125 blood test (standing for cancer antigen 125) often used to measure levels of ovarian cancer. Many women exhibit high levels of this protein without having cancer (a level under 35 is considered normal), and quite a few women with early stage ovarian cancer do not have elevated levels. While mammograms, MRIs, ultrasounds, and needle biopsies can discover cancerous growths in the breast before they can be felt by fingers, no reliable screening tool for ovarian cancer exists. Tests for cancer of the ovaries— bimanual rectovaginal examinations, transvaginal sonograms, and blood tests—tend to produce false positive or misleading or indeterminate results. Nor does the disease silently advance only in older, post-menopausal women, as Gilda Radner's case proves. A groundbreaking biophysicist who contributed to the discovery of DNA, Rosalind Franklin was thirty-seven when her death from ovarian cancer made her ineligible for the Nobel Prize awarded to Francis Crick and James Watson. Forty-three-year-old Barbara Creaturo, an editor at *Cosmopolitan* who wondered, "Is there no end to the indignities imposed by this disease?" endured the "torture" of four years of aggressive treatment before her death.

No reliable screening device, no cure for the vast majority of patients: what about causes? Low parity has been considered a factor in the occurrence of ovarian cancer or, as it is sometimes called, "poor reproductive performance." Frequent ovulation has been blamed, with some physicians touting the benefits of oral contraception. Asbestos exposure, talcum powder, hormone replacement therapy, and fallout from nuclear testing have been linked by doctors or memoirists to the etiology of ovarian cancer, as have a diet high in fat, fertility drugs (or the infertility that caused them to be prescribed), and a number of the pollutants discussed with respect to other forms of cancer. Occurrence of malignancies appears to be considerably greater in Western countries than in Asia, Africa, and South America. There is no consensus on the causes of ovarian cancer, except in the relatively small proportion of cases triggered by heredity.

Among recent scientific breakthroughs in ovarian cancer research, the one related to heredity can contribute to the anguish of young women. The genetic markers BRCA1 and 2 account for about 10 percent of ovarian cancers. BR stands for breast, CA for cancer. Both BRCA1 (on chromosome 17) and BRCA2 (on chromosome 13)—the first so-called breast/ovarian cancer genes—were discovered in the mid-1990s. Mutations in these genes "render the gene unable to make a key protein" and therefore "can spur cellular reproduction to go awry, launching the cascading process that leads to cancer development." Cancer geneticists agree that women who carry a genetic mutation have a 56–87 percent risk of getting breast cancer, a 16–46 percent risk of contracting ovarian cancer. Women with many instances of cancer in their families may carry a mutation. In the chilling language of the social network FORCE (Facing Our Risk of Cancer Empowered), such a woman has become "a cancer pre-vivor": "a survivor of a predisposition to cancer." "Jewish people of Ashkenazi (Eastern Europe) descent have a one in forty chance of having a BRCA mutation," a fact that should be better broadcast in the Jewish community.

Is presymptomatic testing a good idea? Should healthy girls spend their young adulthood worrying themselves sick over whether or not to be tested for a mutation? Mounting anxieties about testing may plunge them into the ranks of "the worried well," as Thomas Couser puts it. What about those women who decide to test and get a "positive" result? They must deal with the "psychological distress" of "dealing with the threat of cancer paired with the uncertainty of if and when it'll strike." With each and every doctor's visit, anxious pre-vivors "would always be ill until proven healthy, and then . . . have to prove it all over again in another month or two": so attests Marsha Gessen, a self-identified "genetic mutant." Additionally, genetic counselors and ethicists fear a "facile reclassification" of body parts "from 'at risk' to 'diseased.' " In other words, women testing positive may leap to the conclusion that risk statistics constitute a preordained fate. Of course, risk percentages only estimate statistical group probabilities, but they can trap an individual into the horrific conviction that she is doomed.

Mourning a great-aunt dead from ovarian cancer at thirty-nine and a mother at forty-two, the breast cancer patient Sarah Gabriel, who feels stalked by death "in the form of an inherited predisposition to cellular malfunction," excoriates the "wretched gene that would very likely kill her unless she amputated large chunks of herself; that threatened to leave her children in the same parlous condition she was left in herself." When Diane Tropea Greene learned that she had inherited a mutation that had killed her mother and her mother's siblings, she knew a "curse" had befallen her family and imagined BRCA2 as "a time bomb that ticked within them." In another family with HBOC (hereditary breast and ovarian cancer), a young woman also refers to her and her sisters' ovaries as *time bombs*." Andrea King Collier, who has pointed out that "African-American men and women were not included in clinical trials at the same rates as other patients," hears her "own little time bomb, ticking so loudly some days that I could hardly hear myself think." Though parents know that children are hostages to fortune, how can mothers bear to realize that they have unintentionally tendered their daughters a curse, a ticking time bomb, or a seed of death? Is it true about girls from "cancer dynasties" that some of them "hate their mothers"?

Offspring of a mother with a BRCA genetic mutation have a 50 percent chance of inheriting it. And the later age at which a mother develops cancer does not predict the age at which a daughter might find herself coping with the onset of the disease. "While breast cancers usually develop later in life," Barbara Katz Rothman explains, "the breast cancers associated with BRCA1 and 2 often occur in women in their thirties and forties." Joanna Rudnick's pioneering film about her own and other women's efforts to deal with BRCA testing illuminates the anxiety and grief each decision spawns. As documented in Rudnick's *In the Family*, younger women who discover a mutation face a frightful double bind with respect to the threat of ovarian cancer in particular. They can opt to screen their breasts (though all such screening carries a level of uncertainty and discomfort); however, they must decide whether to remove their ovaries or confront the likelihood of an undetectable and often incurable gynecological cancer.

Jessica Queller's memoir about the "impossible choices" she faced and the website Bright Pink suggest that the specter of premature menopause during one's thirties, the time when removal of the ovaries is recommended, can terrorize single women with the prospect of infertility or rush them into getting pregnant. An oophorectomy (removal of the ovaries) for BRCA carriers "lowers the odds of getting breast cancer by almost 50 percent and ovarian cancer by about 80 percent." But Marsha Gessen, who decided "the 40 percent risk of ovarian cancer was knowledge I could live with, and the 87 percent risk of breast cancer was not," lists "the unpleasant effects" of "early surgical menopause": "risk of heart disease, high blood pressure, osteoporosis, cognitive problems, and depression—as well as inelastic skin and weight gain." And ovarian surgery cannot completely eliminate risk. "Ovarian-type cancers can occur in the peritoneal cavity lining the abdominal wall even after oophorectomy," Mary Briody Mahowald states, and therefore "prophylactic oophorectomy is not an absolute safeguard against ovarian cancer."

A second medical advance in ovarian cancer research,

announced in May 2010, promises progress in early detection. Dr.
Karen Lu at M. D. Anderson Cancer Center used the CA-125 blood
test over a period of eight years to screen post-menopausal women
in order to establish (through the pattern of their individual scores
over time) which women were at low, middle, or high risk: low-
risk women received the test again in a year, middle-risk women
in three months, high-risk women were given vaginal ultrasounds.
No invasive tumors were missed, and most of those found were in
early enough stages for successful surgical interventions. Because
of Dr. Lu's small sample, unfortunately, American women will
not receive annual standard testing. A larger British study should
appear in 2015. Given the poor cure rates of advanced cases, one
can only hope that such sustained testing will generate tracking
instruments and that various ongoing experiments, for instance in a
"gene therapy-based vaccine against ovarian cancer," will eventually
pan out or that "the use of contrast agents along with ultrasound"
will save women's lives by picking up earlier and smaller lesions.
Meanwhile, as some scientists continue to experiment with emerging treatments—immunotherapy, neoadjuvant therapy, and gene
therapy—others speculate that there may be many different types
of ovarian cancer that should be treated differently and that gene
sequencing will provide an individualized approach to each case.

With warning signs easily ignored or misread and descriptions
of the disease's progress marginalized in cancer literature, ovarian
cancer—whether or not it is genetic in origin—establishes a series
of issues quite distinct from those of breast cancer. No visible, external body part gets sliced off the ovarian cancer patient in surgery.
She need not mourn an amputation and ostentatious scarring on
her body, nor the loss of an erogenous zone that also may or might
have suckled her babies. Nor need she display or conceal (by means

of prosthetic devices or reconstruction surgery) the ravages of her cancer. Except for a vertical line of stitches down the belly and easily covered by panties, the wounds remain inward, invisible, though they can rob younger women of their fertility. Many breast cancer survivors today, writing about the "miracle of medicine," believe that *"If you've got to have breast cancer, it's a good time in history to have it."* The same claim cannot be made about ovarian cancer.

Marsha Gessen calls ovarian cancer "breast cancer's poor neglected cousin" in part because breast cancer is "imagined as a disease that can be overcome," whereas ovarian cancer remains "intractable, unimaginable, unspeakable." "You hear about breast cancer all the time," one ovarian cancer patient points out, "but you never hear about ovarian cancer." An editor of a collection of testimonies, Diane Sims Roth agrees about "the paucity of information on ovarian cancer." According to one British patient, "For the average person who is not a hypochondriac, or a reader of medical journals, ovarian cancer seems one of the best kept secrets in the medical world." Most people refrain from describing (or find it impossible to describe) physiological conditions recalcitrant to heroic stories about individuals triumphing over the adversities of disease. It is hard to find happily-ever-after stories about ovarian cancer; it is hard to read stories without happily-ever-after endings.

There are very few personal accounts of dealing with ovarian cancer not only because it is difficult to narrate progress within a cheerful recovery framework but also because such stories would inevitably address still stigmatized (and thus hidden) bodily afflictions. Who, in search of inspiring or comforting assurances, wants to buy, much less read, a yucky downer? Breast cancer, which has received much more attention and research money and afflicts many more women, has its own patron saint, St. Agatha, who offers her sliced-off breasts on a platter and who weirdly morphed into the bakers' patron since her breasts often looked like rising cakes or breads. To my knowledge, there is no patron saint of ovarian cancer, and most people could not name the color of its ribbon (teal). Many ovarian cancer support groups, national coalitions, and electronic alliances instruct women to become more aware of their symptoms and more assertive about advocacy for research that will discover new monitoring processes for earlier detection. But there is no analogue or equivalent to *Dr. Susan Love's Breast Book*. The state of medical responses to ovarian cancer corresponds to the state of medical responses to breast cancer half a century ago.

Of course no one person can represent all the women struggling with ovarian cancer. Nor can I, a privileged professor at a university that provides me job security as well as health benefits. I would seem to be well placed to defend my life by means of sophisticated medical interventions as well as an informed fighting spirit. Those who credit their survival of ovarian cancer to "positive thinking, trust, and hope" may judge me defeatist or worse—complicit in my illness. Yet after my diagnosis and despite my hunch about the disease's fatality, I did undergo all the operations, therapies, and interventions specialists advised. Given my love of life and of the people in my life, it seemed wrong simply to submit to the cancer's inevitable progress, to succumb passively and helplessly to the determinism of a preordained death. I had to embark on doing what could be done against the disease—even if, even *though* it would eventually terminate my existence. To treasure the gift of life and the people in my life, I wanted to take responsibility for dealing with a condition admittedly beyond my control. Like many people with cancer, I sought to cultivate acceptance while consulting and following the advice of medical specialists.

Unfortunately and surely to their chagrin, the exceptionally able physicians who treated me confirmed my conviction that the miseries with which I contended were hardly idiosyncratic and that, regardless of the good intentions and skilled exertions of researchers and practitioners, the current treatment of ovarian cancer is deficient and debasing. At many times, my initial equanimity at the diagnosis failed to safeguard me from anger at the dehumanizing medical practices with which the employed and the insured are treated or, illogically, from sorrow over the dreadful fates of those not covered to receive such interventions. Most people diagnosed with ovarian cancer, whether or not they are using advanced medical methods to contend with their disease, die of ovarian cancer, and the process can be isolating as well as devastating.

A number of ovarian cancer patients, despite the unique problems we confront, struggle with the same issues facing other cancer patients and would confirm the sentiments voiced by the poet Audre Lorde, who wrote after her mastectomy in the 1970s, *"I carry death around in my body like a condemnation. But I do live. . . . There must be some way to integrate death into living, neither ignoring it nor giving in to it."* I hope to raise awareness about a form of the disease that has not received sufficient public attention, but unlike many memoirists and essayists I am less concerned with fighting the good personal fight against cancer than I am with some of the complex emotions that can buffet or sustain us in the very midst of dealing with a condition that will probably lead to death. "It isn't a very nice exit," one patient has testified about ovarian cancer, "but it is an exit." Soon after the diagnosis, I worried about the burden a not-very-nice exit would place on my beloved husband and daughters and thought that by integrating it into my consciousness I might lighten their load.

When at sixty-one years of age I agreed—after many years of living together—to marry my partner, then approaching eighty, we both had to acknowledge death's ability to part us before, after, or even during the two-minute civil ceremony at the county building that houses a jail (without, I hope, any sinister portent). Fast friends, we were plighted to be with each other through thick and thin, sickness and health, until death did us part when the inevitable struck and ruptured one from the other. Now parting looms imminent as death takes dominion over that place in the body framed and famed for giving birth to life. Despite my antipathies toward current treatments, all are designed to make death delay its dominion over the center of the body. My husband, a man of stubborn integrity, put his faith in each and every effort to force death to relinquish its grip on my being. Don, I suspect, dedicated himself to an attempt to contest death—not in a war against cancer but through the unwearied attentiveness with which he tended his ailing first wife and with which he now daily engages with me. I will never forget how furious he was when Mary-Alice died, how this preeminently gentle man cursed the fact that he had no longer kept death at bay.

Yet intimations of mortality whispered something else in my ear—namely, that I will love my family and friends until death departs, and since death will never depart, I will love them always and forever. Until death departs: the garbled phrase arrests me. I pause to reconsider, could death depart? Might love survive into that unforeseeable time when the dead live, the living die, and music shall untune the sky? These phrases about resurrection, from John

Dryden's ode to the patron saint of music, resound with beauty, but alas not with faith I can share. Should Don or I die—how stupidly put!—*when* Don or I die, the physical departure would be, will be devastating. Yet surely that devastating physical separation cannot leave us or others bereft of our persistent relatedness to each other or of a profound and ongoing awareness of our persistent relatedness to each other. The location of that awareness remains nebulous in my mind, but not therefore less manifest. After the diagnosis and quite spontaneously, I found myself earnestly promising one and then the other of my distressed daughters, "I will love you beyond my death. I will love you from another space that you will palpably feel, and feel to be me loving you." Albeit confused, that declaration seemed to speak of the intense emotions sustained by the urgent desire to continue loving the beloved until and after death. I want to live as long as the people I love live. We will live so long as the people we love remember we love them.

Which thinkers paved the way for such intuitions? Gnomic Epicurus, often quoted, does not appear to be addressing the same issues. "Where I am, death is not," he famously postulated, "where death is, I am not." The puzzling axiom sounds a tad avuncular and solipsistic to my ears. Did Epicurus believe that when he died, death did too? What about those who survived him? If after physical death there remains not my usual "I," but a mote of my sentient being in my daughters' minds, in my friends' and students' psyches, can I adopt the belief of the seventeenth-century physician Thomas Browne, that "there is something in us, that can be without us, and will be after us"? Nancy Mairs, a contemporary thinker about disability and dying, wrests with "the psychological 'undeadness' of the dead—a consolatory consciousness of the beloved as present though elsewhere." Such a conviction reflects faith in death as

the end of personal consciousness but the beginning of a translation "into an existence no less authentic for my inability to read
it." That this paragraph bristles with so many quotations—from
Epicurus, Browne, Mairs—indicates that for quite some time I was
unable to frame the sort of sentences about death that my future
experiences might shape. Toward a comprehension of these thinkers, I felt myself journeying. On the cover of one of Nancy Mairs's
books, a mysterious painting by Frida Kahlo keeps on waylaying
my attention.

It seems to ask, how can those of us without firm religious convictions integrate the awareness and actuality of dying and death
into our living? Most contemporary authors of books about disease would reject the question as unhealthy. Hester Hill Schnipper,
writing about increasing numbers of women surviving many years
after treatment of breast cancer, believes that "the goal must be to
live as though the cancer will never return. Living any other way,
mired in anxiety and sadness, means that the cancer wins, whether
it recurs or not." Understandably less optimistic and yet just as tenacious, some patients view their recurrent ovarian cancer as a chronic
condition requiring continuing counter-treatments. The two doctors who published *100 Questions & Answers about Ovarian Cancer*
conclude the 2006 edition of their book by counseling patients to
combat the disease: "Anyone diagnosed with ovarian cancer must
want to fight it and must trust that treatments are available and
successful and can give you back your life."

Do such admonitions spawn the guilty suspicion that the anxious or distrustful patient is responsible for her own decline or
demise? The character dying from an environmentally produced
ovarian cancer in Richard Powers's novel *Gain* frets, "if she dies,
it'll be her own fault. It'll be because she doubted . . . let negative

thoughts poison her." But current mortality statistics buttress and justify negative thoughts about ovarian cancer. With three-quarters of those diagnosed doomed to death, don't the odds disprove the assertion that available ovarian cancer treatments are "successful" and can "give you back your life"? Just as important, do the fighting words of lucky survivors and plucky specialists reflect the vision of those who have put on "the rose-tinted spectacles" worn by all narrators of stories about recovery, rebirth, and redemption?

Cancer patients dedicated to an epic struggle against their disease reject any "surrender" to it as an act "of conspiring" with it. When I could bring myself to watch the testimonials on the DVD *Surviving Ovarian Cancer*, distributed by the Ovarian Cancer Research Fund, the courageous resolve of women dedicated to their own survival moved me to tears. I honor and admire them for their bravery—without sharing their optimism. Other people, because of the advanced stage of their disease or their age or their refusal to put on "the rose-tinted spectacles" of redemptive narratives, may agree with me that no amount of fighting "can give you back your life," that it would be a lie "to live as though the cancer will never return," and that therefore it is necessary to find a way out of the proposition that if you are not hopefully battling your own cancer, you are somehow rooting for it.

I cannot possibly bring myself to wish for others that they discover the " 'clarity' an illness might bring," as the poet Jason Shinder apparently once did; however, his perspective—"Cancer is a tremendous opportunity to have your face pressed right up against the glass of your morality"—rings true. I am composing this book while in the midst of living this process, and therefore not as a retrospective educator, autobiographer, or critic (though all these voices will undoubtedly emerge), but rather as someone always interested in the tug of life and death in the midst of our consciousness of being—our joy in life but also our inextricable entanglement in and even desire for the obliteration of our individual existence with its infinity of compromises and conceits, its manifold disenchantments with the world and the self. Today a number of scientists, looking for the fountain of perpetual youth, seek to make death depart from the human condition; however, it seems to me, as I now confront mortality at closer proximity, that intimacy with the mortal body educates us. Cancer and its treatments teach us, or have taught me after two years of coping with bizarre consequences, that life without the finitude of death—the inconceivable finality of one's own death—would be intolerable.

Marie de Hennezel, a French psychologist who works with the terminally ill, believes that "the person who can say to someone else *'I am going to die'* does not become the victim of death but, rather, the protagonist in his or her own dying." Those words, silently rehearsed on a hospital gurney, infused my moment of release upon first hearing the diagnosis of advanced ovarian cancer, but not everyone wants to speak them. Many people cling to the hope of a cure and many others believe that they *should* cling to the hope of a cure, even when it appears to be a deceptive disservice. According to the surgeon–author Sherwin B. Nuland, "Almost everyone wants to take a chance with the slim statistics that oncologists give to patients with advanced disease. Usually, they suffer for it, they lay waste their last months for it, and they die anyway, having magnified the burdens they and those who love them must carry to the final moments." I want to apply to myself the discouraging statistics that oncologists deliver patients with advanced ovarian cancer, knowing that I will suffer from the disease but aspiring not to subject myself to pointless and expensive and painful procedures, wanting not to lay waste my end time or magnify the burdens of those traveling with me to the final moments. The question is, will I be able to hold on to this conviction, when so many factors conspire against it?

Especially because *"I am going to die"* is a sentence not everyone wants to hear, it makes its way into passages in the following pages about graphic and sometimes gross physical incidents that not everyone will want to read, but that cannot be excised from reflections on the current treatment of ovarian cancer. Unseemly descriptions of infrequently discussed tribulations of the body derive in part from my wish to attain the veracity at which many memoirists aim, though such truth-telling also unnerves me. I do name the real names of physicians, nurses, relatives, and friends while attempting to convey my understanding of them accurately. But throughout subsequent chapters I also impugn my reliability because my impressions are just that, subjective. Under stressful circumstances, I surely misunderstood some of the directives and descriptions of physicians who spoke in lexicons not always comprehensible to me. The panic that accompanied much of what I experienced impaired and may continue to impair my comprehension. I apologize to those I have injudiciously or falsely represented, but I wanted to capture in writing fleeting feelings that could not be voiced because they clash with my fairly rigorous notions of decorum, of what can and what cannot be articulated in social situations.

Motivated by a desire to tackle a writing problem that Virginia Woolf believed the literary women of her generation had failed to solve—telling the truth about the experiences of the female body—I sought to record precisely what I could not or would not speak to most of my family and friends. At times, I exhibited an almost pathological unwillingness to go into details, especially so as to shield my girls from ghastly complications (which they will, unfortunately, read about here). My older daughter, Molly, fully aware that my reticence or self-censorship frustrated her and her sister's efforts to help in my care, sees my attempt to write the truth about the body as a rejection of what she calls "cultural dishonesty" about medical side effects and end-of-life issues. Too often, it seems to me, squeamish euphemisms glamorize the fight against cancer and thus bracket or inhibit efforts to deal with suffering and degradation, deterioration and death. Why I can report on a computer keyboard what I cannot bear to say aloud remains a mystery to me, but so it goes. Maybe my inability to speak propelled the obsessive reading and writing.

Of course I will not be able to write during the time when death comes to depart *with* me because the first whiff of death's proximity must mean that I cannot sit at my computer, my fingers won't work on the keyboard, my brain won't focus on the paragraphs needing to be framed. So these pages address the questions that, as I dealt with ovarian cancer and its treatments, remained foremost in my mind. What are the standard treatments for ovarian cancer? Would I be able to exert some control over them or at least over my response to them, and for how long? How might my mind and spirit cope with the responses of my family and friends, the closing of my professional career, and with assaults on my body? In anticipation of that time when death departs with me, can my preparations to attain acquiescence and patient loving-kindness prevail or will impatience, anxiety, depression, and peevishness inundate my beleaguered psyche? Will I be able to forgo pointless, painful procedures when I realize that my state may be beyond repair? What sort of hopefulness sustains existence when hope for a cure has been extinguished?

Since death departs eventually with all of us, we human beings have to grapple with it not simply as a border or frame but as a durable cord interwoven in the fabric of our psyches and our relationships with one another. May the chapters that follow be a lasting testimony to a resilient network of family and friends who grace me with the ability not to rage against the dying of the light, who help me glimpse, if only momentarily, how to go gently into that unfathomable night. Let this record redound not against my personal fate but against an undetectable and then unfixable condition that continues to threaten the health and welfare of future generations. Women need to heed the muted or misunderstood symptoms of ovarian cancer and to agitate for early detection tools. We must save our successors from a diagnosis synonymous with death and from current medical responses that are debilitating as well as ineffectual: gutting, draining, bagging, and the poisoning many patients with other forms of cancer also receive as chemotherapy. A framework for the pages that follow, gutting, draining, bagging, and poisoning—standard protocols undertaken not to eradicate but to retard metastases or to help the ailing body function—damage the lives of many ovarian cancer patients.

But first, before the gutting, draining, bagging, and poisoning, a station break from our sponsor, an introduction to the ovaries—if not your ovaries or mine, then the generic ovaries as they have been packaged and presented to women in obvious need of an owner's manual, for it was only after the diagnosis that I began to grapple with my own collusion before the diagnosis in the insidious progress of the disease that would consume my life. Chapter 2 was composed later than the more personal parts of this book, but I place it next because it explains earlier lapses in my judgment, repressions and denials that may also bedevil other women not fully conscious of the ovarian cancer cells multiplying within their bodies. It took me a number of months to answer the questions, why had I not sensed or experienced the invasive cancer spreading in my abdomen and why had I not gone directly to a gynecologist? These are questions that must plague most victims of the disease, specifically the 75 percent whose cancer is found in later stages of development. Since my answers require a recitation of the quirky history of the ovaries, those addicted to muting commercials or fast-forwarding to the gory scenes should skip the next meditation so as to land directly at the massive surgery that would end up blighting my remaining days and ways. As the title of a series of children's books once put it, choose your own adventure.

· 2 ·

OVARIANA

I s t h e s i l e n t killer really and always silent or have women
been deafened by a noisy bombardment of misinformation about
our bodies? Judging from personal testimonials, quite a few people
experience no symptoms or barely discernible symptoms during the
onset of ovarian cancer. Yet after the diagnosis I spin with guilt,
acknowledging my share of blame for the advancement of my disease. "We are all culturally constructed," some academics used to
like to insist, as if that adage would somehow free us to transcend
culture. But at my own peril I was a dupe of the various cultures that
constructed me. Why did I not hear or heed the warning signs? My
answer to this question takes a circuitous route through the icono-
graphic history of the ovaries, a road that may at times look antique
but that leads with various twists and bumps to my arrival at the
gurney in the hall of Bloomington Hospital's emergency room. I am
moving backward, far back in time, so as to take the hospitalist's
advice and progress forward to an operation I very much wanted to
postpone indefinitely.

The ovaries do not have a stellar reputation. Though these almond- or olive-shaped organs contain all the eggs in the complete course of a woman's fertility, though the two ovaries take turns releasing eggs to travel down the fallopian tubes where they may or may not be fertilized to produce babies, though the ovaries supply the hormones that keep aging bones and skin, heart and sexual desire supple, they have received bad press for ages—especially from medical experts but from literary types too. And apparently they don't look too great either. Even a fair-minded science writer like Natalie Angier thinks that the healthy ovary, "dull and gray" and "lumpy," looks "sickly and drained of blood, as though it had given up hope." No wonder it was "no almond of joy" for earlier investigators. Yet couldn't the same claim be made about innumerable body parts, male as well as female? Angier goes on to praise the efficiency of these small, if unattractive, gizmos, whereas most writers from earlier times blame the ovaries for all the ills to which women were apparently heir. Paradoxically, the ovaries were held culpable sometimes for superfluous, sometimes for deficient or deviant female sexual desire. Over the last two centuries especially, lewd nymphomaniacs and prudish spinsters apparently needed quite a bit of help dealing with their ovaries, for a considerable number of experts believed that ovarian disease targeted over- or under-sexed women who deserved what they got.

Like Americana, Ovariana can strike one as kitschy, over-the-top, though it continues to exert a deleterious influence on all of us, certainly on me. In the case of the ovaries, a rich folkloric and cultural heritage may have originally accrued from their hidden but potent and unknown nature. In the olden days, as undergraduates sometimes generalize about historical periods before the present, women did not have ovaries. Instead, that obscured organ was conceptualized as the "inferior, internalized" version of "the male testes." Until the mid-seventeenth century most thinkers assumed that female anatomy should be understood to be the second-rate inverse of the default position, male anatomy: "The vagina was an inverted penis, the labia a foreskin equivalent, the uterus an internal scrotum, and the ovaries a woman's testicles."

Throughout the medieval and early modern period, investigators who followed Aristotle argued that "the male seed" alone creates the form of offspring, while others who followed Galen believed that "the woman's semen [emitted by the female testes] actively enters into the formation of the fetus." Yet "Galen concurred with Aristotle in deeming the female's role to be vastly inferior to that of the male." Greater emphasis was usually placed on the uterus as the paradigmatic female organ and on the female body as a passive receptacle, whereas "the male seed stamped the father's impression on the mother's menses like a seal on soft wax." Especially during the rise of a medical profession that managed to make the ovaries visible not only through autopsies but also through surgical operations, they were singled out to account for and deal with the sickening subjectivity allotted the female of the species. Punitive definitions of ovarian disease have penalized women until fairly recently, as have treatments.

"Ex ovo omnia": "all that is alive comes from the egg," William Harvey reasoned in 1651. The concept of "the egg's self-regulation and innate principle is one of Harvey's most remarkable breaks with Aristotle and is the central point of his entire understanding of the

embryo." More than a decade later, Johannes van Horne identified the testicles of women with the ovaries, where eggs could be found, and in 1672 Reinier de Graaf—studying the ovarian follicles still called Graafian follicles—"provided the first experimental evidence that eggs are released from the ovary." Their combined research contributed "to the credibility of the egg as the undisputed source of life." During the seventeenth and eighteenth centuries, when feminine testicles turned into ovaries, these organs were first recognized as producers of eggs (*ova*) and played a major role in the discussions of so-called preformationists.

Advocates of preformation proposed that "all living beings existed preformed inside their forebears in the manner of a Russian doll, put there by God at the beginning of Creation." Quite a few of its proponents "held that God had encased all life within the ovaries." Arguing with "spermists," who believed that God had encased all humans within the testes of Adam, the "ovists" relied on the perfection of the spherical shape of the egg to make a case for the ovary of Eve as the origin of humanity, a claim that nevertheless ran into difficulties because of the assumed inferiority of women. According to Clara Pinto-Correia, "as perfect as eggs might be in their form, the theory that the ovists had to defend could not avoid the disturbing fact that God had chosen to put His most perfect creation inside the body of a lesser being."

While the controversy between spermists and ovists raged, they implicitly agreed on the ovaries as the central symbol of a womanhood always in danger of uncontrollable surfeit. The Enlightenment scientist Albrecht von Haller "attributed uterine fury to excessively large ovaries. [His contemporary] Rousel reversed this causal connection, suggesting that large ovaries were the result of excessive venereal desire. The repeated reading of erotic literature, for example, would increase the size of the organs." Before the introduction of anesthetics and antisepsis, before 1827 when Ernst von Baer discovered the ovum in the ovary, before 1875 when Oscar Hertwig observed the fertilization of an ovum by a sperm cell, ideas about the functioning of these pesky nodules remained mixed and confused. Yet scientific belief in preformation began to give way to faith in epigenesis, the idea that organisms develop through cell differentiation. It is startling to realize that researchers did not comprehend the roles played by the ovaries and their eggs in human reproduction until late in the nineteenth century, early in the twentieth, and of course it took some time for that knowledge to filter down to authors of popular advice books and common citizens. The ovaries were difficult to study and remain difficult to test and treat because they are so deeply embedded within the body.

For this same reason, in the less rarefied world of practical medicine the ovaries took center stage in the emergence and evolution of surgery. In 1809 the Kentucky surgeon Ephraim McDowell removed both ovaries and the fallopian tubes of one Jane Crawford to relieve her of a cyst weighing more than twenty-two pounds. A few decades after 1824 and the first British so-called ovariotomy, the German surgeon Karl Thiersch discovered "my" type of cancer—cancer originating from epithelial cells. Doctors in this period associated women's complaints with diverse deviations from standard definitions of femininity and blamed them on the ovaries. "Normal ovariotomy" began to be deployed on women in order to manage "disorders" ranging from " 'excessive' sexuality to 'eating like a ploughman' to 'simple cussedness.' " Additionally, removal of the ovaries might be prescribed to cope with menstrual problems or the shrinking or enlargement of sexual organs thought to be brought about by unseemly education or foreign travel.

A 1996 play, *The Waiting Room* by Lisa Loomer, features a tightly corseted Victorian character (named Victoria) who is treated for hysteria which has been diagnosed as "a disease of the ovaries" caused by reading, especially the reading of "Romantic novels," and "a desire to learn *Greek*": "erotic tendencies," Victoria explains, "are one of the primary symptoms of ovarian disease," for which she has already been treated with "injections to the womb" and the placing "of leeches on my *vulva*." In other words, like the womb (etymologically related to the root *hyster* and thus to hysteria), the ovaries were defined by the nineteenth-century medical establishment as the source of inveterate and unladylike cravings and ambitions. Diseased ovaries, according to Victorian physicians, signaled psychological disorders to which women were especially vulnerable.

And, yes, even though *The Waiting Room* is obviously a contemporary look at the Victorian period, there is abundant evidence that leeches were actually deployed along with tapping (to drain fluid), purging, and blistering. According to an often reissued 1868 medical textbook by Edward Tilt, a president of the Obstetrical Society of London, "Leeching the womb is the best way to relieve the congested ovaries, particularly when the menstrual flow has lessened," specifically by applying "four leeches to the cervix a day or two after the flow has ceased." The leeches had to be counted because a leech lost in the body could produce frightful pain. It is tempting to ascribe resistance to some of his unfortunate patients. Consider, for example, his account of placing "eight leeches over the ovarian region, with little effect" on one woman and then "four leeches to the womb": she "immediately left treatment." Dr. Tilt agrees with the "eminent obstetricians" of his day that "Of all the organs of the human body, scarcely any seem so prone, either to functional or organic diseases, as the ovaries." Quite a few physicians believed that most female complaints stemmed from the ovaries, which exerted a powerful sway over women's lives.

According to the doctor-historian Ann Dally, "Virchow, probably the greatest pathologist of the nineteenth century, wrote, 'Woman is a pair of ovaries with a human being attached; whereas man is a human being furnished with a pair of testes.' " The French physician Achille Chereau argued that "it is only because of the ovary that woman is what she is." Two typical documents provide some proof that the reproductive organs of women were assumed to contribute to the extreme volatility of female psychology. In *Suppression of the Menses* (1873), Henry Maudsley claimed that "The monthly activity of the ovaries which marks the advent of puberty in women has a notable effect upon the mind and body; wherefore it may become an important cause of mental and physical derangement." From his perspective, "the mania [that arises from] a sympathetic morbid effect of the ovarian and uterine excitement" causes female patients to become "elated, hilarious, talkative," but then produces depression, with such cycles of extreme emotions recurring until "there are no longer intervals of entire lucidity." Maudsley's *Nymphomania* (1873) linked "the irritation of ovaries or uterus" with "the direct occasion of *nymphomania*—a disease by which the most chaste and modest woman is transformed into a raging fury of lust."

If women's desires and disorders are ascribed to "faulty sexual organs," the historian Ben Barker-Benfield postulated so as to uncover the logic of Victorian physicians, "why not destroy the sickness at its source?" After the introduction of anesthetics, rapid advances in surgery "came largely through the ovary," although one physician observing an ovariotomy could not have been idiosyncratic when he was repelled by the sight of "the bowels rush[ing] out of the wound," which brought to mind "the fate of Judas Iscariot."

During the 1880s, the widely performed (and aptly named) "Battey's operation" removed normal or healthy ovaries "not in response to any organic disease," but because "they supposedly elicited one or several nervous symptoms." The popular diagnosis of "ovariamania" sprang from a conviction shared with Dr. Robert Battey that, as he put it, "Insanity is not very infrequently caused by uterine and ovarian disease." Especially in the United States, physicians also used oophorectomy as a response to a host of menstrual aches and pains and to sexual "transgressions" like masturbation and orgasm. Eugenicists who wanted to purify the race could rid society of the so-called unfit through sterilization. For this reason, administrators at state hospitals debated whether or not to set up wards for madwomen to be subjected to Battey's operation. "One estimate in 1906 was that for every one of the 150,000 doctors in the U.S. there was one castrated woman; some of these doctors boasted that they had removed from 1500 to 2000 ovaries apiece." Soon feminists and antivivisectionists protested against the credo "when in doubt, take them out." Both "the great increase in ovariotomy, and its extension to the insane" were attributed to the surgeons' *"prurigo secandi* [itch to cut]."

The woman whose ovaries had been excised was described as castrated or spayed or unsexed, no longer a "real" woman, unable to menstruate or reproduce—which may have had its benefits, given the view of many specialists who conflated menstruating women with animals in heat. In 1877, one of the "laws" Dr. Mary Putnam Jacobi listed as axiomatic among her colleagues was the proposition that "the menstruation of the woman corresponds to the phenomena of excitement, which is manifested at the rutting seasons in various animals." Another proposition taken as evident: "Fecundation is in constant relation with menstruation; therefore in the human species it is easy to rigorously establish the intermenstrual epoch at which conception is physically impossible." While Jacobi took issue with some of these "laws," as the nineteenth century turned into the twentieth many birth controllers assumed ovulation occurred "at or just after menstruation" and thus flummoxed women with the promise that sex would be safe when taking place midway between monthly periods.

Was I being driven batty by researching Battey's operations and the axiomatic "laws" of early gynecologists? I find myself worrying that I have taken on the characteristic features of "the *facies uterine*" or "the *facies ovarian*," as described in the 1886 publication *Diseases of the Ovaries* by the acclaimed physician Spencer Wells. Have I begun to exhibit "the long compressed lips, the depressed angles of the mouth, and the deep wrinkles carving round these angles"? Were the itch to cut out the ovaries and belief in "the *facies ovarian*" propagated by the sorts of views expressed by Havelock Ellis, an otherwise progressive sexologist who championed the rights of so-called inverts (or homosexuals)? His 1894 *Man and Woman* describes the morbid psychology "liable to occur" in menstruating women, including hysterical and epileptic fits, erotomania, dipsomania, kleptomania, and suicide. Then he concluded: "These facts of morbid psychology are very significant; they emphasize the fact that *even in the healthiest woman a worm*, however harmless and unperceived, *gnaws periodically at the roots of life*" (emphasis mine). Surely it was time to refresh myself with the progressive views coming from later in the twentieth century.

Curiously, however, as the twentieth century advanced, ovarian disease took on an antithetical significance, more frequently signifying not female desire on hyperdrive but rather female eroticism repressed. Sterility became not only the effect but the cause of the disease. Diseased ovaries still represented a deviation from standard femininity, but a differently defined femininity. If nineteenth-century women were thought to develop ovarian disease because of too much libido, their twentieth-century descendants apparently had too little. During the 1930s, gynecologists disagreed about whether or not to remove healthy ovaries during hysterectomies, though increasingly they became aware of "the menace of ovarian carcinoma in the ageing woman." But misdiagnosis continued to pose a major problem: "between 1945 and 1949 only 27% of ovarian cancers were adequately diagnosed, and during the period from 1965 to 1969 the figure was only 28%." A 1946 publication on gynecology explains that "The prognosis with carcinoma of the ovary is almost invariably bad." With medical debates proliferating and increasingly technical, literature and film best reflect the prevailing evolution of Ovariana.

No poem better illustrates the link between ovarian disease and prudish sterility than W. H. Auden's "Miss Gee" (1940), whose thin, small protagonist exhibits "no bust at all," who resides "in a small bed-sitting room," does "a lot of knitting," and fearfully dreams of "a bull with the face of the Vicar" of her church "charging with lowered horn." Barren Miss Gee—passing by "the loving couples" on her bicycle, praying to be "a good girl"—goes to the doctor because of an internal pain, only to be asked, "Why didn't you come before?" In this ballad of the ovarian cancer patient as a desiccated spinster, Auden ratchets up the satiric contempt when the doctor explains the etiology of the cancer:

"Nobody knows what the cause is,
Though some pretend they do;
It's like some hidden assassin,
Waiting to strike at you.

"Childless women get it,
And men when they retire;
It's as if there had to be some outlet
For their foiled creative fire"

According to Auden, cancer should be blamed on the blocked victim and specifically on the blocked victim's childlessness and her analogous suppression of her own "creative fire." She is constitutionally incapable of making babies and of making art, of procreation and creation. Therefore the crime of ovarian cancer seems to deserve the punishment Miss Gee receives:

They laid her on the table,
The students began to laugh;
And Mr. Rose the surgeon
He cut Miss Gee in half.

Miss Gee, presumably killed by this operation, devolves from a medical magician's laughingstock to a pedagogical specimen or butchered cut of meat when she is wheeled away for an anatomy lesson:

They hung her from the ceiling,
Yes, they hung up Miss Gee;
And a couple of Oxford Groupers
Carefully dissected her knee.

Gee whiz, Miss Gee (Auden might seem to be saying), you really did yourself in. If you had only trusted the G-spot and the joys of sex, your miserable fate might have been quite different. My collaborator Sandra Gilbert conveys the larger implications of the poem's conclusion: "It's hard to imagine a terser summary of the abjection that every patient fears—abjection linked to a process of medical reification that transforms a person not just into an object, not just into an object of indifference, but even into an object of indifferent laughter and scorn." Of course a number of reformers decried what Auden spoofed, but they also provide proof that medical treatments must have felt painful and degrading. In an account of an experience in a 1930s Paris hospital ward, one Maxence van der Meersch witnessed a woman "dangling upside down" and "disemboweled like an animal hanging from a hook in a butcher's": she tells her story while a doctor bends over her, "tearing out the ovaries and sponging blood from the bottom of the pelvic cavity, as though from a bucket of flesh lined with muscles."

If Auden's cancerous old maid exemplifies repressed desire, the central character of Thomas Mann's *The Black Swan* (1954) signifies desire gone amok. A post-menopausal mother of grown children, Rosalie von Tümmler attributes the return of her menstrual cycle to awakening desire, only to discover that the bleeding actually results from advanced ovarian cancer. About the postwar period, the medical historian Patricia Jasen notes "growing fascination with the hormone-producing granulose cell tumour, even though it was a much less common form of the disease": "These oestrogen-producing tumours . . . affected post-menopausal women who might briefly and unwittingly welcome their 'feminizing' effects." Thomas Mann's widow, delighted that she is blooming again, is fifty years old when her surgeons see "murderous cell groups," all "started from the ovary," in the pelvic organs, the peritoneum, the glands of the lymphatic system, and the liver. Mann himself claimed to be fascinated by the ironic hoax nature plays on a child of nature. Yet the narrative plot effectively punishes the affectionate but aging widow for unseemly desire, unhinged from reproduction and obsessively directed toward a man young enough to be her son.

Such responses to ovarian cancer, viewed as the result of erratic or atrophied eroticism, sound offensive to most of us now, even though they occasionally resurface. The deliberately outrageous media personality Camille Paglia has judged ovarian cancer to be "Nature's revenge on the ambitious, childless woman." Vicious as it is, Paglia's comment reflects a current medical consensus that "continuous or 'incessant' ovulation, uninterrupted by pregnancy or oral contraceptive use, has the strongest correlation with the disease." Whether based on such a consensus or not, stereotypes of the barren spinster with ovarian cancer at times recycle in a more submerged manner that nevertheless qualifies otherwise powerful texts. Margaret Edson's play *Wit* (1999), for instance, forcefully criticizes dehumanizing medical approaches to ovarian cancer. Yet *Wit*'s central character, Vivien Bearing, bears not only the indignities and painful procedures inflicted by her physicians but also the marks of "the ambitious, childless" stereotype Paglia exploited.

An uncompromising scholar, never married, childless, Vivien has only one visitor during a lengthy hospitalization for experimental chemotherapy. She remains as isolated in the hospital as she was in her life. The ingenuity and intellect she prizes in poetry cannot save her from the ingenuity and intellect of the doctors who reduce her to a text, a specimen to be interpreted and endlessly manipulated. Like the doctors, she had dedicated her career to erudition; however, during her dying she eventually discovers that compassion and simplicity remain the fundamentals she had scorned but really needs. At first sardonically and later pathetically, Vivien Bearing learns that she had "ruthlessly denied" her students "the touch of human kindness she now seeks." By the end of the play and the end of her life, the previously introverted and cerebral academic—finally on palliative care for pain management—receives words of wisdom about compassion and simplicity from her visiting teacher, a great-grandmother who cradles her while reading aloud a children's book, Margaret Wise Brown's *The Runaway Bunny*, about an all-caring and all-knowing mother: " 'If you become a bird and fly away from me,' said his mother, 'I will be a tree that you come home to.' " The elderly teacher interprets the story as "a little allegory of the soul. No matter where it hides, God will find it."

Since the God-like figure takes the form of the runaway bunny's eternally solicitous and endlessly inventive mother, the story may also serve as an allegory of the health and survival secured by devoted mothering. Moving as Edson's text and Emma Thompson's performance are, *Wit* raises a disturbing question. Had its heroine received sufficient mothering or pursued less intellectual, more maternal roles in her living, might she have been spared the excruciating pain of her early dying? Was ovarian cancer Vivien Bearing's punishment for criminal neglect: her resistance to a properly dutiful motherhood?

For the most part, troubling stereotypes like these have been laid to rest by a revolution in feminist approaches to women's bodies that has transformed public understanding and medical education. They have been powerfully challenged, too, by Susan Sontag's critique of the ways in which "Patients who are instructed that they have, unwittingly, caused their disease are also being made to feel that they have deserved it." For centuries, ovarian cancer patients were effectively told that their aberrant sexuality caused a disease they deserved. Might historic prejudices against ovarian disease have contributed to the miserable state of ovarian cancer treatments today? Sometimes I think, probably not; sometimes I think, you bet. For didn't Ovariana retard and deform scientific investigations? Didn't it shape the mind-set of physicians who, until quite recently, were generally men? Doesn't the disease for the most part affect a subsection of the population—older, post-menopausal women—with little cultural capital? *Wit* concludes with the ethical and spiritual maturation of Vivien Bearing, but the doctors who treat her remain unregenerate to the end—callous, callow, and self-congratulatory about research that issues in protocols worse than ineffective since they reduce the patient to a tortured lab animal. Images of a malevolent or ineffectual medical establishment continue to proliferate in popular media that rarely focus on the post-menopausal women most likely to be diagnosed with ovarian cancer.

In the few films made about ovarian cancer, if not in fact, medical authorities emerge as morally bankrupt or useless. Produced to protest bigotry, the prizewinning movie *Southern Comfort* (2001) documents the last year in the life of a female-to-male transsexual dying of ovarian cancer. Fifty-two-year-old Robert Eads makes peace with his biological parents and children while he gathers around him his adopted son, his new lover, and several other couples in the small town of Toccoa, Georgia. Puffing on his pipe, thin as a rail in his blue jeans, he philosophizes about the members of his "chosen family" as he entertains and feeds and counsels them outside his trailer. Eads, having been turned down by some thirty doctors who found it embarrassing to treat him, refuses to hate but declines to forgive negligence. About the gynecologists who barred him (as a male patient) from their waiting and examination rooms, he says, "They didn't want to lose one or two clients to save my life. I'm expendable." Though anger would seem to be amply justified, it does not characterize his response to the surgeons who told him earlier, during his transitioning, that he did not need to have a hysterectomy. "It's kind of a fool joke," he shrugs. "That last only part of me that was really female is killing me."

Robert Eads—ironic, brave, and courteous—is portrayed by director Kate Davis with a dignity related to his integrity and courage but also to the nurturance he gives and receives from a support network composed mainly of gay and transsexual people. With transparent serenity, he refuses to allow fatalism about his terminal disease to poison the intimate relationships he has sustained and that continue to sustain him through his dying. *Southern Comfort,* named after an annual convention of transsexuals that Eads is determined to attend before his death, comforts me through its affirmation of community. Part conference and part prom, the celebration to which Robert Eads manages to travel serves as the joyous climax of the film and of the end of his life. In marked contrast to Vivien Bearing's torment, Robert Eads's tranquility raises an eerily ironic question: might he have lucked out? Is it possible that his equanimity has been facilitated by the *denial* of treatment?

Another movie about ovarian cancer, Isabel Coixet's *My Life Without Me* (2003), also intimates that the happiest outcome for people dealing with the disease involves staying away from doctors. Again set in a trailer in a rural and impoverished region, its narrative also focuses on a character determined to check off "Things to Do Before I Die." The twenty-three-year-old heroine of *My Life Without Me* responds to a terminal diagnosis by hiding the information from her family as she sets out to do what she wants with the few months she has left: recording birthday messages for her two little girls, having an affair, finding a future wife for her husband, eating pineapple cheesecake. By the end of the movie, Ann (played by Sarah Polley) has intensified her sense of being alive and therefore feels ready to die. Taken together, both films evince skepticism about what the medical establishment will or can do for people with advanced ovarian cancer (as well as optimism about what such people can do for themselves). The same claim can be made about *One True Thing* (1998), a movie based on Anna Quindlen's novel about a daughter moving back home to care for her dying mother.

As might be expected, a television dramatization of ovarian cancer in the series *Thirtysomething* concludes with a complete remission, with the character of Nancy Weston (played by Patricia Wettig) saving herself "because of her own inner strength." Unlike most women, who are diagnosed with late-stage disease, creative and youthful Nancy contends with stage 1C. Yet various episodes in the third and fourth seasons (1990–91) realistically emphasize the strain cancer puts on caretakers, friends, and children; the "massive burden" cancer patients feel they must strap on their shoulders daily; and the degradation of hair loss, nausea, and weight loss during chemotherapy. Don, watching the DVDs with me, says, "Friends try to help her out, but they don't really know what to do." "Yeah," I agree, "it's the banana bread syndrome—bake and bring, serve and eat." Unnerved at being the center of everyone's attention, at becoming the means by which others grapple with their fear of death, Nancy observes how cancer and its treatment shrink her world and herself.

Throughout this process, Nancy and her husband generally find her physicians remote, rushed, and insensitive. After a series of tests, her surgeon delivers the diagnosis by tragically intoning Nancy's name, as if the word "cancer" cannot be spoken. The next scene—showing Nancy seeking information on ovarian cancer in a library's microfilm archive—suggests that patients cannot rely on their doctors for guidance. A woman undergoing chemotherapy in Nancy's cancer support group fantasizes about traveling to Hawaii in order to perform a ceremony: throwing an oncologist into a volcano. When, in response to failing sexual desire after a hysterectomy, Nancy consults a female and a male doctor, both belittle her complaint, dismissing it as self-induced and offering "to play" with her estrogen. But she feels "castrated" and shouts at the male doctor, "If that happened to *you*, you'd call it the end of your life." Angry, she resents "the song and dance" of physicians who "insult" both her intelligence and her body. What can account for these derogatory representations of the health-care establishment, if not the circuitous evolution of Ovariana and the miserable by-products, or the ineffectuality, of medical responses to ovarian disease?

It is worth remembering that mortality rates for ovarian cancer have not dropped dramatically over the past twenty years, as they have for lung, colon, testicular, and cervical cancer, as they have for leukemia, lymphoma, and some types of breast cancer. Women are not living appreciably longer with the disease. After being diagnosed, a neonatal intensive care nurse admits that she "was absolutely overwhelmed by statistics and the feeling that 70 percent of women die within two years, and the other 30 percent die within four years, and that it's exceptional to find someone who lived more than five years." Although she prided herself on "recognizing symptom change [in premature babies] from one minute to the next minute," it took her "three months of being tired to go and do something about it. I had every excuse in the book. I thought, I am just constipated, or I haven't been running quite as much, or maybe I need a multivitamin, or I didn't get a full serving of vegetables this week."

How to distinguish the general noise of the midlife or aging body from meaningful signals that portend danger? In difficult-to-obtain books published primarily by small presses or self-published, the testimonies of women underscore the need for an early detection tool, given the vagaries of symptoms. Jo Ann Schmitz, diagnosed when she was fifty-three, explains that she "was concerned about my thickening middle, which appeared despite my three to four times weekly aerobic exercise. I was disgusted . . . nothing seemed to fit and I didn't like the way I looked. That was all. No other signs, no symptoms, no warning that everything in my life as I knew it would change." A woman who wishes to remain anonymous testifies, "I was thirty-seven and I never saw it coming. The symptoms were there, bloating, cramps, erratic periods. Of course, I attributed them to something else. Why wouldn't I? There was no history in my family."

Patients' stories include multiple accounts of medical mistakes too: women not informed about ovarian cysts apparent on ultrasounds, misadvised by doctors who did not send them to a gynecologic oncologist surgeon, directed to forgo genetic testing despite evidence of cancer in the family, advised by primary care physicians that abdominal pain was the result of a pulled muscle or pregnancy or a dermoid cyst. One woman whose ovarian cancer was misdiagnosed first as menopause and then as diverticulitis states, "My key message to all my friends and family is to listen to your own body. Don't listen to the doctors if they say it is nothing. Just keep pushing." Another patient who spent fifteen months with misdiagnoses exclaims, "One thing I really want to happen before I die is for doctors to be correctly educated to the early symptoms of ovarian related cancers." Still considered a silent killer by some patients, ovarian cancer receives a small percentage of governmental research funding and very little public attention. The teal ribbon, rarely displayed, remains for the most part unrecognizable.

Legal, commercial, and psychological factors continue to hinder progress. For many years, Myriad Genetics, which gained a series of patents, controlled the specific test used to identify the presence of BRCA1 and 2, the genetic mutations that predict a high risk of breast and ovarian cancer. As a monopoly, Myriad could set unreasonable prices and limit accessibility of services by denying certain types of insurance. Though genetic patents are being debated in the courts today, the profit motive continues to curtail available responses. Currently a number of drugs proven effective with ovarian cancers cannot be obtained because the companies that created them seek (through further testing on other populations of patients) wider markets. Activist patients, who have been so successful with other types of cancer, must contend not only with the debilitation caused by treatments and potentially beneficial yet unavailable drugs, but also with drug shortages and the short time span of remissions. In addition, modesty or reticence, related to gastrointestinal problems at onset of the disease or the bowel obstructions advancement produces, continues to inhibit patients from recording their experiences. With respect to protocols, especially the initial surgical intervention of the so-called debulking operation, women with ovarian cancer are offered little or no choice and few options, given the urgency of dealing as quickly as possible with looming mortal threat.

In my case of ovarian cancer, there can be no doubt about the deleterious effect of Ovariana. While I became interested in women's

lives and therefore in the history of gynecology, any faith I might
have had in its practitioners eroded. Back in 1979, Sandra Gilbert
and I completed *The Madwoman in the Attic*, partly a meditation
on how the culturally induced invalidism of nineteenth-century
women rendered them invalid as advocates of their own destinies.
Physicians played a prominent part in rendering women invalid
invalids. At the time of the book's publication, I dealt with flooding,
and my gynecologist advised a radical hysterectomy. I did not trust
his opinion. Like many women of my generation, I doubted the
popularity of an elective procedure which manifested, I suspected,
the propensity of mostly male doctors to regard women's reproductive organs as diseased or abnormal. In part because of feminist
publications like the ones I was coauthoring, widespread skepticism
had mounted about how routine hysterectomies were becoming,
something like 560,000 a year in the United States, often performed
on women with benign conditions who then suffered from various
consequences of the operation. In the early 1980s, did the feminism
to which I dedicated my life lead me astray? Or, many years later,
did my friend Ilinca's fierce insistence that I drop this particular
gynecologist—he had misdiagnosed her ovarian cancer, despite a
panoply of appointments and tests—buttress my earlier prejudices
against the medical establishment?

Worse yet, had shame or misplaced priorities retarded my realization about exactly what was going on in my body? Only after
the diagnosis in November 2008 did I think back and realize that
for quite some time I had kept to myself a series of digestive tribulations that I tenaciously attempted to minimize or simply ignore.
At the onset of the ovarian cancer that would kill Ilinca in 2005,
she had complained of a swollen abdomen, but never mentioned
indigestion or bowel problems or a feeling of being too full to eat.

Between 2005 and 2008, how many times had I overlooked or trivi-
alized bouts of constipation and then diarrhea that sent me rushing
into restaurant bathrooms or stopping at gas station restrooms? I
remember being horribly sick when visiting Oberlin (hiding in the
library), once in New York (retreating to a Barnes and Noble), once
in Berkeley (searching out a Mexican restaurant). I recall too many
delicious meals that I could hardly touch. But I had work to do,
miles to go before I slept, responsibilities to shoulder that ought to
take precedence over such banal and disagreeable matters. I thought
at the time, who wants to be a wimp or a whiner? Just deal with
it, I told myself.

At the start of the twenty-first century, during exactly the
period of time when activist patients were protesting that the so-
called "silent killer" really "whispered" and that women "should
listen" to what their bodies were telling them, my body yelled out
repeatedly, loudly and clearly. "It's not a whispering disease. It's a
shouting disease," one interviewed woman has declared. Was I deaf
or deafened by mortification or a deranged work ethic? Despite
Ilinca's private communications, was I blind as well and insensitive to the fit of my clothing? Photographs taken a month before
the diagnosis show my midriff larger or sort of swollen, a pot belly
apparent beneath my pants.

No matter how eccentric or misguided, no matter how under-
standable or justified, my persistent denial of symptoms and my
qualms about gynecological practices will probably result in my
death. I squirm at the thought, consoling myself with the notion
that feminist rhetoric today has become more nuanced than it once
was and that writing about the disease will provide recompense for
my earlier reticence. While goading myself with nagging personal
regrets or fulminating against widespread silence about a silent or

whispering or shouting killer and the failure of the medical establishment to find causes and detection tools and cures, I ponder the
mythologizing of those small factories of hormonal production and
maternal reproduction whose industry can give life with the same
inexorable tenacity as they take it away.

3

THE MOTHER OF
ALL SURGERIES

HAVE YOU EVER heard of a debulked woman? Have you ever seen one? I am one such living, breathing, debulked woman, though no one ever explained to me how such a being comes about, what such a condition means, or how it would feel, so I'm still finding my own debulked ways of being in a decidedly bulky world.

Going in for a debulking is not like hospitalization for a hernia, a gallbladder operation, a broken bone, a mastectomy, or an organ transplant—at least not for the ovarian cancer patient to whom, for whom it is decreed. In those other cases, people are generally told exactly what will be done to them, when, and how. Upon waking from anesthesia for a hernia or gallbladder operation, a broken bone or an organ transplant or even (occasionally) a mastectomy, the patient may be informed that the problem is on its way to being solved. The debulked woman, however, rarely hears such information or assurances. Nor is she encouraged to rest and relax during convalescence. Why do these seemingly sound practices not pertain to the individual with ovarian cancer?

The answer, to my mind, has everything to do with the unpredictable nature of the operation and thus the reticence of physicians. Impossible to anticipate the extent of the surgery until the body has been sliced open from navel to pubic bone. Who knows if malignancies have spread from both ovaries over the fallopian tubes, the uterus, the cervix, the appendix, the bladder, the liver, and parts of the intestines or lymph system? The silent or whispering or screaming but ignored killer has advanced unimpeded. Days after a CT image finally identifies the ailment, immediate measures must be taken that cannot be fully estimated or assessed until a long incision discloses the internal organs on the operating room table. There and then, efforts to stop the cancer's growth require surgeons to get up the gumption to gut a seemingly vital woman, removing many of her internal organs.

Horrible as the idea of gutting may be, debulking is considered a marked improvement over the "peek and shriek" operations of the past, when a doctor who glimpsed cancer stitched the patient back up and put her on sedatives. Personally, I kind of relish the sound of "peek and shriek" with its typecasting of the voyeuristic physician as a sort of drama queen, while the term "debulking" (if only to my ears) conjures up a censorious *debunking* of a patient's massive flab (bulk mail, buying in bulk, bulk food) or hulking muscle (bulking up). Debulked: what an ugly adjective. A surgery that can take six to eight hours, that entails a high rate of postoperative complications, debulking has earned the nickname MOAS from surgeons: Mother Of All Surgeries. As was the case four or five decades ago with breast cancer and with the earlier "peek and shriek" approach, the woman to be debulked is denied the chance to know beforehand what will be done to her or to participate in any surgical decisions.

Think of debulking as evisceration or vivisection or disemboweling, but performed on a live human being. It is considered "complete" if there is no visible tumor left after surgery, "optimal" if the residual tumor is less than one centimeter, and "subopti-mal" if larger than one centimeter. Gynecologic oncologists, the specialists who perform this operation, know that as many as half of the debulking surgeries completed in the United States end up rated "suboptimal"—visible lesions of cancer remain in the body, increasing the risks of recurrence. A 2007 British publication states that the "proportion of *completely* cytoreduced [cancer-reduced] patients [has been] reported as 42% only" and "the real explanation of this poor success rate is unknown" (emphasis mine). Whether the high percentage of suboptimal debulkings is the result of more aggressive tumors or less aggressive surgical approaches, gyneco-logic oncologists must worry, how can they embark upon an inju-rious physical intervention *that will not cure?* For such specialists fully realize that microscopic cancer cells inevitably survive even optimal debulking and go on to migrate throughout the abdomen and elsewhere. Debulking, which undoubtedly extends life, simply removes visually contaminated tissue so as to begin the also debili-tating process of chemotherapy as soon as possible.

By the time debulking is arranged to dislodge metastasizing tumors, a number of other medical measures have proven inadequate or beside the point. Diagnostic MRIs for back pains, ultrasounds, Pap tests (effective for detecting cervical, not ovarian disease), exercise regimes, drugs for indigestion or urinary tract infections, massage, antidepressants, and over-the-counter constipation meds may have been prescribed but proved to be indecisive or inefficacious. Frequently misdiagnosed, abdominal bloating or fatigue or indigestion finally gets explained by a CT picture of cancerous masses, probably deriving from the ovaries. There's no talk of clean margins in these domains or of counting lymph node involvement, at least not to this patient. There's no talk of a discrete tumor the size of a lemon or grapefruit either. At a glance (if the cancer is advanced), technicians will immediately deduce from the CT image that debulking must be done immediately—if not, as in my case, at the local hospital which handles few such complex operations then in the nearby research institution where I am sent with dispatch. Advice books urge patients to search for the best possible gynecologic oncologist, but I was told to drive immediately from Bloomington to Indianapolis where a surgeon would be assigned.

A woman about to be debulked will be informed that she is undergoing a hysterectomy—removal of the ovaries, uterus, fallopian tubes—accompanied by the possible removal of the omentum (a membrane lining organs in the abdominal cavity), parts of the involved bowel (which may require a bowel resection), and cytoreductive surgery which excises as much as possible of the visible cancerous tissue in the area. In my case, debulking surgery—scheduled as an emergency on the Saturday morning of November 8, 2008—took about four hours. Because "ovarian cancer sneaks up on women," experts agree that "after a short period of subtle complaints—often ignored because of their ubiquity—the cancer is typically diagnosed as stage III or IV, essentially incurable, ovarian cancer."

"I was aware that something was happening," Martha Stoddard Holmes explains about her condition before surgery, "but none of it added up to anything definite." Self-diagnosis, which tricked

Holmes into positing her own impending menopause, led me to propose irritable bowel syndrome, which I studied for remedies on various websites. But one night before consulting my family doctor, I lay down on my bed and felt beneath the palm of my hand intense spasms in one section of my intestines, rapid and forceful pulsations that were followed in the coming days by constipation. Even though I thought I could feel a knot on the left side of what I took to be my bowels, IBS stuck in my head as the proper name for my troubles. Indeed, I set upon proclaiming it as a sort of talisman. I rarely reveal medical information on forms for YMCA classes, but that fall I wrote next to a question about prior physical conditions "irritable bowel syndrome," as if to convince myself that this and only this was the nature of my problem, which would be cured by dietary changes along with yoga relaxation, breathing, and stretching.

My family doctor took the same tack as I did, originally. Before ordering the CT scan, she prescribed laxatives and then a recipe for "Healthy Bowel Habits": a few spoonfuls every day of unprocessed wheat bran, one cup of unsweetened applesauce, one small can of prune juice. Sadness on the face of the youthful doctor who read the CT image in the ER burst this particular bubble. The physician sees on the CT scan what the woman herself can neither see nor feel nor imagine. This explains why the medical establishment may appear to be more directly engaged with the disease than the person whose body contains it.

The first surgical intervention will further convince the about-to-be-debulked woman of her ignorance of herself in contrast to the expertise of doctors who can view (first on the scan, then on the operating room table) what she neither sees nor feels nor imagines within her. Even if I had been handed the scan before the operation, I would not have had the expertise to interpret its images. It would have remained opaque, unreadable. With or without copies of their scans, patients find ovarian cancer "a disease of primarily nonvisual symptoms," a condition "hard-to-visualize." One visual artist with ovarian cancer finds herself altering "ovarian charts, creating surreal images of bulls or deer": "I make horns and antlers of fallopian tubes, and turn uteri into animal heads and noses," intrepid Annie Smith explains about the days before her debulking. But even Annie Smith, who uses a cartoon bear as a surrogate for herself in a book about her treatments, does not draw the cancer which she describes as a tribe of malicious gremlins within her.

The night before surgery does not bode well in my case, for the nurses' preoperative bowel preparations do not seem effective. Unable to imagine what has gone wrong within the interior of my body, I will know immediately the debilitating effects of the surgeon's first foray in the war against cancer. "With the patient's body considered to be under attack ('invasion,')" Susan Sontag explains, "the only treatment is counterattack." The battle between ovarian cancer and the doctors is waged not with or by the unknowing woman but on and over her body. Physically, immediately after the surgery I will suffer from what the counterattacking doctors do against the cancer, rather than from the disease itself. The hardly noticeable symptoms of cancer pale in comparison to those produced by the surgeons determined to excise it. The physicians' greater knowledge as well as the misery produced by the operation can confuse the debulked woman about the interface or exchange-ability of the medical establishment and the cancer, the malignancy of the illness and its treatments. But of course, given the anesthesia, the surgery itself remains a blank or gap in consciousness, though I remember a freezing, windowless storage room, technicians or nurses in scrubs and colorful caps, and some of my final words about not wanting to wake up to a colostomy.

Cancer is paranoia's dream come true: there's something in there that I cannot see or feel or imagine, trying to murder me. What was inside me, requiring gutting, that I could neither see nor feel but might attempt to imagine? The rapidity with which debulking gets done masks a longer period of time in which cancer, unbeknownst to its host, has begun to inundate the core of a woman's abdomen. William Blake's poem "The Sick Rose," ostensibly about the insidious effects of jealousy, risks the sentimentality of a floral personification of femininity to capture the stealth with which an indiscernible incubus infiltrates itself into the vulnerable body:

> *O Rose thou art sick.*
> *The invisible worm.*
> *That flies in the night,*
> *In the howling storm;*
>
> *Has found out thy bed*
> *Of crimson joy:*
> *And his dark secret love*
> *Does thy life destroy.*

From the alienating world of ferocious nature ("the howling storm"), an unseen maggot penetrates into the private sanctum of personhood and passions ("thy bed / Of crimson joy"). Scholars of Blake explain that the cankerworm does not actually fly "in the night." Its stealth attack on the Rose has been imagined by Blake to envision "the invisible agents that cause human ailments": "Jealousy destroys love, disease destroys 'life.' "

Disease destroys with "secret love" by devouring the healthy tissue upon which it thrives. From its very inception, cancer has stuck to and been nurtured by the woman unconscious of the growth inside of her. Like a worm eating away at a fruit, cancer consumes what it spoils, cankers what it ingests. After being diagnosed, Lynette Walker "imagined a lovely golden and rosy peach with a little dark spot in it": "I'm the peach," she thought, "not the black spot." It is the continuous feeding upon flesh—the cannibalistic spreading of "this internal alien" or "enemy from within"—that terrifies victims of the disease who feel as if they are being eaten alive, consumed by metastases. Siddhartha Mukherjee titles his book about cancer *The Emperor of All Maladies* because of the cancer cell's voracious megalomania. Traveling cancer cells, proliferating by means of "pathological mitosis" and by suppressing genes that would put an end to such growth, become "immortal." To do so, they acquire "the capacity to draw out their own supply of blood and blood vessels."

Putting aside for a moment the imperial rule and dominion of the "emperor" of disease, consider first its cannibalism. According to medical authorities on ovarian cancer, before a woman's operation and perhaps for months, "feeding the cancer [has drained] calories and other essential nutrients from her vital organs." When the poet Alicia Ostriker discovered her breast cancer, she prayed, "Let me not become swallowed up by cancer. I don't want to be eaten alive." Another patient, struggling with the recurrence of her breast cancer, consulted the psychologist Martha Manning because "the cancer is eating her up from the inside out, resulting in ulcerations all over her chest." "Being eaten away from inside" by cancer, a dying Gordon Stuart says, "there is something not me in me, an 'it,' eating its way through the body." One woman whose breast cancer metastasized to her bones wept, "I know the cancer's in my neck and it's so close to my brain—it's going to go to my brain! It's eating me alive." The symbiosis between the proliferating cancer and the human body upon which it feeds can resemble a destructive and covert parasitism.

Blake's painting of "The Sick Rose" in *Songs of Innocence and Experience* encircles the verse with the thorns and leaves of a single stem from which the flower itself droops onto the ground at the bottom of the page. Out of the opening petals of the Rose, a woman appears emerging from the blossom with a snaky tail entwining her torso. Blake's cankerworm reappears in Reynolds Price's description of the cancer concealed in his spinal cord, a "*lethal eel*" rendering him as vulnerable as other "cancer hosts." Blake's "dark secret love" brings to mind the cancer cells' intimacy with healthy organs, their tenacity at replicating speedily and invisibly to infest and deflower the "bed / Of crimson joy," if not like a worm or eel then like a malevolent fetus in the womb or a voracious bug or thug in the house.

Metaphors of cancer, especially of ovarian tumors, register horror at a grotesque pregnancy. About her mother's cancer, Anne Sexton explained, an "embryo / of evil" grew in her "as simply as a child would grow, / as simply as she housed me once," an anti-fetus or satanic succubus in the place of the beloved baby in the barn. Jackie Stacey, hearing her surgery described as a "monstrous birth," worried that her malignant tumor was an "unnatural and twisted offspring": "germ cell tumours, in particular, can produce all sorts of tissues because the tumours originate from the egg cell whose function it is in pregnancy to produce differentiated cells that form other body parts." Although upon removal a discrete tumor may be described as a lemon or grapefruit, the heroine of Margaret Atwood's short story "Hairball" thinks of the growth on her ovary as a hairy coconut, with "fragments of bone" and "a scattering of nails, toe or finger. There were five perfectly formed teeth." The germ cell tumor called a teratoma, a less common form of ovarian cancer, often contains hair, bones, or teeth. Atwood's heroine pictures this "flesh of her flesh" as "her warped child, taking its revenge": "what it tells her is everything she's never wanted to hear about herself." In the 1994 production of *Sistahs*, a play by Maxine Bailey and Sharon M. Lewis, an African historian with advanced uterine or ovarian cancer worries about her daughter's future without her, for "This gift from my womb, and this . . . this thing in my womb" cannot coexist much longer (ellipses theirs).

Despite Susan Sontag's admonition against illness metaphors, images insist on creeping back. "Ovarian cancer is like a cockroach, defying an arsenal of poisons," the fashion editor Liz Tilberis declared about her sense of infestation. Systemic, cancer can morph from a cockroach to an astrological crustacean to an insane avenger. "Cancer was the crab, grabbing hold, eating away, destroying from within," according to one sociologist. The Greek word *karkinos* means "crab," which is how cancer looked to the first ancient physicians. Christina Middlebrook explains that the shifty and mobile crab-cancer "never takes the direct path, preferring to move sideways and furtively": a sneaky but tenacious interloper. Reynolds Price, whose doctor spied malignant "cells 'looking wild and ugly' under a microscope," resolved to turn body and mind "against a guest who'd become a kind of lethal twin." Similarly, Sherwin B. Nuland, the author of *How We Die*, describes cancer as "berserk with the malicious exuberance of killing." Nuland views cancer's first cells as "bastard offspring of unsuspecting parents, who ultimately reject them because they are ugly, deformed, and unruly. In the community of living tissues, the uncontrolled mob of misfits that is cancer behaves like a gang of perpetually wilding adolescents."

Meredith Norton also associates her stage III inflammatory breast cancer with "a crowd of looters" and a "blood-thirsty little doppelgänger." How can cancer be a "lethal twin" or a "doppelgänger," this last a word that the oncologist-author Siddhartha Mukherjee also uses? "This image—of cancer as our desperate, malevolent, contemporary doppelgänger—is so haunting because it is at least partly true," writes Mukherjee. He comes to this image of the double through the trope of colonization: "Cancer is an expansionist disease; it invades through tissues, sets up colonies in hostile landscapes, seeking 'sanctuary' in one organ and then immigrating to another." With its unbridled growth, the "emperor" of disease "is a phenomenally successful invader and colonizer in part because it exploits the very features that make *us* successful as a species or as an organism." Spreading and adapting at an alarming rate, cancer cells "are more perfect versions of ourselves" or "an enigmatic, if somewhat deranged, image in a mirror."

To another doctor facing multiple tumors in a recurrence, any medical intervention resembles "trying to lasso a wild horse." The women in Doris Brett's online support network "refer to ovarian cancer as the 'Beast'—a ravening, devouring monster," though she imagines "a bumbling, confused lout who postured a lot but hung around the home." The heroine in Gail Godwin's novel *The Good Husband* pictures her ovarian cancer as a "gargoyle" munching on her internal organs. To Katherine Russell Rich, cancer becomes "a panther, voracious but willing to bide its time," but also "a cellular part of you turned wild, ungovernable. It is you divided against yourself. It is your body made sinister, made into its own assailant—its own assassin." In one of Lorrie Moore's stories, cancer—"a lump of wild nothing"—hurtles toward "its mad, ambitious desire to be something: something inside you, instead of you, another organism, but with a monster's architecture, a demon's sabotage and chaos." A cankerworm, eel, embryo, or cockroach; a wilding twin, bully, emperor, beast, assassin, or demon, cancer strengthens itself at the expense of the weakened and unsuspecting human being whom it attacks and within whom it lodges to gain in strength.

Blake's Rose cannot but bring to mind innumerable painters following Georgia O'Keeffe who depict women's genitals as flowers. When the modern poet H.D. sought to describe female erotic and reproductive potency, she envisioned a goddess with a perfect and perfectly sufficient rose between her marble thighs:

> There is a rose flower
> parted wide,
> as her limbs fling wide in dance
> ecstatic
> Aphrodite,
> there is a frail lavender flower
> hidden in grass;
>
> O God, what is it,
> this flower
> that in itself had power over the whole earth?
> for she needs no man,
> herself
> is that dart and pulse of the male,
> hands, feet, thighs,
> herself perfect.

If we keep H.D.'s perspective in mind, Blake's Rose sickens from a deadly intruder who lodges within the very origins of life itself. Women's sex organs have "power over the whole earth," H.D. affirms. Yet the dart and pulse of Aphrodite's ecstatic dance of life devolve into a macabre dance of death. For the goddess of love has been befouled by the "dark secret love" of an evil embryo cloning into the demonic assailant within her.

So how does the debulked woman, no goddess of love, feel after radical surgery embarked upon with barely one rushed conference (during which she may have been in shock or sedated for shock since she has only days before received her diagnosis)? First, an odd and seemingly trivial problem of dry mouth arises. The night after surgery, one thoughtful nurse brought me a popsicle stick with a triangular-shaped sponge at its tip which was plunged in a Styrofoam cup of ice chips. Attached then to what was probably morphine, I later recall that long night as the rhythm of dipping and swabbing, dipping the sponge into the ice and swabbing my mouth. Dry mouth attended my nights and days for almost two weeks after surgery. Neither water nor juice, neither tea nor hard candy refreshes the aridity of the caked palate. Even a vigorous tooth- and tongue-brushing barely makes a dent. Will subsequent treatments of cancer similarly choke and muzzle the patient?

But by all means let's get to the more blatantly incapacitating symptoms, also unmentioned by physicians, a series of surprises in the hospital and then after the return home, some hard to anticipate. Simply to sit down on a chair (or get up), to turn on one's side (or lie back) in bed feels patently impossible. There must be millions of invisible stitches holding together the intestines, knotted around the removed uterus or ovaries or fallopian tubes. Impossible when reclining to move one's hips two inches to the left in a chaise. Nigh impossible to get out of bed, regardless of upper or lower body strength. Only huge spurts of determination enable brief, excruciating moments of standing or walking. How many muscles have been sliced through? At a later time, I learned from *Diary of a Zen Nun* how a forty-seven-year-old woman with ovarian cancer responded to having "all the machinery below the navel . . . disconnected": Nan Shin understood "where the *hara* was," the very "center of energy and activity" from which "all movement, even of the fingertips, has its origin."

After her debulking, Maureen Ryberg lamented, "I'm an empty shell. A gutted fish." The ordinarily resilient and cheerful Annie Smith says, "They had gutted me. I was pretty empty." On the sixth day after surgery, "I looked—and felt—like the victim of an axe murderer." Andrea King Collier's mother woke to a colostomy: "It was a billboard sign that pointed to the beginning of a loss of dignity. She couldn't do a thing about it. It had happened without her permission."

Less related to immobility, more associated with a loss of dignity, my next worst symptom is bloating. As a debulked woman, I have been hollowed at the hub, but my legs swelled into mighty oak stumps and my ankles tripled in width. When I hobbled to the bathroom, I jiggled—the flesh around my bones jogged up and down. At a frantic visit to a nearby clinic, a scale proved that I had gained thirteen pounds, presumably in retained water. In a reflex of vanity I had taken off my shoes to be weighed when I heard Molly's bemused voice, "Mom, you really are an anorexic!" But my daughters' hoots compensated only momentarily for the miseries of bloating. The indignities and pains of not being able to excrete or of excreting too much anyone can imagine, given all the drugs poured into me, not to mention the seven inches of bowel taken out of me. But who would have imagined an eviscerated trunk borne along by ballooning extremities?

Reformed, the debulked woman has a new sensitivity spot on her body. The omentum—a lacy yellow "apron" or sheet of fatty tissue hanging in front of the intestines from the bottom of the stomach to the pelvis—has been peeled away. Without a layer of fat behind it, the skin over the lower abdomen is taut, tender, and seemingly translucent. Crisscrossed with horizontal stripes of tape, a series of vertical stitches start a few inches above the reconstructed belly button and move down deep into the half-shaved pubic hair: a sort of cellophaned zipper. Through this six-inch incision, all those compromised organs must have passed out of the body into the pathology buckets or bags. Curiously sensitive to the touch, the belly feels defenseless, vulnerable, puffed out a bit (not bloated as before), but very delicate, uncannily skin-deep for the first time, instead of cushioned by a pad of flexible fat. Impossible not to place the pinky right above the pubic hair and stretch the thumb up toward the reconfigured belly button to sense under the palm a new bump (is that the bladder?), a series of wiggly tentacles (rearranged intestines?).

Because of the new sensitive area on her belly, the debulked woman may not sleep as she did previously. Old physical habits die hard, but curling on one's side like a spoon around one's lover, partner, or husband would set off all those internal tweakings and twinges and put a strain on the flesh traversed by the incision. Though I never took sleeping pills before, they seem essential now, as does my new way of going to sleep which must look like a corpse pose. Flat on my back, I clasp my hands together down over my pubic bone and tuck one foot beneath the other. Part of the idea is to generate warmth in extremities always slightly frozen, regardless of the thermostat or the layers of blankets. But I also seem to be miming the arrangement of limbs in a coffin or stone sculptures of the dead displayed recumbent on medieval tombs, though I expect to be cremated so my remains can fit into my husband's plot or near it in the local cemetery, waiting there for him to join me.

Frida Kahlo's painting *The Dream*, depicting a bed with its wooden canopy functioning like a double-deck, relates to my bed posture. On the lower bunk, a fleshly and nightgowned Kahlo lies sleeping in the corpse pose. Or she's a bit more on her side than I can be, overlaid with an appliquéd blanket of green leaves that sprout into new shoots beyond its borders. The artificial plant on the quilt, less passive than she, puts out new tendrils growing around the sheets, pillows, and nightgown near and surrounding the sleeper's head. On the wooden canopy or upper bunk, a skeleton shelved on its side clutches a bouquet of violet flowers. He looms larger than she, looms over her. The parallel figures of life and death have two pillows beneath their heads, as I do. The sightless black holes on the skeleton's eyeless skull and its bared teeth contrast with the closed eyes and mouth of the dreamer. Kahlo's reverie on death and the maiden suspends their bed high up in a cloudy sky. The only planet the artist sees consists of the bed in which she lapses out of consciousness under the spell of ever-present death. With a pill, sleep comes fast, but ends early—I sneak out of bed in the dark at five o'clock—to usher in another day of too much attention placed on my physical miseries.

The Yiddish word *kishkes* was used in my family to signify those sloshing and dark organs within the body that rule mind and spirit without ever being seen or understood. Now my *kishkes* had to rearrange themselves, and they felt somehow unsettled. Given the intestinal resection, a bowel movement comes to feel like a dire threat, a bit of gas like a poison dart, diarrhea or constipation a dreaded form of physical torture, and what if I do not make it to the bathroom in time? Fear of soiling myself tethers me to spaces in close proximity to a bathroom. Have my bowels been twisted as well as foreshortened by more than half a foot? When I spend more time thinking about stool softeners than about conversation at the kitchen table, the tyranny of the body—the treachery of the body—comes into focus: how the sick or dysfunctional body trumps not only mind and heart but also volition or will. I no longer "have" or "relate to" a body. This injured body rules me. There is no chance that I will be able to pluck from the diagnosis an opportunity to compose "a little obituary of my soul history," like the central character of Gail Godwin's novel *The Good Husband*. The gross details of case history, not the spiritual configurations of soul histoty, would absorb all my attention.

Rarely discussed, physical complications like mine may be embarrassing and boring; however, they put temporality on a speed track, functioning like a kind of accelerated time machine, for they effectively plummet me into old age. Although at sixty-three I have never experienced any serious illness or disability, overnight I become an old woman. Worse, I have become my mother with all of her ninety-three-year-old frailties. Like her, I step very slowly and advance at a snail's pace, bent over double. Like her, I cling to railings, taking one stair at a time. Like her, I find it hard to get out of the passenger seat of a car. Like her, I worry aloud about whether fiber or fruit might aid digestion. It is horrible since I had resented my mother's dependency. It feels as if some sadistic god were turning the tables to declare, "Well, see how it feels from *her* perspective, you idiot!" The debulked woman, plunged into a mimicry of old age, judges her frozen extremities, her feeble inability to handle insignificant weights, her exhaustion levels rising after minuscule exertions, and finds herself ludicrously wanting. How could she possibly have been the active professional she thought herself to have been a few days ago when she had juggled teaching and research, grocery shopping and cooking, traveling and lecturing, mentoring and the chairing of administrative committees? Those selves have been peeled off and lie discarded in a litter of ruin behind me.

In the mirror, the debulked woman looks at a body that has lost most of its strength through eyes that recede from the sockets of a pale crone's visage. Anyone undergoing a hysterectomy must experience the extreme fatigue coupled with the loss of estrogen that can plunge patients into depression at aggressively quick aging. After my friend Mary Jo's hysterectomy, she was so weakened that she felt as if all the water in the bathtub of her self had been sucked out in one fell swoop. The debulked woman has been told that besides the removal of a number of her organs (and the hormones they generate), some sort of gadget—perhaps a miniature vacuum cleaner, she wonders—has been used to sweep up and dispose of all evident cancers (though unseen cells undoubtedly remain "to shed" and "to seed," forming new tumors in the abdomen and elsewhere). A midlife obsession with trying to eliminate what my kids used to call my "pillow"—a pronounced protrusion between my pelvic bones after pregnancies—has found an unforeseen solution.

But I feel taxidermied now, with my stuffing removed, like a caved-in fowl or a dead animal awaiting batting. Since I had already undergone menopause and have two adult children, I can only guess what such a state must feel like to a younger woman deprived of estrogen and fertility. What of women debulked before they have the opportunity to conceive children? In Ava Vanyo's novel *Sarah's Rain*, I encounter a younger patient diagnosed with epithelial ovarian carcinoma who weeps and frets that after the operation she will no longer be feminine, will no longer be a woman. Vanyo generously bestows all manner of good things on her heroine, but surely debulking must horrify younger women plunged into premature menopause. Other anxieties, related to those less lucky than I, continued to plague me.

For what about debulked women without relatives capable of arriving to oversee postoperative recovery for the first few critical days at home? Simone, my younger daughter, delegated the tasks of her job in New York City. She and her sister, Molly, who shelved her responsibilities at the University of Pittsburgh and her husband and baby son, devoted themselves to the laying on of hands—oh! the creature comfort of tender pats and hugs, but also of these particular arms to lean on, granting the timeless physical intimacy possible with those whose proximity dates back to their earliest existence. Though Simone and Molly would start to make a salmon dinner only to discover that somehow they had lost or left the salmon at the grocery store, their loving-kindness was palpable, as was the affection of a succession of colleagues who signed up for "meals on wheels" after the girls' departure.

Motivated by the intimacy of small-town communities, schooled

by a limited number of good restaurants, male as well as female colleagues outdid themselves with chicken stir-fries and savory tarts,
roasted vegetables and baked fish, soothing soups and smoothies,
each arriving at six or seven o'clock in the evening and each returning for me the previous cook's containers or pots. But the real horror of women without such familial or social networks involves the
number of debulked women without money and insurance and
the assurance that work responsibilities can be ditched and ditched
entirely. The fearful state of such women seems beyond pathos to
me, almost inconceivable. How would they manage to find the will
to make the money to pay the bills? And what would the bills come
to without adequate insurance?

During the four to six weeks it takes to recover from debulking, one day might bring a bit more strength to sit on a cushioned
chair at the kitchen table—with flesh wasting away, the cushion
became essential—to gag down a tablespoon of noodles in broth;
another not. TV, novels, e-mail, CDs, Netflix, and knitting relieve
the tedium only intermittently, for as the debulked woman creeps
through the enlarged corridors of her house, she harbors her time
to realize what has happened to her. The rapidity of the surgery
has left her in a stunned state so she can explain quite calmly, for
instance, that she has advanced ovarian cancer, yet it has not fully
sunk in. Thus, for me the writing becomes an effort to catalog the
physical and mental states through which I am passing, with the
hope of then comprehending their significance. Nothing nearly
as heroic as the writing that strenuously seeks to control Anatole
Broyard's disease: "It forces the cancer to go through my character
before it can get to me," Broyard boasted in his book *Intoxicated by
My Illness*. However, cancer has definitely gotten to me before my
character could grapple with it through the self-reflection of prose.

Not at all intoxicated by my condition, I also do not agree with Broyard's view that "stories are antibodies against illness and pain." More like sedatives, perhaps.

Unfortunately, sedation impedes the two tasks the debulked woman has been told explicitly that she must accomplish immediately in this very state of enervation: gaining strength and researching her medical options. Not rest and relaxation but physical and mental toughening seem to be what is required to withstand what awaits the debulked woman, namely the trials of chemotherapy which (given the advanced state of the cancer) should begin as soon as possible. She must bulk up because she will soon be weakened not once but once every three weeks for a total of six sessions of toxic drugs intravenously poured into her. Perhaps there are other diseases that put comparable pressures on patients, but I do not consider them. "Ovarian cancer treatment is aggressive and at times unrelenting for the patient," Virginia R. Martin and Carol Cherry state.

After three nights in the Indianapolis hospital, upon my return home I begin to receive importunate phone calls from relatives in Pennsylvania, friends in California, and family in New York—all with the same message: "You must immediately locate the best oncologists and research trials for your specific circumstances and get a second opinion. Time is of the essence." The gruesome hilarity of this injunction has everything to do with my not knowing a thing about my "specific circumstances." No one has told me the extent of involvement, the name or type or stage or grade of my particular kind of ovarian cancer, the narrative of the surgery, or any details related to the pathology report. Callers intone lists of suggestions—a pioneer at Sloan-Kettering, a hotshot with results at M.D. Anderson, a researcher at Dana-Farber. These are hotsy-totsy specialists in famous faraway research centers, about which I know nothing. In a state of health, I could Google away, but not with the decrepitude that has affected me so profoundly.

Either to accept the usual chemo cocktail from a local Bloomington oncologist or to go with my Indianapolis surgeon's research trial—this way of putting the decision is assumed to reflect crass ignorance on my part, parochial incompetence, or lazy tomfoolery since the first treatment always would be the most important and shouldn't one therefore find the most expert of physicians? How to locate a specialist dealing with my particular case (which I did not myself fully know)? Would a face-to-face interview be required (the idea that I was supposed to get to an airport and on a plane seemed inconceivable) or could a conference phone call be arranged? All these details eluded me, while I suspected that the urgent directives issued from people prejudiced in favor of the know-how of those residing on the coasts over and against the know-nothingness of those presumed to be unwillingly marooned within flyover states. With some 22,000 American women a year diagnosed with ovarian cancer, why can't a beneficent computer guru simply supply each unfortunate with a list of the five top programs within a hundred-mile radius?

Besides, I put it to myself at my most cynical, fifty years hence doctors will look back at the treatment of ovarian cancer today and judge it medieval. Were leeches and blistering then more gruesome or punitive than debulking and chemotherapy are now? Margaret Edson's play *Wit* encapsulates what most people intuit: a succession of poisons are hurled at the ovarian cancer patient in a series of so-called therapies that may kill the patient before the disease does. If the cancer is destroying the woman by eating her up, the chemo will murder fast-growing cancerous cells by blocking their replication. With the cancer attacking the woman, the physicians warring against the cancer, the woman again dwindles into a bystander at the massacre or the scarred no-man's-land on and over which it takes place. Since there is no question in my mind that the doctors have hurt my body more than the cancer has done so far, my recurrent fantasy involves rejecting chemotherapy altogether, especially because the statistics are so discouraging. Should the chemo be mandated, a fallback resolution begins to form: just one round of chemotherapy, not any more than that. As doctors Mary L. Disis and Saul Rivkin explain, "Most patients diagnosed with more advanced stage disease go on to develop disease recurrence." With my two girls having had to go back to work after my first week home, every day a phone call from one asks if I shouldn't hire a therapist—I must be depressed—or an e-mail from the other urges me to try Greek yogurt and maybe Ensure. Meanwhile friends Google and phone around like mad, while e-mails and gift baskets and cards arrive in flurries.

The debulked woman, understanding how embarrassed many people become at the thought of death or dying in their midst, must cut some slack for those most discombobulated by her condition. "Hey, hi, how ya doin'?" my brother roars into the phone. "You gave us quite a scare, but we're glad you're back home now, safe and sound!" Cheery e-mails proclaim, "Congratulations on your speedy recovery! Can't wait to see you back at work soon." Stuffed animals arrive, as if I was receding backward into infancy rather than hurtling forward into decrepitude. Or people tangled in their own doubts painfully confide on flowery Hallmark cards, "I would pray for you, but unfortunately I no longer believe in the power of prayer."

Inexplicable gestures start early, in my case the day after the operation, when my surgeon Dr. Stehman arrived at my bedside to hand me a copy of the poem "In Flanders Fields," stapled to printouts of other websites on veterans and the Tomb of the Unknown Soldier:

> *In Flanders Fields the poppies blow*
> *Between the crosses, row on row,*
> *That mark out place, and in the sky*
> *The larks, still bravely singing, fly*
> *Scarce heard amid the guns below.*

Was the doctor keen on the poem because it was composed by a physician, actually a surgeon—one Lieutenant Colonel John McCrae, MD? Or was the day of the surgery, or the day after, Veterans Day? Or did he want me to think of myself as a warrior in or veteran or casualty of the war against cancer? Or, unlike those people who worry aloud about their grammar around English professors, was this Dr. Stehman's way of saying that he, too, relishes the grandeur of verse? But even the most sensitive of callers can seem eerily distant to the debulked woman whose mortal sickness turns her into an alien in her native land.

Each friend bustles into the house bristling with energies and affections in abundance, brimming with a multitude of attachments to the bulky world of parents and children, professions and hobbies, civic commitments and artistic activities. Given the debulked woman's ontology—a state of being now decidedly attached to remissions and recurrences—she can only marvel at how embedded her visitors are in existence, how passionately devoted they are to their views on this actor or that politician, how zealous about their diets or their home improvements. Overwhelming and fearful distress about the present body's frailty and the future body's degeneration loom so large in my mind that it becomes difficult not to zone out, not to switch into silent movie mode and watch without hearing the succession of guests. Like an autistic child who experiences other people as threatening or incomprehensible, I engage in what Oliver Sacks calls "pseudosocial conduct," going through the motions of conversational exchanges without being engaged with their emotional dynamics or intellectual content. Yet the last thing I would want is a series of monotonous conversations about me and my woes.

During the following days, a surrealistic cancer salon evolves in my living room, populated by visitors not denying the reality of my condition but rather affirming me *because* of it. On the couch, I seem to be holding court to a succession of voyeurs. While my intimate friends adopt designated roles in the arduous treatments to come—Jan will shave my head, Jayne offers driving, Mary Jo will investigate hospice—it seems that for another succession of visitors I am the designated victim whose illness imbues her with a sort of reigning celebrity. Put on display as a person about to encounter precisely the suffering they seek to ward off, I am an icon, a fetish. A touch of my hand, the feel of my cheek, and the exclamation, "You look great!" accompanies an air kiss hollowed out by bodies withdrawing so as not to hurt me in a tight clasp or so as not to be contaminated by the evil that lurks within me. The buffer around me thickens. I avoid eye contact and direct answers by repeating decorous phrases of welcome.

Even the meals-on-wheels so carefully organized by caring colleagues turns into a hassle. What an ingrate I am becoming as I get impatient with not knowing how long I will have to converse with people pandering to a pathetic shut-in. My disgust with orange soups escalates as thick, sweet carrot and butternut squash and pumpkin compotes multiply. Increasingly I do not ask these generous people to take off their coats and sit down. Instead I try to hurry them into the kitchen and then out the front door. But if I succeed, others arrive to visit and stay. I must rehearse the surgery and the plan of the chemo to those who keep on assuring me that I look great and that I have strong determination that will see me through. Irritation or pique is no doubt misdirected at guests. But I am helpless against being visited, being fawned over, and the silent movies (I am watching conversations without hearing the words spoken) and the autistic "pseudosocial conduct" (I am miming rote reactions) isolate me from the bulky world.

Although or maybe because I am recovering from the surgery, my mind swerves from guests talking to one another and to Don, for it seems inconceivable to me that cancerous cells continue to germinate and multiply throughout any number of my organs. Yet as my own incredulity and vexation spiral, the glum assessments and glib convictions of my guests do too, for they cannot help but gauge my sallow complexion and halting movements to assure themselves of their own resplendent vim and vigor. Or perhaps they twinge in guilt at their own resplendent vim and vigor. Each moment they waste of my precious time, though, brings me closer to poisoning. Despite the ice cream and the yogurt with which I am plied, a ring falls off my finger while I am making the bed. I remove all the rings—my maternal grandmother's diamond and the three thin rings signifying my marriage—and enlist as a nun of cancer, a novitiate of chemo, but alas not a cloistered one.

Visitors and phone callers mean well, but they are propitiating a future that they want to eliminate from their own lives. Or they are stumbling through a series of tangible gestures manifestly inadequate and inappropriate to their needs and mine. Contiguity to death fills me with a ghastly surplus from their point of view. I am ghoulishly visible and poignant. Mutely, they seem to mouth the tactless inquiry of the intrepid husband of one guest: "How does it feel to be so proximate to death, not theoretically but actually?" If they have themselves had cancer, I spark recollections of what they went through, and they goad me to gird my loins. If not, I am a fearful reminder of what they might go through, and they assuage me as if to repress their own vulnerability. They telephone with cancer stories which, as Kathlyn Conway notes, quell anxiety and "draw a circle around the threat of cancer," a targeted circle that I am in and they are not. "Treated to the details of someone's cousin's death and even an acquaintance's friend's mother's death," Conway knows that "People dispel their anxiety by ridding themselves of these stories, giving them to me. Now I hold the fear they cannot bear to feel." Why do I allow myself to become so annoyed? Why can't I simply say, "Sorry, I can't speak with you now," or take the advice of my daughters and get caller ID? Our Lady of Ovarian Cancer holds court in a shrine always strewn with bouquets of flowers, knowing that she is sneering at precisely what others would consider the luck of an energetically supportive community. Not just exasperation but irritation with my irritation abounds aplenty.

No matter how surreal they seem, friends and colleagues are keen on my survival, so I must be too. The monochromatic days float

by—of resting on the sofa and consuming multiple mini-meals—
as I move through a recovery that is supposed to strengthen me to
endure the horror of being poisoned. "No superfluous calories—not
sugar, but protein and fiber! A longer walk outside each day!"—a
well-meaning relative bellows into the phone, while I lie on the
couch cocooned in a quilt of my own making, one modeled on
one of my favorite Mark Rothko paintings. Brochures from the IU
Cancer Center deploy a similar tone of insistent militancy: "Cancer
means the time has come to look more aggressively to the future."
Aggression characterizes the treatment of cancer, just as it characterizes the cancer itself. But aggression has little to do with my
exhaustion or with the mildness of the impassive quilt. Nor do the
brochure's other adages pertain to my values or goals: "View cancer
as a blessing, rather than a curse"; "Be a good example"; "Put your
trust in God"; "Try to believe that miracles sometimes happen."

As you may know, Rothko's most somber canvases were often
monochromatic rusty reds or shades of black. But like his brighter
works, paintings with dimensions that recall the size of a full-size
bed quilt, the blanket enfolding me was fashioned to display three
stacked blocks of colors. In the case of the quilt, I sewed together
small diamonds of blue at the base, a narrower band of yellow in
between, white at the top, each horizontal panel created out of a
spectrum of barely distinguishable colors very slightly variegated
in tone and vibrancy, for I had pieced the diamonds together from
hand-dyed swatches ordered from the Web. At the bottom, satu-
rated dark blues modulate up into royal blues. The narrow central
strip is composed of deep golds mutating into egg yolk, daffodil,
and then paler yellows. The largest and most variegated top third
of the quilt displays my sense of the ineluctable motility and mobil-
ity of the huge Midwestern sky—batiks of light blue, lighter blue,

blue-toned white, mottled white, rose-colored white, white-on-white, yellow-hued white, grayish white reflect the palette of ever-changing clouds and shafts of pellucid light above and streaking across the horizon. In the middle of the country, I often reflect, the overarching atmosphere of modulating cloud formations filtering or flitting within the rays of the sun acts the way the ocean does on the coasts—putting trivial human pursuits into a vaster perspective.

I leave the cocoon of the quilt reluctantly—for example, to get a haircut with a youthful stylist who tears up asking me, "Who is your doctor now?" I have no answer. My family practitioner in Bloomington never phoned or wrote after my return from the surgery, nor should I have expected her to. My Indianapolis surgeon did call once with a perfunctory summary of the so-called "path report"—papillary serious stage III cancer involving all removed organs—and instructions to see him in a month for a post-op consultation. While still drugged in intensive care, I vaguely remember being told that a "shelf" of cancer remained lodged on my bladder. Does this mean the operation was suboptimal? How clueless I am. I consider tossing the buckets of glossy brochures sent home with me from the hospital. In a matter of days I do. Despite the promises of the *Johns Hopkins Patients' Guide to Ovarian Cancer*, I do not feel "quite comfortable with the language of the disease as well as the treatment philosophies." Repelled, I fret: for how many months or years or decades have I unconsciously been infested by a worm or an embryo of evil, then stalked and sabotaged by a wilding assassin?

Were the microscopic "seeds" beginning to sprout when I went to Israel last June to celebrate the first gender studies textbook in Hebrew? Had the "shedding" started to germinate when I was directing a graduate seminar on women's literature at the

University of Kansas later that June, or had tumors mushroomed in July when I met my British cousin and his wife in New York City, or in September when I felt too exhausted to see the Frida Kahlo exhibit on display during my trip to San Francisco for the joyous festivities of the marriage of Simone's best friend, Emily, and her partner, Wendy? Dr. Susan Love, explaining that "it takes 100 days for one cell to double and become two," writes that "most [breast] cancers have been present for eight to ten years by the time you can feel the smallest of lumps." Does this slow growth pertain to the three types of ovarian cancer—epithelial, germ cell, and sex cord-stromal tumors—specifically to the first and most common type which I apparently have? When Andrea King Collier asked about her mother's treatment for ovarian cancer, a doctor told her, "Once it gets going, ovarian cancer is very fast-moving."

Fast- or slow-growing, how do I begin to imagine the cancer that was within me before the debulking operation? It starts to bring to my mind not a crab or a fetus, not an assassin or a beast or an emperor, but mucky seaweed clinging and clogging and swelling as it lodged in and over my internal organs, creeping rhizomes sending out circuitous tubers and gnarled nodes and octopus shoots, venomous suckers and blades of kelp slicking surfaces with the olive-green slime of slippery moss. Impossible to know the cancer cells' stealthy forays, disorienting to picture the masses of growth they seem to have laid down, unbeknownst to me, at the center of my being. To get some answers, a solicitous administrator at my school made an appointment for me in Indianapolis with an eminent specialist who would discuss the once and future nature of my disease. Though it turns out that this man has himself retired because of progressing cancer, he sends me to an up-and-coming colleague, and I must marshal if not aggression then at least a list of cogent questions to look like a viable candidate for her concern. Perhaps Daniela Matei will become my doctor. Perhaps she will help me shut the door on the dreaded chemotherapy.

Before the debulking, my mother had been kept in the dark about my condition. While I was still in the hospital, however, Don informed her of the disease and the operation. And when (a few days after surgery) the girls arrived to help at home, they explained separately and together, on the phone and in person, the state of affairs. How can one expect a ninety-three-year-old woman to take in this gruesome twist of events? So one sunny day after lunch, more than a week after my return from the operation, I phoned my mother at her nearby assisted living quarters to try to explain why I would not be able to invite her over for Sunday dinner or take her on an outing to the mall in the coming weeks. In her excellent nursing facility, she would be well taken care of.

"Hey, Mom. How are you?" On and off since my dad died in 1960, my mother has struggled with depression.

"You haven't phoned," she pouted.

"Do you understand what has happened, Mom? What the girls explained?"

"I know," she said in a formulation the family mimics as her effort to assert proficiency without learning a smidgen of information about anyone around her. But in this context it must have sounded a bit lame even to her own ears so she added, "You're having chemo."

"No, Mom, that may happen in a few weeks. Now I'm just recovering from surgery for . . ."

"Susie," she interrupted, "someone's at the door—I know you don't like to hold on so I'll let you go now."

"OK, Mom," I said. "Have a good afternoon."

Such an anecdote, left on its own, would only contribute to the self-pitying woes of the debulked woman, were it not for the one figure I have omitted from this description of how two weeks of post-debulking got negotiated by a sixty-three-year-old who had bulked up her earlier life by means of an insatiable appetite for reading and writing books, making friends, teaching literature, quilting, knitting, cooking, partnering, collaborating, and mothering, never put in any particular order, but all nicely jumbled together like the bits of fabric in a quilter's stash. For if debulking means anything it signifies the subtraction of all those interests, now subsumed by an overriding and offensive obsession with one's own physical vulnerability. This, too, threatened to remake me into a double of my mother, were it not for the voice responding to my account of her blatant attempt to get off the phone and off the hook of understanding what her daughter was in fact going through.

"Must be a big bingo game about to start in the rec room, or maybe wheelchair tai chi," Don joked. I looked at his crooked grin, silently rehearsing my nicknames for him. Outwardly undemonstrative, Don has no nicknames for me, but I spill over with affectionate endearments since Don sounds to me more like the name of a colleague than a beloved: Donner, D-est, Mr. D, (less predictably but with a formality suited somehow—who knows how?—to his seniority) Frederick, and (most devotedly) Bear. How these nicknames came about I have no idea, for he is tall, handsome, and fit, markedly younger-looking than his eighty-one years, not stout or hairy, but with the sly grin of a lizard. Except he is upright, a man with backbone. During the dreadful years of his first wife's degeneration and dying, the strength of his character took not a bombastic or showy but a domestic turn. He had three rules—make the bed every day, never eat before the TV, and always use a place mat—not one of which I had the resources to follow when in miserable loneliness I was going through the breakup of my first marriage.

Or so I mused as I considered the debulked life he now lived—lending me a hand into the shower, bringing me tea, gathering logs for the fireplace, answering the phone with reports of my progress, setting and clearing the table, doing the laundry, tossing dead flowers and gift baskets. I fretted that he had "been there, done that" decades before and with the steadfast patience he had shown his dying first wife. It grieves me to observe a grief in him that cannot but reopen this earlier passage of grieving. That long-ago and difficult period of devoted caretaking in his life had spun me then and there out of friendly fondness for him into a passionate adoration of the very fiber of his being; and how strange that we had been given the gift of having a real life together—eighteen years of a companionability about which I had never even dared to dream—during which time we daily share trivial and momentous feelings, intuitions, thoughts, impulses, jokes, sights, gossip, music, news stories, historical tidbits, all tempered by passion and esteem that even now seem to fill the empty cavities at my core, leaving me not for one second grateful to or angry at cancer but full of wonder at the abundant magnanimity of human concord and consanguinity.

This, just *this*, I soon determined to determine, must be the emotion to which I would cling if I couldn't avoid the bumpy road into treatments as bad as or worse than the disease. It was an affect that brought me back to my sense of what I valued about a self I have often judged and found severely wanting in most other regards. Not faith in my ultimate survival but rather my passion and esteem for Don, and for my daughters, and for my many friends and students would be my gauge of personal integrity. Should I be able to keep my heartfelt affection for them intact—despite reversals and setbacks, physical suffering and mental confusion—what mattered could take center stage in the drama to come: not the disease but the fiber and fabric of a life we had stitched together with a patchwork of individuals whose variegated temperaments, ideals, and investments form a shifting kaleidoscope of patterns that, I hoped, would continue to enhance each and every one of us.

4

STARTING "INFUSION"

"IT'S A VERY common form of epithelial ovarian cancer, but the debulking was suboptimal. A ledge of cancer lodged on the bladder has not been removed." Dr. Daniela Matei examined my file after an initial delay in our appointment caused by a "Code Blue in Infusion" announced on a loudspeaker. Don and I were sitting in a barren hospital cubicle with two upright chairs, one stool, charts on the wall staging ovarian disease, and the usual paper-lined gynecological contraption. Rushed but intensely concentrated on making eye contact, Dr. Matei proceeded to answer all the questions on the list I had brought to the brand-new Melvin and Bren Simon Cancer Center in Indianapolis, as she rolled closer to decipher it.

—Parts of the colon have been removed, along with the appendix and all of the omentum, because of involvement also apparent in the drained abdominal fluid.

—Carboplatin and taxane are administered to all

participants in the stage III government trial she helps to administer. Starting with the second session, a blind two-thirds also receive a third drug (bevacizumab or Avastin) which has had good results with other cancers.

—Concern about perforated bowel reactions had worried the research group initially, but generally pertains to more advanced cases and the statistics are not yet in.

—She will e-mail a colleague at Sloan-Kettering for confirmation, but believes that other trials (in which chemo is administered directly into the abdomen) are no longer applicable if the surgery is suboptimal.

—At the start of the chemo sessions, every three weeks for six sessions, side effects should be minimal. Symptoms like nausea (threatening to someone five feet, seven inches and now down to 113 pounds) can be controlled by prescription drugs, and neuropathies in the hands and feet can be treated with vitamin B6. (I'm scribbling madly, but leaving blanks that must be filled in later by Don since I listen without hearing or hear without apprehending much of what Dr. Matei says.)

—Without chemo, women in my condition would probably live a few months; with it, maybe three years or, if luckier, three to five years.

I had come seeking competence and honesty, not wisdom and certainly not bland assurances. Given the power dynamics of cancer's medicalization—the authority draining away from the unknowing cancer patient into her knowing physician—I had been put off by the jocular tone of my surgeon who had responded to my last question (about the consequences of not pursuing further treatment) with the admonition that such a decision would make him "very angry." In contrast, Dr. Matei's answer hits home, for I realize that my daughters cannot possibly be ready to part with me in three or four months, that I could not possibly be ready to die in that brief span of time. Like so many people with cancer, I face a double bind: either lethal metastases or treatments with side effects worse than those produced thus far by the disease. Deciding to undergo chemotherapy makes death depart from my immediate neighborhood, if only for a sabbatical, as I enter a liminal zone—a betwixt and between bracketed by the surgery receding into the past and the chemo looming in the near future—without a clue about what exactly I should be thinking or feeling about either.

A woman, an immigrant, probably two decades younger than I: these features of Dr. Matei buoy me up. They could not possibly level the playing field between authoritative doctor and plaintive patient, but they might embolden me to ask for time-outs or explanations about the game plan. There was nothing to do but consent on the spot, to imprint on my brain that the second syllable of Dr. Matei's name rhymes with "gay," and to initial twenty-four pages describing the methods and risks of the government-sponsored research trial. After quick urine and blood tests, Don and I felt guilt and perplexity falling away on the hour-long car trip home from Indy. The decision has been made. No need to schlep to Boston or New York. There is a plan and, as my father relished intoning, "Without a plan, one cannot survive." Yet of course Daniela Matei—so young, so Romanian, and so forthright about how much

my cosmopolitan friend Ilinca Johnston chafed against her advice—
had mentioned neither the word "survival" nor the word "cure."
Wearing a short pleated skirt and loads of rings on sturdy fingers,
she gazed intently at me as she rehearsed rates and percentages of
remissions and recurrences, which was probably why Ilinca (whose
Paris doctors tiptoed around mortality) disliked precisely the candor
that drew me toward a youthful physician with bouncy brown curls
framing earnest brown eyes.

Still, our satisfaction at having found a truth-telling oncologist
in whom we could place our trust and at participating in a scientific
study that might benefit other women did not mask the disturbing
information she had conveyed. "That's terrible news, that the operation was not optimal, that so many organs were involved," one and
then another daughter fretted on the phone. The experts agree with
them about the importance of the quality of the debulking: "there is
absolutely nothing the doctor can influence, including choosing the
type of chemotherapy, that affects a woman's chance of surviving her
ovarian cancer as much as the quality of her initial surgery . . . Sadly,
however, only between 30 and 50 percent of the women with ovarian
cancer in any given geographic region will have optimal surgery."
I am now someone within the majority covered by that "Sadly."
Visible lesions, larger than one centimeter, had not been removed.
Needless to say, the probable impediment to optimal debulking must
have been the advanced state of my tumors, as the surgeon himself
intimated directly after the operation, rather than his incompetence
or attitude toward minimizing risk or, for that matter, his effort
to heed my final admonition. In any case, a suboptimal debulking
lowered my chances for survival.

The Online Ovarian Cancer National Alliance furnishes statistics pertinent to my case. "Approximately 80–85 percent of patients

with stage III ovarian cancer who are suboptimal (a large volume of residual tumor remains after surgery) will have a recurrence." Receiving this information, other women strengthen themselves by determining that "there was no reason why I could not be among the 15 percent that survived." Indeed, in *Ovarian Cancer* Conner and Langford assume about their readers, "you've probably been holding on to the hope that you would be one of the lucky women who does not recur." But in limbo-land the odds sound bad to me. Anxiety about the information conveyed by Dr. Matei on November 24 teetered against relief at committing to a plan with a trustworthy physician. Precisely this juxtaposition of worried apprehension and appreciation for a brief reprieve before chemo characterized the emotional seesaw of my moods after I signed up for a trial that sounded as hazardous as Franz Kafka's. Though I tried to stay in the present with all its blessings, jittery trepidation about the future threatened to permeate the waiting, even though waiting is what patient and impatient patients have to do.

Two weeks hence, would I find the chemotherapy as innocuous as the term "infusion" makes it sound? Infusion involves the act of pouring and changing a liquid, as in Jesus's transforming water into wine. By soaking or steeping, we infuse a cup of water with tea or dissolve soluble substances into other liquids. In early times, a priori ideas of divine grace were thought to be infused by God into the human mind or soul. Therefore the word "infusion" came to mean the pouring on of water in baptism, as opposed to complete immersion. Whether I would eventually judge the first session to be chemo or infusion, I would quickly discover my expectations overturned by a set of events that beleaguered me and threatened to erode a sense of equanimity already strained by the debulking operation. I kept on trying to strengthen the frayed filament of composure to which I had clung at the diagnosis and to which I had hoped to cling afterward, but it began to unravel.

Kafka's novel *The Trial*, but also his parable "In the Penal Colony," had been haunting me. The grisly short story was especially easy to translate into language pertinent to my ominous sense of the chemotherapy. *About to be attached to a remarkable piece of apparatus, the condemned woman tastes fear rising off her tongue as she finds herself led forward into a maze of equipment, but is assured that the machinery should go on working continuously for six hours or six days. If anything were to go wrong, it would only be a small matter that could then be set right at once by the uniformed technician.* So my variation begins. *Positioned on the bed, she gets attached to various IVs, ports, tubes, and monitoring devices. After each session the woman will learn on her body which sentence has been passed, and has no chance of putting up a defense.* In the perverse scenario replaying in my head, the torture has to be staged and restaged, for as long as it takes, since *guilty cells cannot be tolerated.* A needle penetrating the skin, an upside-down plastic bag, the beep beep beep of a box on an adjacent pole, the drip drip drip of venomous solutions, and then dreadful side effects—all would knock out the isolated victim until she no longer had the strength to protest or scream. *When Enlightenment comes at the end of treatment, she deciphers it with her suffering, for now she realizes that the fight against the disease has ended. What else is there for her to do but to give up on being damaged and get on with the practical and protracted business of dying?*

Allusions to Kafka's fable flit through accounts of chemotherapy, perhaps because of his description of a brutal apparatus comprised of needles recurrently piercing the skin of a condemned prisoner. As decreed by long-standing law and tradition, the tortured victim of "In the Penal Colony" is manacled to a bed while needles puncture and scar his body in a public forum administered by lesser authorities answerable to higher-ups. It takes quite a few hours for the penal writing machine to imprint its message on the uncomprehending prisoner's flesh. "In the Penal Colony" surfaces in Marilyn French's discussion of her doleful state after strenuous medical interventions. Her "misery and helplessness" resemble "the fault tattooed on one's body by acid-dripping needles that prick it as the sinner is turned around and around on a huge rotisserie." Similarly, Juliet Wittman likens the repetitive imprinting of her chemotherapy protocol to "the punishment machine Franz Kafka describes."

Quite a few cancer survivors believe that "Used in another context, on prisoners, say, chemo might be regarded as torture, not therapy." After a recurrence of ovarian cancer, the mother of TV journalist Betty Rollin protested against another prescribed bout of chemo: "I expected a death sentence. I didn't expect torture." In *The Wounded Storyteller*, a book about illness narratives, Arthur W. Frank notes that "chemotherapy fits with disturbing ease into Elaine Scarry's definition of torture as 'unmaking the world.'" Hyperbolic or melodramatic as it might sound, both chemotherapy and torture damage people; they produce an injurious effect on the human subject. Like chemotherapy, torture does not kill an individual outright but rather mimes or truncates murderous assaults that wear down and tear down the human being. A violation of the boundaries of the body and the self, according to Jean Améry, torture "transforms the person into flesh" and "while still alive . . . a prey of death," as does chemotherapy when patients suffer debilitating or dangerous repercussions. During the infliction of pain, Elaine Scarry explains, "the created world of thought and feeling, all the psychological and mental content that constitutes both one's self and one's world, and that gives rise to and is in turn made possible by language, ceases to exist."

But of course no oncologist is motivated by a malicious effort to exercise unchecked dominion over patients who, in turn, would never voluntarily sign up for torture. Especially those people dedicated to healthy diet and exercise regimes find the idea of injecting poisons into the body hateful. In chemotherapy the condemned person must stifle her aversion and enter into the process *for her own good*. This point has been made in a number of testimonials (about a variety of cancers and chemical treatments). One breast cancer survivor recounts lying in bed, thinking, "I was crazy to have *chosen* to do the treatments. I thought a lot about quitting and wondered what kinds of risks I would be taking if I stopped. I didn't stop; I was too scared of the alternative." Right before Diane Tempest received the diagnosis of stage III epithelial ovarian cancer, her daughter explains, she determined that "if the tumor was malignant, she would choose not to have chemotherapy." In her early fifties, the mother of this Mormon family soon felt she had to reverse her decision: "I told myself I would not let them poison me. But now I am afraid not to." After eleven months of chemotherapy, radiation, and various surgeries, she died at home, still in her early fifties. One husband of a woman who died of ovarian cancer felt that her death certificate "would have been more accurate" if it had stated "death due to chemical poisoning."

How can something bad—those toxins and their miserable side effects—be good for you? Cognitive dissonance takes over, the confusion of trying to hold two contradictory ideas in mind simultaneously. Perhaps a better analogy would be warfare, as Susan Sontag originally noted. For chemotherapy was a brainchild born of World War II, when mustard gas exhibited the "capacity to decimate white blood cells" and thus inspired scientists to deploy it strategically by targeting "*malignant* white cells." According to Elaine Scarry, "in war, the persons whose bodies are used in the confirmation process have given their consent over their most radical use of the human body while in torture no such consent is exercised."

War, which can be defended on ethical grounds, resembles chemotherapy because both set out to wreak massive injury (against other nations, against cancer cells), even if collateral damage may inadvertently be inflicted (on innocent civilians, on noncancerous cells). In the contest or battle between chemotherapy and cancer, in which there can be only one winner and one loser, the supporting army on the chemo side should be comprised of valiant volunteers dedicated to "a good war," for the foe takes as its goal nothing but extermination. Yet since I'm revolted by the destructive methods exploited by higher-ups (napalm, Agent Orange), I'm back in the seventies, wanting to burn my draft card. Or when I consider terrorist cells breeding fervent suicide bombers in too many impoverished and faraway lands, I'm in the present, uncertain that any measures (no matter how drastic) can be efficacious.

Dread draws a solid line around the contours of my self. Life outside the mark goes on as usual. Rigidly outlined, however, I am divided from its realities, now incomprehensible or irrelevant to me. Not wanting to advance into the chemo colony, I resemble autistic children who stare at stuffed animals or blocks without reaching out to play or who stand at the edge of the schoolyard unable to interact with other kids. Like the caring mother of an autistic child, I try to tell myself "social stories" to prepare for fearful events: reassuring accounts about smart doctors controlling side effects, about the supportive friends on whom I can count, about my luck at not having to go to work on a daily basis, about my determination only to endure the six sessions of one cycle of drugs. I have freely consented to the trial, but it threatens to change me and my body in unforeseen ways. I do not feel the disbelief, anger, numbness, shock, denial, guilt, and devastation all the brochures sent home with me from the hospital attribute to people diagnosed with cancer. Aversion splits me off from everyone else.

Not dread of cancer or death but rather dread of cancer treatments has me in its thrall. Throughout my life, I have feared doctors, hospitals, testing procedures, and just about everything related to better living through pharmaceutical chemistry. My intense alienation may have been one of multiple reactions against my mother, who prided herself on being a doctor's daughter and whose most prized social outings still consist of visits to her umpteen physicians. While my mother boasted of the innumerable medications prescribed by her internist, kidney specialist, eye and heart doctors, dentist, rheumatologist, and podiatrist, the only concession I had made to my general practitioner was to embark on a low cholesterol diet so as not to take one of the widely advertised drugs on the market. Now, however, I am facing the slow drip of carboplatin plus paclitaxel once every three weeks for six sessions, not to mention the possibility of the mysterious third drug. All the books concur on the effects of the first two: nausea and vomiting, fatigue, loss of appetite, numbness and tingling in extremities, hair loss, and diarrhea or constipation. A wimp and a coward, I find it hard to believe that I would freely go forward with what will not diminish so much as destroy my QOL, as the technical manuals term quality of life.

Why did trepidation about what I assumed would be the

inevitable failure of the trial (at least with respect to my particular case) consume me, when so many people recounted tales of miraculous cures and so many others apparently pursued even the most inauspicious methods with so much hope? How aberrant I felt, given the memoirists of cancer who respond to treatment as Barbara Rosenblum did: "being on chemotherapy gave me the sense that I would not have cancer as long as I was taking my injections and tablets. I became what is known as a 'chemo junkie.' " Marilyn French, who "never absorbed the fact that *no one survives metastasized esophageal cancer*," subjected herself to intensive chemotherapy and radiation, fully realizing that "simply to treat cancer means [physicians] must violate the primary tenet of their code: First, do no harm." A number of self-proclaimed survivors interviewed on YouTube, including the actress Kathy Bates, have recorded their optimism about fighting against and surviving ovarian cancer. Unlike such patients, I am convinced that chemotherapy will simply forestall the inevitable, while making me very sick indeed.

Because of the death of my friend Ilinca and because I have begun to consult the books piling up in my study, I know that "between 50–80% of patients with advanced ovarian cancer relapse after achieving a complete clinical response to regimens such as paclitaxel plus carboplatin, and most of these patients are incurable." Why should one submit to nausea and vomiting, fatigue and loss of appetite, numbness and tingling in extremities, hair loss and diarrhea or constipation when chances are they will only preface a recurrence? And even before a recurrence, under such fraught circumstances reading and writing might well be impossible, as would loving and teaching, mandating an existence inconceivable to me. My aversion to the toxicity of harmful drugs cannot be countered, as it is in many other forms of cancer, with faith in their success rates. Describing "the bizarre roller coaster" of chemotherapy on testicular cancer patients, Arthur W. Frank wonders about "the only real issue: would it be effective? Would I be one of the lucky 80 percent who come out alive?" Antithetically and fatalistically, I ask myself, would I be one of the majority of women worn down by an eighteen-week process that leads to humiliating and incapacitating side effects and then an incurable recurrence?

"Are you drinking enough water?" the girls kept on e-mailing daily. "There are options after chemotherapy." *A Guide to Survivorship for Women with Ovarian Cancer* confirms their judgment, explaining that treated ovarian cancer "goes into remission for a while and then returns, is re-treated, goes back into remission, and so on." But at some point the chemotherapy stops working: tumors metastasize in the liver or breast, bowel or brain, lung or bone. I've read the chapters on second-line and experimental treatments as well as their hideous consequences. Not a few people pursuing draconian procedures eventually feel the despair of Liz Tilberis: "With the bone marrow transplant I had endured the worst kind of assault, a frightening, tortuous experiment, and it had all been in vain." In later stages of ovarian cancer, carcinomatosis (the proliferation of tumors throughout the body) frequently causes ascites (fluid obstructing the diaphragm), bowel obstruction (requiring a PEG or percutaneous endoscopic gastrostomy tube to provide continuous drainage), abdominal blockage (requiring an NG or nastrogastric tube), lymphedema (fluid retention in the lymphatic system), kidney obstruction (requiring nephrostomy tubes or stents), fistulas (abscesses), dyspnea (difficulty in breathing), and malnutrition— all convincing oncology nurses that care after unsuccessful chemo should become palliative, though proactive doctors may resist such judgments. My inability to pronounce these arcane terms, like my need to look them up in the dictionary and translate them, contributes to what the manuals might call my dysphasia (speech impairment) and dysphoria (anxiety).

Toward the end of a terminal recurrence, I would be lost in space under the ever-present imminence of death, like Kahlo's sleeper, but not in a serene dream because tethered by plastic ropes to a hospital bed cluttered with invasive equipment. Before Deborah Rose Sills died of ovarian cancer, she lamented, *"treatment is really a pact with the devil."*

I peer at the miserable reproduction I have of Kahlo's painting *The Dream* which is sometimes called *The Sleep* or *The Bed*. Google Images blows it up so I can perceive the electrical wires connecting the sticks of dynamite lodged inside the skeleton's limbs, threatening to explode and break every joint, bone, appendage of the remains of the corpse. This ammunition-bearer must reflect Kahlo's dire condition after a terrible accident in her youth. Or does he—he does look male to me—manifest her anxieties about a destructive masculinity, a manhood hardwired for violence? A suicide bomber, the figure of death might set off a series of blasts that will surely smash into smithereens the fleshly sleeper on the lower bunk. Horizontal on their double-decker, the recumbent figures could be allegories of the embodied present and the skeletal future, ephemeral being and the bare bones to which it will be reduced. Given the tranquility of the dreamer below, cradled within her quilt and the green vines growing out of it, I want to defuse the metal connectors in the skeleton, remove the dynamite, or dislodge the fraught upper canopy from the lower bed, float it away in a Chagall windstorm. Though larger than Kahlo, the skeleton looks lightweight, precariously posed on his side, flimsy enough to topple off the top bunk. How to decouple the violence of death, the wired skeleton, from the repose of the fleshly sleeper beneath her quilt? How to keep alive the dream of peace when threatened by incessant and destructive blows?

Life at any price does not seem a meaningful goal, a conviction that had struck me when I glimpsed the twisted and bandaged catatonics parked, glassy-eyed, in wheelchairs along the corridors of my mother's Health Pavilion. Did the presence of these ancient subterraneans (as the attendants call them) weaken my resolve to creep into old age, to do whatever it takes to prolong existence, or was the state of ovarian cancer treatment or the cancer itself shedding seeds of disbelief—that it's better to sleep and even to dream in death than to be kept alive in the tormented body or the unhinged mind? Remembering my first entranced reading of John Keats, I experience myself falling half in love with easeful death as an alternative to the needles and tubes, catheters and leakages, wounds and stinks, ramblings and gibberings of profoundly ill people, their sickening and embarrassing incapacities; even more as a shelter from the dreadful tax levied on caregivers of those sickened and embarrassed dependents. Who does not entertain the flickering impulse to snip life hanging by a thread?

As the weather gets colder and President-elect Obama chooses Hilary Clinton for his secretary of state, his energetic period of transition gets eclipsed in my mind by confusion about wildly veering feelings. Unlike the god of doors, Janus, who impassively looks forward and backward, I tend to wait in limbo-land wearing two successive expressions: a frowning grimace, as I try to glimpse a fearful future, and an attempt at a serene smile, registering the treasured

ephemerality of the here and now in which I memorize those reassuring "social stories." Though the bathroom remains a torture
chamber, all other symptoms from the debulking—fatigue, immobility, weakness, twinges, bloating, dry mouth, a pervasive chill—
have eased during the last week of November, the first week of
December. Despite lowering temperatures outside and huge heaps
of dead leaves filling every conceivable space around the house, I
walk around the woodpile to pick up kindling, negotiate the stairs
to my study without stopping to rest, even go out once to eat with
friends.

Plucked out of ordinary existence, I make an effort to counter dread by cherishing a prelapsarian interlude before the fall into
chemo, giving me a chance to consider my interior state. That I
have the freedom to ponder my reactions has everything to do
with the generosity of the faculty and administrators in the university at which I have taught for more than thirty-five years. All
my responsibilities toward the end of this fall semester have been
divvied up among colleagues now teaching the remaining sessions
of my graduate class and serving on the numerous committees I
ordinarily attend for purposes of recruitment, fundraising, diversity,
interdisciplinary humanities facilities, and faculty governance. A
combination of chairs and deans has determined to keep me on the
English Department's payroll throughout the spring semester since
I will continue working with graduate students at the dissertation
stage, an act of generosity for which I am unprepared. With news
stories about layoffs and plant closings and massive unemployment
proliferating, such unusual material benefits contribute to my ability
to reflect on the oddity of a psychic life of lows and highs, downs
and ups, of teetering between angst about the upcoming treatments
and appreciation for the recess before poisoning.

Not an isolated instance, the relief that flooded me upon first contemplating the diagnosis intermittently revisited me in the two weeks before the start of chemotherapy. Many mothers, I suspect, will understand the grounds of my convoluted but taut sense of the rightness of my fate: namely, that it was I and not my daughters who had to deal with this horrible condition. Of course I worried over the sort of reaction experienced by Terry Tempest Williams: "I look at Mother and I see myself," she writes during her period of caretaking; or worse: "A person with cancer dies in increments, and a part of you slowly dies with them." But my own logic (or illogic) clings to and reeks of magical thinking: "I have cancer so my girls will not." I know too many young women with various forms of cancer—some in remission, some dead—not to give thanks that my daughters are healthy. "Who can contemplate the death of a child, their own or anybody else's . . . ?" Nancy Mairs asks. "It appalls in a way no other death can do because it violates the natural order." As I realize from the tragic experience of friends and from fiction and film, the death of a child inflicts a never-ceasing hurt, hurling its parents into the very pitch of grief: "No worst, there is none." I have had a blessed life; let Molly and Simone have theirs, I prayed, while I also considered the luck of my second marriage, the sustained care I knew I could count on receiving from my husband.

After I survived a divorce and Don survived the illness and death of his wife, after our camaraderie ripened into a staunch passion, we decided to live together and bought a house in the countryside. With its several acres shielding us from neighbors, the house's back windows look out on a wooded ravine. Its front windows frame what we dubbed "the circle of beauty," a plot of land within a circular driveway that contains lilac bushes as well as two imposing evergreens, pines sixty feet high that must be half a century old and

whose wingspans interweave their weighty lower branches. Neither
Don nor I could have afforded such a place independently or at any
earlier stage in our careers. While we weeded hostas and lilies eaten
by the roaming deer, it seemed to us a pastoral idyll juxtaposed to
Don's lively youth in Chicago, mine in New York City. The day-
dreams of a troubled urban adolescent in a novel by Peter Cameron
revolve around finding dream houses in the Midwest that resemble
ours: "Made of stone, real stones that aren't identical, with screened
porches and birdbaths in the front yards, front yards with big old
trees rising above the house, trees that might be struck by lightning
during a thunderstorm and collapse upon the house, but probably
not." In our bucolic retreat, Don and I never had to struggle against
the physical disabilities or psychological disorders that plague Nancy
Mairs as well as some of my students. Nor for the most part did
my girls, who have not yet lived long enough to enjoy many of the
opportunities I have relished. Infinitely better me than them: this
was my overwhelming conviction. Or to more vengeful powers, I
might mutter, "Take me and let them go."

Intermittent composure was real, then, and sustained by my
close friends. Being a somewhat capricious person, I need gritty
realism from some, casual insouciance from others. During her
visits in these days, Mary Jo engages matters of mortality that have
punctuated some three decades of our evolving and eccentric conversations. Jo, having retired from teaching American Catholic history, possesses a contemplative soul, prays two hours every morning,
and keeps diabetes, high cholesterol, and high blood pressure at bay
with rigorous exercise and diet management. Given her absorption
with anticipation and upkeep, many of our wayward discussions
had invariably devolved upon dying and death, our own. No later
idea trumped Jo's first plan (decades before my diagnosis) which

continues to intrigue me: we trek to the northern tip of Alaska to embark on an ice floe with a large bottle of scotch. With the nicely aged liquor, she reasons, we'd never feel the chill of the polar expiation, no less of death itself. Now, with the exception of my lawyer, who immediately provided the legal papers the hospital will need not to continue my life under intolerable circumstances, no one else would confront end-of-life issues, as if naming them could make them not simply conceivable but inevitable, which of course they were and are for each and every one of us. It was a great relief to me that Jo linked up with Bloomington's hospice and never once shied away from discussing how we might manage the breakdown of my body and the management of pain.

"I've got Thanksgiving under control": to Don's amusement, these are the words Jo trumpeted into the phone, as she orchestrated the usual suspects invited to my annual Thanksgiving celebration, and in the process affirmed the pleasures I continue to receive from my extended family. Joining Simone and Molly with her husband, Kieran, and their two-year-old, Elliot, close friends take upon themselves designated roles in the treatments to come. Jayne, highly sarcastic about her public relations job, sets out to amuse me through stories and websites and a nicely jaundiced perspective on the absurd situations in which we will continually find ourselves. Earnest and efficient Jan and Jon promise to program the iPhone Don has given me for my birthday. To accompany their culinary contributions and with a bit of kibitzing from me, Molly produces the turkey and stuffing that await the usual "turkey parade," strutted to the strict rhythms of a blaring Baroque trumpet recording, so everything begins to seem all right with the world.

My ex-husband lightens our load by transporting my mother in a portable wheelchair so we can give thanks for her recent recovery.

After a heart attack and an operation that placed two stents in her heart, landing my mother in the Health Pavilion, she became convinced that a replica of her room existed in the basement, complete with her name on the door. There were children coloring the privacy curtain near her bed every night, she explained, but the management was changing hands. Just a few days before the holiday, she urged me to come to a bell-ringing concert—she had rehearsed for weeks and admired the conductor—by explaining that "all the other parents" were attending. Still, she seems saner and sounder in her own private room, reading aloud to a neighbor the account of her life that she self-published and posing in her wheelchair with Senior Olympics gold medals slung around her neck. (I recall Molly laughing with Kieran, "That's why we call the Health Pavilion 'the last resort,' Mom.") My mother partakes of the feast, while informing everyone that she has been through what I am going through and "it's not that bad." Presumably she believes that I have had a hysterectomy. I utter not a word of demurral as I determine not to dwell on the word "mother" inside the word "chemotherapy."

Around the T formed by the two tables, everyone else gets a bit tipsy, high on the wine but also the glee that we have pulled off this annual event, despite my incapacities. Notwithstanding my wayward mother, overwhelming joy becomes the emotion each guest sparks in me, even with respect to her. Either her mental confusion or her anger at being abandoned—and she *has* been abandoned, since I used to visit her several times every week—cause me to absent myself in felicity for a while. Raising a glass of wine, I "bless us, each and every one," and make my way out of the noisy dining room, back to the quilt on the living room sofa. There, in one of those precious pockets of stillness that a crowded party can contain, I study with little Elliot his cherished Richard Scarry book,

a pictorial encyclopedia of every conceivable conveyance, construction tool, foodstuff, and critter imaginable. When I sit down on the
floor beside him, the slow-motion brought about by concentrating
on a delightful moment manages to thin or smudge the marker
outlining my boundaries.

While I admire my grandson's thick, dark eyelashes (the sort
that people used to say were wasted on boys), we stop at a page with
a picture previously under dispute. Elliot points to a bowl containing
pink worms and says, "Pasta?" I recall that his father had previously corrected this interpretation, insisting fairly emphatically that
it was a bowl of ground beef, and then I begin savoring the illicit
pleasures of grandparenting. "Pasta in tomato sauce," I grin, nod-
ding in assent. He pauses, a conscientious child with a phenomenal
memory. "Pasta and tomato and ground grief too," he laughs, hop-
ping up and down, beginning to make a song that we start chanting
over and over again, as I marvel at the patent pleasure Elliot finds in
language and at the beneficence of grief ground up into such a fine
powder that it can be blown away by a song and a dance.

But it is the person who washes all the dishes and sweeps up
after the guests leave who fills me with exaltation, especially when
I recall watching Don putting on his socks that very morning, and
pretty much any other. Often an atmosphere of pathos descends
as he sits with both feet on the floor, both socks in one hand. Can
the effort be made, he must be brooding. Can he will the upper
body to bend over, the foot to come up, the hands to reach down,
and of course they do, one foot at a time, both arms at a time, but
with a pause between each sock as if to mark the effort the eighty-
one-year-old frame must put into a process that will only lead to
another laborious task of struggling into often painful shoes. When
I think of the strain that the cancer and its treatments will place on

him—of the multiple hour-long trips to Indianapolis and of care-taking in general—I worry about its toll. As the terrorist attacks on Mumbai fill the television screen, I realize how encapsulated I am within a network of care that has removed me almost entirely from the outside world. I suspect that chemotherapy will further contract my sphere, but gratitude fills my days of recuperation after Thanksgiving when I receive e-mails, letters, and cards from many former students and colleagues scattered around the country.

Quickly, however, I discover that the shock of the unexpected will punctuate my future days and ways, for the least feared of events casts me into a pit of exhaustion and depression, admonishing me now to expect the unexpected from any medical contact. Scheduled halfway through the pre-chemo period of reprieve, the trip back to the Simon Cancer Center should be, if not a lark, at least a blip on our radar screen since the standard chest X-ray, EKG, and CT scan take only a few minutes each. I have read about how terrify-ing these "machines with penetrating calibrating vision" can be to other patients, when they become "the ultimate arbiters of truth," but I am not hopeful about results and thus dispassionate about the assessments of the machines. Yet the moment I set foot in the hospi-tal, I am chilled and anxious. The proper papers don't seem to have been forwarded to the proper authorities. There remain questions about the order of these various procedures. One entire side of the ground floor of the sterile new building consists of nothing but glass and I feel the frigid air infiltrating all the waiting areas.

And of course mostly we wait and wait and wait first in the

chest X-ray waiting area, then in the EKG waiting area, then in the CT scan waiting area. There are many apparently poor people wearing mouth-and-nose masks, or with oxygen tubes and portable tanks, or without teeth, either too fat or so thin they look shrunken and breakable. They, too, wait. I will wait and turn and bend and lean and breathe and hold my breath on the tables and gurneys for the procedures as well. "The patience required to be a patient demands of those who have less time (both because they may not live long and because being ill is time-consuming) to spend it in waiting: waiting for test results; waiting to see the doctor; waiting for the next appointment; waiting for the medication to work; waiting for the painkiller to kick in." The preparation for the CT unexpectedly turns out to be horrifically invasive. Shivering in my winter coat as I move from one waiting area to another, I clasp a paper bag with four large vials of what looks to be red Kool-Aid which must be drunk every half hour starting at 12:30. By two o'clock, I find myself running repeatedly to the bathroom with ever more explosive results. Perhaps the amount of the Kool-Aid has been calibrated for overweight Hoosiers, I worry.

I fear that I will not be able to stay on the CT stretcher, keeping my hands up clinging to an iron bar hanging above me, long enough to be infused through the veins with one dye and then another (that produces the sensation of "having to pee") without soiling myself, the linens on the stretcher, the massive machine itself. As I am rolled halfway into the tube so the machine can take pictures of my abdomen and groin, as the machine informs me (in a mechanical woman's voice) first to hold my breath and then to breathe, again to hold, again to breathe, I contemplate the irony of this unexpected resolution to the recurrent constipation inaugurated by the surgery or postoperative drugs. "Take an Imodium," the attendant advises, little foreseeing the stops-and-starts at gas stations on the way home, or the next day, when wiped out by the rhythms of too many trips to the toilet I sleep away one of my precious prelapsarian mornings.

But even before the next day, intimations of all that could and would go wrong with every trip to the hospital become all too evident. Breathless with anxiety, Dr. Matei phones as soon as we walk in the door of our house: "The radiologist is very concerned about a buildup of fluids in the lower part of the abdomen. Do you have any fever or back pains? Here are my numbers. Should they eventuate, you must phone." Exactly where was this "buildup of fluids" and what does it portend? While I am worrying about my oncologist's reference to future scans, my brother makes one of his cheery phone calls. Undertaken as a familial duty, his upbeat and rushed shtick revolves around staving off any intimation of what ovarian cancer means and hanging up as soon as possible.

"Just standard EKG, X-ray, and CT tests," I explain.

"Correct!" he asserts. I never have understood his propensity for this particular verbal tic, which I find distracting.

"But the stuff they make you drink for the CT made me sick."

"Barium! Correct! Lets them see inside."

Though I was explicitly told that the fluid did not consist of barium, I couldn't remember the name of its arcane compound so I simply said, "The radiologist found a fluid collection."

"GREAT," my brother enthused. "A sign of healing."

In every family, there must be those who find it easier to spin their way toward the most optimistic of scenarios, instead of confronting the unpredictable course of any individual's condition. My brother's bravado masks a barely concealed disquietude about his kid sister.

After that phone call, I have a nightmare. Crates of small pellets of gas and huge gas canisters arrive in heavy covered trucks with uniformed attendants informing me that the chemotherapy has been moved up two days, hastened by the fluid deposit near the back of the bowel. On each and every pellet and canister, in block Gothic letters, the words "Zyklon B" have been stamped. Through a loudspeaker, a heavily accented voice orders all the bald or shaved women in Chelmo to line up. Chelmo, chemo: my dream mind has conflated my future treatment with the horrors of the concentration camps. As the offspring of German-Jewish immigrants, I know that such facile analogies should be avoided or judged immoral. But the stunned passivity of my days has brought back one passage in Primo Levi's *Survival in Auschwitz*, about the inmates whose "wisdom lay in 'not trying to understand,' not imagining the future, not tormenting ourselves as to how and when it would be over; not asking others or ourselves any questions."

Does history stop for the cancer patient, as it did for the prisoners of concentration camps? "Cancer is not a concentration camp," Siddhartha Mukherjee cautions, "but it shares the quality of annihilation": "it negates the possibility of life outside and beyond itself; it subsumes all living. The daily life of a patient becomes so intensely preoccupied with his or her illness that the world fades away. Every last morsel of energy is spent tending the disease."

One Sunday afternoon, I receive a visit from my dear colleagues Mary and Andrew, whose two children—my godchildren—bake a challah for me and decorate get-well cards with plastic moving eyeballs. Mary, with her boyish cap of hair setting off the delicate bones of her face, and Andrew, with his rougher good looks, have produced two delightfully creative and (oddly for me as their god-mother) perfectly Aryan-looking offspring, now in the lovely levity of latency—eight and ten years old or (it is hard to keep up) nine and eleven. Near a brightly burning fire in which the kids roast marsh-mallows, Mary companionably knits and we all gossip or urge each other to read some especially engaging novel. Later Andrew e-mails me a letter that speaks about his awareness of the grotesque cancer salon. First he quotes a passage from one of Virginia Woolf's essays:

> There is a virgin forest in each; a snow field where even the print of birds' feet is unknown. Here we go alone and like it better so. Always to have sympathy, always to be accompanied, always to be understood would be intolerable.

Andrew then adds that reading these words has made him imagine "that you must be feeling both more intensely alone with this illness inside you and also more intensely with others around you, Don of course but also all those people visiting, writing, bring-ing you meal after meal, kids, grandkids, friends, colleagues . . . I think I would feel both more lonely and more crowded." Yes, I do feel more lonely in the forest of myself and more crowded in the cancer salon. Woolf's snowy field where "we go alone" reminds me of her injunction at the end of *A Room of One's Own* that there is "no arm to cling to." How "intolerable" it feels always to be given sym-pathy, always to be accompanied and presumed to be understood.

Andrew's note helps me struggle out of derisive mockery and self-mockery into a weird sort of stoicism that I need to cultivate by and for myself. If it remains impossible to control my meals and my visitors, a measure of quiet self-possession might be attainable. A

solution comes into focus and may be within my grasp. The passage
Andrew quoted by Virginia Woolf comes from her odd essay "On
Being Ill," which she originally published in 1926. Directly after it,
she explains that invalids "become deserters" in contrast to those in
health who "march to battle":

> We float with the sticks on the stream; helter-skelter with the
> dead leaves on the lawn, irresponsible and disinterested and
> able, perhaps for the first time for years, to look around, to
> look up—to look, for example, at the sky.

Again I am reminded of the conclusion of *A Room of One's Own* in
which women are admonished to look past all the rules and regula-
tions framed about them by the authorities of the past, and instead
to perceive the contours of the sky from their own perspective. The
paradox of meeting reality's most obdurate and inordinate demands
with dignity and in one's own singular person, while becoming
"irresponsible and disinterested": Woolf's words return me to the
teachings of the ancient philosopher Seneca.

What good can anger or fear, self-pity or dread achieve, once
it becomes clear that disaster surrounds us and those we cherish
all the time, that there remains no place exempt from its malice?
It was a lesson I had learned as a child growing up with refugee
parents. Uprooted and impoverished, my father and mother perpetually mourned the deaths of their relatives and of their prior
lives in Germany. According to Seneca, "Fortune gives us nothing
which we can really own" because "We live in the middle of things
which have all been destined to die." Thus my parents learned that
they did not really "own" their parents and cousins and grandpar-
ents, their citizenship and rights to existence. For this reason, but

centuries before the Holocaust, Seneca declared that "No yoke is so grievous as not to hurt him who struggles against it more than him who yields to it: the only way to alleviate great evils is to endure them and to submit to do what they compel." One should surrender to, rather than fight against, the inevitable. One must submit by bowing to necessity, for the struggles of a wild animal "only pull the noose by which it is caught tighter." Tugging in the wrong direction, a bridled or harnessed horse, a dog on a leash can get hurt or strangled.

I equivocate about Seneca's judgment with regard to my parents, for it was their will to resist Hitler and to struggle against the tightening Nazi noose that made possible for them a new, albeit diminished and haunted life in America. But relinquishing optimism about my particular case of advanced ovarian cancer and of the outcome of its treatments could free me not to hurt myself further. Quietude might be achieved by meditation, especially by meditating on or anticipating the mortality decreed by the diagnosis. And isn't the later death promised by chemotherapy preferable to a sooner death? What might it mean to pull toward the fearful therapies that threaten to hurt me so profoundly, even without any faith in their ultimate efficacy? The leash was about to be fastened around my neck. How I accepted it would depend on me. My fingers on the laptop's keyboard began taking me to websites on how to twist scarves into turbans and cowls. Maybe with some dexterity and training I could begin impersonating those fundamentalist Islamic and Jewish women against whom I had generally railed and from whose resolute habits of mind, I now suspected, I might possibly have something to learn.

With a mantra or meditation serving as a prayer practice, might it be possible to bypass anxiety altogether, throw it off? It is of course a traditional Buddhist aspiration: to watch and interpret our feelings, to interrupt the indulging of our emotions, "to catch the emotional reaction and drop the story lines." Only then, Pema Chödrön explains in a book given to me by Mary Jo, do "we feel the bodily sensation completely." Is it true that "a life-threatening injury or disease makes Buddhists of us all"? The Buddha's quest, after all, was motivated by a need to deal with the fact of suffering in the world. Perhaps I could feel all the fears about cancer treatments but forget the libretto, the specificity of the events that fueled them. Perhaps feeling the fear intensely would be cathartic, would cause it to release its grip. As a narrative junkie, I find it hard to believe, but nevertheless tempting, even inspiring. I studied underlined passages in the dog-eared pages of Pema Chödrön's *The Places that Scare You* while being driven to the hospital's infusion facility for the first chemotherapy on December 11, 2008. And yet upon arrival, the Shakespearean stage direction *"Enter, fleeing"* echoed like a refrain in my head.

What a relief that not one side effect accompanied the first session. Within a commodious room furnished with leather recliners partly screened by sliding opaque screens that formed airy cubbies across from curving windows, it was possible to look beyond a fake fireplace decorated with Christmas stockings in the center and out the windows, without being seen by anyone except a solicitous nurse. With a mantra in mind and, should it fail, all my toys in place—iPhone, laptop, knitting, novel—there was no need to turn on the adjacent flat-screen TV, with earphones thoughtfully supplied. It seemed churlish to complain about the day-long treatment: no allergic reaction, no immediate nausea. Dr. Matei, still concerned about abdominal fluid apparent on the CT scan, prescribed a repeated bout with the red Kool-Aid in the near future (with half the usual amount). In the days following, I could handle the fatigue as well as diarrhea or constipation and hair loss, I determined, for the upcoming holidays would bring the girls home, a tree into the living room, a menorah on the kitchen countertop, and all the festivities we could summon to celebrate our still being together.

Despite subsequent fatigue, diarrhea, constipation, and hair loss, I would try to make the holidays festive. I thought of Terry Tempest Williams's caretaking—"I look at Mother and I see myself"—and of Betty Rollin's insight: "Disease may score a direct hit on only one member of a family, but shrapnel tears the flesh of the others." Doris Brett, a clinical psychologist who dealt with a recurrence of stage I ovarian cancer, puts it best for me: "One of the cruelest aspects of illness is the way you become the unwitting cause of suffering to people you love most dearly." My heart went out to my daughters, so I would put on makeup, earrings, a sufficiency of layers to look fatter, and comb my hair to hide the thinning spots. In the days following the first chemo, I resolved to stock up on the cereals, crackers, and other staples they would want in the house, including the ingredients that my son-in-law Kieran would need for his fragrant Christmas curry and that my stepdaughter Julie would need for her ornately decorated Christmas cookies. But had I exulted too soon about the lack of side effects, I worried when it dawned on me to consult Dr. Matei about constipation.

Four days after the first drip, an instantaneous response from my oncologist informed me that I "must take immediately steps" with "Mag Citrate (green bottle)." "Worked immediately, thanks,"

I briskly e-mailed back with relief. But the next day, when my husband and I set out to do some grocery shopping, I find myself in a miserable quagmire. The neighborhood supermarket has been recently renovated, blown up as if with a huge hydraulic pump, into what looks to be a humongous multiplex, so I have miles to go between the fresh vegetables and the fish, the cheese and the bread. The lettuce and avocados, asparagus and beets start glistening with a sinister aura. I note that all the energetic people pushing carts, young and old, are not desperately seeking a stray chair or bench on which to rest. "The physical world is altered for the ill person," the philosopher Havi Carel muses. "Distances increase, hills become mountains and stairs become obstacles rather than passageways." At Kroger's, I am taught by chemo the lesson she learned from sickness: "My illness is stronger than my body, stronger than my will." The public space induces agoraphobia. I will become "nervous about leaving the house and going to unknown territory."

I can barely put one foot in front of the other as I choose scallions and tomatoes, and then waves of cramps shoot through me, and of course I have no idea where the restrooms are located. Will I make it? Might it be better to sit down on the floor and simply clench up? Surely, though, I would look like some sort of nut. I can't bear the thought of soiling myself, but have no idea what else to do. The vulnerability of the ill in public places comes home to me. I do not belong in this normal space. I am disabled, deficient, unable to predict what will incapacitate me in a second and turn me into a shivering refugee among the healthy hordes. The cancer or the chemo's effect on the cancer drags me through the supermarket. The cancer or the chemo takes the upper hand. I am merely its battered envelope, a conveyance of crap upon which many writers have sermonized or snickered in a series of distant and not-so-distant meditations worthy of a short detour from the scene in Kroger's since they surely inflected my experience there.

Excrement, the inert deposit of a body that will also ultimately be dumped or incinerated like waste, has long exemplified filthy and sinful corruption. Worse yet, it "raises ideas of death, putrescence, and dissolution." In Dante's *Inferno*, flatterers, plunged in a ditch, flounder in feces poured from human privies. Still, often in a comic mode, famous thinkers have mocked the spiritual or aesthetic aspirations of human beings bound to fail since we are all mired in the loam of dung. From Rabelais to Bakhtin and Philip Roth, creative and critical authors have dwelled on the down-to-earth, carnival humor of "foul play," though shit tends to exude not from them but from those they observe at a remove. Samuel Beckett's characters exhibit some of the sadistic, mercenary, and exhibitionist behaviors Sigmund Freud assigned to the anal drive. Beckett's Lucky struts "the hard stool," stuttering about "Acacacademy," while Beckett's Krapp plays with his "spools" and his Molloy bends over a heap of muck, seeking to disgust himself with eating.

I have looked through the works of women writers, especially of so-called illness narratives and cancer memoirs, but cannot come up with anyone who goes beyond vague mentions of "plumbing problems" to deal with the defections of the body through defecation, though almost all accounts of chemotherapy mention diarrhea and constipation.

Is this reticence a reaction against the age-old identification of women with waste that dates back to the time of the church father Tertullian, who defined woman as a "temple built over a sewer"? In the tenth century, Odon, the abbot of Cluny, purportedly exclaimed, "If men but saw what is beneath the skin, the sight of women would nauseate them. When we cannot bring ourselves to touch with our finger a spit, phlegm, or a trace of dung, how can we desire to embrace that bag of filth?" Possibly because of monthly menstruation or vaginal discharge or lactation, the female body in the West has recurrently been imagined as a seeping, secreting viscosity. Throughout the history of civilization, "accusations of dirtiness have been consistently leveled at women, with men devoted to scrubbing out yucky female contamination, often armed with powerful detergents in the form of rituals, taboos, and religion (with its numerous purity rites)."

Maybe the ancient connection between females and filth explains why women rarely bring up the topic. Since for centuries theologians and philosophers contrasted embodied females to disembodied males, women writers tend to eschew a subject that might just deny them incorporeal transcendence or spiritual stature. Not apparently troubled by the status of women, the psychoanalyst Dominique Laporte nevertheless wants to break the taboo against scatology and exonerate shit by pinning its bad reputation on capitalism, as would any self-respecting Continental theorist. To detonate or derail embarrassment about excrement, Laporte asks, "Who will write the history of Saint Jerome, advisor to the ladies of Rome from 382 to 385, who warned against the practice of smearing one's face with shit to preserve a youthful complexion?" Not me, I know. Squeamish, I rarely discuss bowel issues aloud, or even hint at them. My friends would laugh or fret or research solutions, and I would be ashamed of myself. Despite my inbred reticence, I forge ahead with this writing by keeping in mind a purported comment of Roland Barthes: "when written," Barthes once remarked, "shit does not smell." But why am I resorting to academic quoting of academic quoting here? This long-winded digression is, after all, easier to sustain than a description of my fretful, then fraught quandary inside Kroger's.

Literature, of course, has contributed to the association of women (and Jews and the poor and foreigners) with the stinky contents of the latrine. Does the connection between vilified women and material waste derive from Augustine's justly famous insight—that we are born "between feces and urine"? Interior bodily cavities evoke more pollution anxieties than external organs, psychologists tell us in their discussions of "the taboo on the apertures."

When the modern poet William Butler Yeats imagined a bag lady talking back to bishops like Augustine, he reached for a subversive insight into what it means to be born "between feces and urine." Yeats's Crazy Jane responds to the traditional dichotomy between the "heavenly mansion" of the soul and the "foul sty" of the body by refuting it: "Love has pitched his mansion in / The place of excrement." After being conceived between the urethra and the anus, we come into the world with the piss and poop of our crowning mothers. Often, apparently, we leave for the hereafter with piss and poop in our pants. Actually, it turns out, most of this fascinating mini-cultural history ends up having little to do with my dilemma in Kroger's. More to the point (and completely unrelated to gender) is Mark Doty's observation upon caring for a beloved partner stricken with AIDS. "Like death," Doty explains, "excrement is the body's undeniable assertion: *you will deal with me before all else, you will have no other priorities before me.*"

Between the wine racks and the shelves of the deli, the sewer begins backing up with shaking knees, a light sweat, and a stomach- or backache before cramping begins. A rushed trip to the lavatory— miles away beyond the checkout lanes—brings massive explosions. Certainly this is not the place or time to fulminate about public bathrooms with their latchless doors, empty toilet paper dispensers, and unflushable or eternally flushing toilets. I know that I must sit in the car while Don brings packages out and we make our way home where, I surmise, there might be a box of baby wipes. The humiliations of urinary incontinence can be hidden with panty liners and even diapers, but the stink and filth of shit spills out to splash me with self-loathing, a numb sense of my own stained, sullied being.

Of course the next week it is no better coping with constipation. Not unlike the constipated figures I could conjure—John Osborne's obstructed Luther and miserably impacted Henry James—I resemble nothing so much as a blocked crypt. No matter how I strain on the toilet, bracing my legs, holding my breath, pushing—nothing happens. Walking up and down the aisles at the drugstore, I am trying to deal with the nausea of being clamped or locked up. Just think of yourself filling up with whatever you call it in your family and the pressure weighing your consciousness "down there" all the time so there is really nothing else to feel except extreme impatience for that blessed moment when it does finally descend and you praise the Lord, knowing that whatever gods exist could not give a damn about your stool and that there are children and parents, as well as American soldiers, dying in Iraq or Afghanistan. Exactly how diminished has my field of vision become? It feels vulgar to dwell on such matters, but the unrelieved pressure whittles away at consciousness until one realizes the truth of Don's insight while nursing his first wife: not exactly the selfishness of the sick but rather the selfishness of sickness which leaches consideration, perspective, and humor, making the sick selfish. The misery of constipation seems matched only by the horror of diarrhea, and both spell the effects— supremely embarrassing but all-absorbing in their discomfort—of the debulking operation and also of chemo's side effects thus far.

Uncontrollable intestines have been the worst punishment visited upon nefarious villains, from biblical times on. According to

Luke's gospel, Judas the betrayer had been possessed by Satan before
he sold out Jesus and witnessed the explosion of his own innards:
"falling headlong, he burst open in the middle and all his bowels gushed out." In my book about Judas I had reprinted medieval
psalters and paintings depicting Judas with his abdomen slit open,
his intestines tangled and dangling out over his midriff. Reading
a book about Frida Kahlo, I am astonished to discover Judas in
her painting *The Dream*: "Her skeleton is made of papier mâché
rather than bones and is a distinct product of Mexican folk culture.
Judas figures, based on the composite Catholicism of Mexico, were
exploded on the Saturday before Easter, their bursting bodies recalling the violent suicide of Christ's betrayer."

Seeing Judas on the upper bunk requires reassessing a painting
that now seems connected to my earlier scholarship. In the gospels, Judas does not explode *and then* commit suicide or vice versa.
In Matthew, he repents the error of his ways and commits suicide
by hanging himself, whereas in Luke he explodes, unregenerate.
Which is worse? Many communities conflated the two versions of
the traitor's demise since Judas deserved the very worst fate imaginable. In their depictions, Judas hangs himself from a tree while
his bowels explode: the patron, the icon of brute despair. Not the
tranquil sleeper in the lower bunk of *The Dream*, I have devolved
into a descendant of the figure of death on the upper shelf or his
mail-order consort.

Explosive, my body has become an excremental and execrable
traitor. My offense is rank; filth has fouled my nest. There is a reason why a sinkhole widens behind my house in the backyard, or
so I decide as I gaze from a window at the gaping breach in the
patio during the aftermath of what I now definitively judge to be
not the first "infusion" but instead the first chemo. In April, the

construction workers will have to smash concrete blocks, dislodge the birdbath, uproot the myrtle. If our bodies are indeed ourselves, my self shames me with its interminable or un-voidable waste.

Kahlo, much more beautiful than I ever was, has her thick hair and her famous eyebrows on display as she sleeps unmolested in the pristine lower bunk. Hooked up to detonators, Judas the bridegroom offers his bouquet of flowers in a salute. He seems to be grinning not at her but at me, as if to say, *"Vale, puella!"* She may be dreaming him, but he addresses me: "You are in for it now, sweetie, no question."

· 5 ·

DRAINED AND BAGGED

BODY ATTACHMENTS: the phrase haunts my sleep. It could refer to something as simple as earrings or nose studs attached *to* the body. Or it might signify the attachments *of* the body to food, to sex, or to its own well-being, its integrity. But the attachments *on* and *in* my body alienate me from desire and from the body itself. Rather, they act like a legal attachment, seizing my body to force some sort of compliance from me; or like a legal writ of bodily attachment, an order issued by courts directing authorities to round up people guilty of contempt—disreputable culprits, despicable bodies.

Is it still particularly difficult for women to overcome inbred modesty and express distressing truths about those parts of the anatomy most hidden and reviled as dirty, obscene, or sinful? Or do the inhibitions of men as well as women stem from a party line about which discourses on disability have been deemed politically acceptable? We read so many recovery accounts meant to be self-affirming, first-person testimonies but critical analyses of them as well.

Undoubtedly, I balked when I recently picked up a feminist book about cancer in literature, one arguing that women—by "employing the trope of leakiness"—can "reclaim their medicalized bodies through acts of resistance or agency." The words sounded offensive and silly to my ears. I hooted at the idea that bodily "leaks can be reconceptualized as a transgressive form of fluid embodiment and ethical knowledge." More revolting than revolutionary, my encounters with "fluid embodiment" involved being drained and bagged in ways that would make me gag for months afterward, though at first my leaks and leavings seemed inconsequential, if distressing.

The freezing temperatures that had knocked down power lines in the Northeast issued in gray mists of dank air in southern Indiana, but they permeated me with a profound chill and an unnerving sense of physical vulnerability. A nightmare woke me the morning I was expecting Simone and Julie as well as Molly and Kieran and Elliot for the Christmas holidays. It involved waiting at a supermarket checkout line not to pay for food but to receive drugs. In the dream, identical medications for each person must and will be administered to all cancer patients so through my blood flows a succession of solutions that I cannot predict and in a jumbled order and dosage pertaining not to my unique needs but to the ailments of millions of others who have eaten the fruits and vegetables made glossy by poisonous chemicals, the milk and cheese, chicken and meat contaminated by destructive hormones and pesticides. So many of us are battling this disease, there is no time to prepare individual remedies. Despite my pleasure in my daughters' presence, peevish irascibility at my enervation and frequent trips to the bathroom estrange me from the normal rhythms of existence. I begin to feel like a member of some intermediate species unable to transition into a decidedly human world of complex needs and demands that I cannot meet.

Recurrent aches and pains especially in the bathroom, the impossibility of teaching or shopping for food, the exhaustion attendant on finding sheets to fit the various beds, the torpor of the invalid resting on the sofa under a quilt concealing a heating pad: all separated me from my former life now put in a decidedly diminished and curiously inconsequential dimension. Paroxysms of exasperation at my own incompetence would arise when I seemed unable to pour a box of chicken stock into a pot without spilling half of it on the stove and the floor. (Forget about the idea of making real chicken stock.) The candles kept on falling out of the menorah. No matter where placed, the menorah looked dwarfed by Don's beauteous Christmas tree. Just helping to decorate Julie's cookies exhausted me and Kieran's curry disagreed with my mother. Little Elliot suffered from a cold that became a stomach flu for everyone else. When Mary Jo slipped on the ice and broke her wrist, I had to be assisted to make it to the emergency room. Folding the laundry weighed me down, and childproof vials of drugs proved impossible to open. I felt like tearing down something or just tearing up. How can I send Don to the drugstore yet again because I have forgotten some needed item? Two pairs of socks, two pairs of pants, two sweaters: I am bulking up indoors, but the freezing cold seeps into my heart.

As Don took over many of my chores, as Israel started bombing Hamas in the Gaza Strip, I reverted to the sofa, now with a new and unfinished quilt. Might quilting furnish a diversion or, to be more realistic, promote a quiet rhythm to pacify the atmosphere? Right before going in for the first CT scan in Bloomington, some intimation of disaster must have convinced me that I would not have the strength in the near future to make the sort of fabric sandwich that precedes the act of quilting. Back in early November, on the largest floor space I could find in the house, I had laid down a queen-size backing; on top of it went the batting or cotton filler; on top of that I unfurled the pieced quilted top. The three layers— backing, batting, pieced top—had to be basted together before one could take out a large hoop and begin the tiny quilting stitches that firmly attach the top to the two layers beneath. In this case, the pieced top consisted of squares sewn together out of fabric cut out of Don's frequently laundered striped shirts. Every day to the office for more than half a century, he had worn under his sports jacket a brown-and-white or blue-and-white or maroon-and-white striped shirt.

On the sofa in the family room during the Christmas holidays, while I began the long process of quilting by placing my hoop at the center of the piecing-batting-backing sandwich, my daughters found a private moment to share their concerns. First Simone wondered if she should ditch her life in New York and return home, for how could she carry on working while I was going to get weaker and sicker from subsequent chemotherapies. Then Molly appeared, fretting that either the prognosis or the dreaded medical interventions would cause me to do something self-destructive. Though the stitches looked crooked and askew, I explained that I would never do anything to hurt them, that I wanted them to live the prime of their lives with passion and integrity and without my cancer warping their ambitions and desires, that the only way I would seek an end to life would be at the very end of my life, when I would in fact rely on their understanding. Squeezed inside what sometimes seems the sandwich composed of children and parents, I found it

harder to deal with the phone calls from my mother explaining
that she had just had her eyebrows done (to arch them, but they
still needed to be colored), and that the manicurist had managed to
erase the mustache (it must be growing on her upper lip because of
the broken bridge), and when would I make the appointments for
her new dentures?

With the girls gone back to their respective cities, I fret about
Don: is my condition contagious? Cancer and chemo have cemented
Don's retirement. He literally retired more than a decade ago, but
my daily trips to school had propelled him into driving me to the
office, and then spending the day in the library where he worked on
an oral history about other retired faculty or various bibliographical
tasks related to his earlier Victorian scholarship. Now, though, he
stays home. When we are invited to a party or a reception, I pencil
it in the date book and urge him to attend, but he has become reclusive, avoiding social situations. When I fall asleep under the quilt,
he snoozes in a nearby chair. When he goes to put a log on the fire,
he may trip on the carpet or bang his head on the mantel. Because
of arthritis, he takes one step at a time downstairs. He still drives
me like a homing pigeon from here to there, but resists going out
to attend an evening poetry reading or concert, as he would have
in the past. While ice slicks all the driveways, porches, and roads, I
sympathize with and profit from his companionable retreat, but it
worries me that this process will accelerate his aging, as it does mine.

As shameful as they seem to me, do my ongoing bowel problems have a dire biological basis? Just days before my next scheduled chemo, it becomes clear that they may throw me out of the
research trial altogether. An "agonized" Dr. Matei phones about an
"abscess" on another CT image, which probably contains infection
and which would be a "mega-problem" if Avastin were part of the

chemotherapy. What does it mean that the mysterious "collection of fluids" has morphed into an "abscess"? I will have to travel to Indy for a Gastrografin enema to see if there is a "perforation" in the colon. When I deliver this information to my visiting friends Jan and Jon, they decide to postpone the head-shearing. I've got enough "on my plate," and even though my hair has thinned into weird patches, I'll be bald for quite a long time. That night (as on all nights), when the lights get turned out, Don and I lie on our backs side by side with his left hand cradling my right. "I worry that this sickness is taking over your life, Bear," I murmur in the dark now permeated by a bathroom nightlight he has just affixed.

"I have no other life," he responds while gently stroking my fingers.

"I don't know what to hope for," I whisper.

"Let's hope for a good summer," he says.

On January 7, 2009, one day before the second scheduled chemo, Don and I drive through light snow to the Gastrografin enema. Another surreal room, the undressing, the obdurate-looking scanning table—flat and hard—with its cameras and monitors above and all the tubes to deliver chemical dyes laid out by an assistant for the physician whose first words upon entering warm my heart: "Those are too big." With a tube in my rectum, I am told to move into various positions, but I have begun to anaesthetize myself to these interminable degradations, and happily the entire procedure takes only fifteen minutes. A few hours later, the result is phoned to me at home by Dr. Matei, who never beats about the bush: "There is a leak, from a little hole on the sutured colon." We discuss my low-grade fever, weakness, chills, and she determines to admit me to the hospital so as to keep the second chemo on track and drain the abscess.

"The drain enters through the buttocks," she informs me.

"How so?" I sputter. "How do I sit down?"

She laughs. "We'll find a way."

There is nothing to do but to submit, though I fear that the malevolent hole and the leak, the abscess and the drain underscore the infernal mechanisms of the medical enterprise into which I have now fallen as well as its indefatigable industry.

The day of the second chemo, right after the Gastrografin enema and Dr. Matei's phone call about the "little hole on the sutured colon," I was hospitalized for three nights. On the Saturday of my release, a nurse dumped on my bed all the syringes and bottles in the huge carton deposited by Interventional Radiology, muttering, "These would be impossible to use. Ridiculous." Tiffany fulminated against the doctors before she went in quest of user-friendly equipment. I was getting out after a grueling stay that made the second chemo a mere afterthought, a postscript to miseries beyond my expectations. Dr. Matei's discovery of a low hemoglobin count and an infection from the abscess led to lengthy blood transfusions followed by a truly gruesome procedure by a very interventional radiologist. During the transfusions, Don had tried to cheer me up with a story about my mother's reaction to my hemoglobin count of six: "When I received transfusions," she had smiled at him, "*mine was four.*" But after I surfaced from anesthesia, the radiologist left me moaning. He had inserted a plastic tube to drain the abscess and help heal the "small perforation" in the "sutured colon." The radiologist inserted the thick tube into the center of my right buttock: in the Midwest, "the butt"; in New York, "the tush"; in the South, "the bottom"; in fancy French, "the derrière"; in pseudo-science, "the gluteus maximus"; on the street, "the ass"; in Don's jokey repetition of the nurse's word, "the bee-hind." Six feet in length from its penetration into my body, the rest of the tube presumably reaches invisibly down into the abscess that lies near my coccyx at the base of my backbone. This tube to heal the hole—was it caused by the cancer or by the bowel resection during the suboptimal debulking?—became the source of my subsequent torment.

I was to receive the standard chemo, but I had been thrown out of the clinical trial because of the perforation—thrown out of the trial like a frantic protestor hustled out through the courtroom back door, like a cheating student disqualified from taking the final exam, like a culprit assumed guilty before the chance to establish innocence. The compliance with which I accepted Dr. Matei's prescription of the drain may have had less to do with her brisk certitude and more with a stunned passivity that began to exert and extend its grip. The oncologist, an expert, had not consulted my judgment. It never entered my mind to get a second opinion. Nor could I imagine beforehand the arcane imposition Dr. Matei deemed necessary. Am I to go home with a tube longer than the length of my leg coming out of the tush, a plight I have never read about in any of the accounts of cancer I have consulted? Since I wear pants, the tube constitutes a major sartorial quandary, unless like a cartoon wolf I cut a hole in the back of my pants, in my case a hole at the center of the right side of the seat of my pants. At the puncture site, the drain requires recurrent flushing and re-bandaging and because I cannot reach it, poor Don has to be given lessons. I am a cyborg, though I'd rather be a goddess—with one organic and one inorganic hole for excretions—and it's no picnic being tethered. Indeed, in a grotesque fashion I'm on Seneca's leash.

Now quite literally, I have become one pain in the ass. I have seen drains from breast cancer and on other postoperative bodies, but a long drain jutting out from the center of the right cheek of the bottom—this comes as news to me, and it is so cumbersome that days go by before I figure out how to thread the tube out of my pants, how to wear underpants. Only the good advice of one of my stepdaughters helps me maneuver the tube beneath and then over the front of my pants to hook the attached bag to my waistband so I can stand and use my hands. A sort of weird sporran, Don calls it—and who else would know the name for a Scottish purse?—this one for filthy lucre. Otherwise, a plastic ball-and-chain drags behind me. Sitting or lying on one buttock is not easy for long periods of time—about that I can testify—so hydrocodone becomes my best friend. Who knows what havoc it will wreak on my digestion as my weight plummets?

To the nurse Tiffany, instructing us upon our departure from the hospital, I wonder aloud about home-care help and force myself to say something that might hurt Don's feelings, to articulate in front of him my fears that he may not be "handy" enough to tackle these plastic connectives. I am thinking about the lightbulbs that have spun out of his fingers to shatter on the floor, his fumbling while positioning a nail on the wall for a photograph, though I know he prides himself in helping in every conceivable way. He has large and expressive hands, which have always thrilled me, but the tubes are tricky and the inter-connectives small. At home, I position myself on the bed, bottom up, cradling my head. Even if I lift my head up and peer down, I can barely see the puncture site so I cannot accomplish the complex procedure for myself. Yoga breathing steadies me, as Don peels off the pads and tape on my bottom, then decouples the tush-tube from the longer tube, though there is very little fluid collecting in that tube or the bag at its end.

Don unwraps one of the prepackaged syringes Tiffany has supplied in abundance, squirts the first abrupt drops of saline up toward the ceiling, presses it into the tush-tube, and slowly "flushes" or "irrigates" the liquid into me. Next he drains the little bit of reddish-brown fluid from the plastic bag into a measuring cup to record output. Finally he reconnects the tush-tube to the longer tube and bag. Lying on my stomach, I quaver, "I worry that this damned treatment is taking over your life, Frederick." He responds, "You *are* my life," patting me on a spot near enough to the drain that a yelp accompanies the tears spurting from my eyes. That night he will repeat the process, changing the bandages around the puncture wound. Then we lie down next to each other—now on each other's side of the bed because of the position of the drain—so his right hand reaches below the covers to cradle my left before he responds to my usual admission ("Bear, I don't know what to hope for") with his standard response ("Let's hope for a good summer"). In my corpse pose, I breathe into the night air, practicing rhythmic in- and out-takes and imagining the coming of sleep as the coming of death, a simple release of consciousness, though lying on a garden hose in your bottom casts an odd light on the story of the princess and the pea.

Bracketed by these twice daily ablutions, our days are taken up by what consumes the time of all sick people and those upon whom they depend as well as those who depend on them: the routines of buying drugs, timing their intake, consulting with doctors and their assistants about flare-ups. In my case, I have to deal with my mother's need to find a notary public to authorize her existence so the German government will continue paying reparations. And I need to solve the problem of a Visa card that won't be honored by her pharmacist and that puts me on the phone to somebody probably in Mumbai. The person who owns the card—no matter how elderly or senile—must consent *on the phone* to the Visa representative's direct inquiries, I am informed. Neither my mother nor I are well enough to visit each other so I hand the receiver over to Don who does a hilarious imitation of *Psycho*'s Anthony Perkins morphing into Norman Bates's mother and then into my mother. Quavering into the receiver, his falsetto recites her date of birth and social security number, information I had jotted down for him, only getting stuck at my mother's mother's maiden name and the rising decibels of my laughter.

After a much-needed head-shearing, I begin to morph in looks from Yentl of the Shtetl (in a paisley scarf) to a mournful Oliver Twist (in a navy cap), each tethered to a long plastic tail and dirty bag. I have to figure out a way to minimize the pain of the drain in my consciousness, maybe by thinking about others worse off: that's the advice I hear in my head, and I consider applying it to the numbers of people whose illness memoirs I am reading, though I might just start feeling sorry for them too. Reynolds Price, paralyzed in his lower body, strikes me as heroic. In a physical state much more perilous than my own, Reynolds Price does not dwell. I was always instructed not to dwell, but alas I generally did and do dwell—never or rarely in conversations with friends who for the most part remain clueless about the specifics of my physical condition, but always in my head. If there weren't so many damned umlauts in Pema's last name—it is a royal pain to find the damned symbol list—she might be worth consulting and quoting, for she believes that "when we encounter pain in our life we breathe into our heart with the recognition that others also feel this." Can I learn to deepen compassion by realizing that my distress is shared, that there are many other people all over the world feeling pain worse than mine?

While I am contending with the drain, sitting at my desk becomes unendurable and my alienation from earlier professional commitments deepens. A research assistant has been assigned to come to the house each week with a box so I can rid myself of the papers cluttering my study. Copies of correspondences, book contracts, and annual reports must go, into the box for the library's archive or into the trash. Busying myself with such housekeeping, I should try to look beyond current physical miseries, to prepare myself for retirement. For, given Dr. Matei's three-to-five-year forecast, as well as the debilitation of treatment, I must not postpone retirement. Though I will see my current graduate students through to their doctoral defenses, it would not be fair to continue teaching large freshman lectures that require a sustained level of stamina and adrenaline on which I can no longer count. In each pedestrian task of tossing or filing, I esteem Audre Lorde's efforts to "*integrate death into living, neither ignoring it nor giving in to it.*" I study the memoir of Deborah Cumming, who acknowledged cancer's insistence that "*we are living and dying.*" I, too, seek to face my impending decline and mortality with "*deeper sources of resiliency, of strength, of joy.*" My collaborator has determined to brave a series of Arctic freezes as well as her own health problems and grief over the death of her partner so as to visit me. She wants us to coauthor two short essays that seem peripheral, if not irrelevant, to my current concerns.

Pema of the many umlauts advises us to observe ourselves so as to nurture kindness for others. When "the sense of being irritated by ourselves and our lives and other people's idiosyncrasies becomes overwhelming," she advises, it is important to emphasize kindness: "Sometimes it's expressed as heart, awakening your heart. Often it's called gentleness. Sometimes it's called unlimited friendliness."

Who more than Sandra deserves my unconditional love and coop-
eration, whether or not the task at hand seems extraneous to my
needs? When in *The Places that Scare You* Pema Chödrön discusses
Tonglen (the Buddhist practice of "exchanging oneself for others"),
she mentions engaging in it for a specific person in an "on-the-spot
practice." The ancient Tibetan exercise has inspired many people
working in hospice environments. "*Tonglen* (the Tibetan word that
means 'to give and to receive') consists of accepting another's suffering and distress, making an offering in return [with] all the confidence and serenity one can muster. This simple sharing of someone
else's suffering means being with him or her, not leaving that person
alone." Breathing in the pain of another, breathing out relief and
release might whittle away at my solipsism. Tonglen is believed to
be "one of the great meditation jewels that offers a way to nurture
the natural energy of mercy and basic goodness."

Could Tonglen help me ignore my dead soles and paralyzed
toes, my uncontrollable diarrhea, weight loss, and inability to manage the drainage without intermittent crises? Might it allow me to
detach my attention from my aching body and achieve instead the
sort of enlightened state in which one can be mindful of the sorrows
of others or gaze at the sky? Buddhist practices provide "an inner
haven which enables a man or a woman to live *with* pain, to take
possession of it, affirm it, and experience a profound peace of mind
in the midst of suffering." A remark by one of Barbara Kingsolver's
characters illuminates an intuition that has come to me when I am
in the corpse pose in which I wait for sleep every night: "when I
thought about it," the narrator of *The Bean Trees* explains, "being
dead seemed a lot like not being born yet, and I hadn't especially
minded that." A series of snowstorms blow from Kingsolver's Kentucky through southern Indiana on their way north.

The snow blanketing all that I can see makes the driveway impassable, insulating me further in attending to the pleasures of making a lemony lentil soup, emptying all the trash cans to a Schubert string quartet, getting Don to list musicians and singers, mostly of jazz and blues, with geographical place names so I can marvel at what's in his head:

Ike Quebec, Illinois Jacquet, Philly Joe Jones, Dakota Stanton, Tennessee Ernie Ford, Mississippi John Hurt, Kokomo Arnold, Irving Berlin, Wilbur and Sydney de Paris, Julie London, Panama Francis, Tex Benecke, Memphis Slim, Houston Person, Georgia Gibbs, Jimmy Cleveland, Tampa Red, Dinah Washington, Grover Washington, Jr., George London, Mound City Blue Blowers, Vi (Virginia) Redding, Memphis Minnie, Ginny (Virginia) Sims, Roswell Rudd, Louisiana Red, Janis Joplin, Blind Boys of Alabama . . .

Against a chalk sky, the thick flakes descend in windblown flurries that can best be seen out the window against the dark trunks of the frosted trees. Never before a domestic hausfrau, I seek stasis, calm, a serene being-in-the-present which is the antithesis of the hectic stamina and adrenaline that fueled my professional exertions.

Despite the constant pain of the drain, I want the quiet concentration of each everyday task to fill me with an active love of living and a passive acceptance of dying, for I remain convinced about a recurrence some brief period of time after the last of the six chemotherapies. The worse the cancer (and hadn't the suboptimal debulking, the abscess, and the perforation signified a bad cancer?), the quicker the recurrence. The shorter the TFI (treatment-free interval), the more unlikely survival, according to most of the books.

Despite the constant pain of the drain, I wish to cultivate the mystic intensity of each moment alone or with others, to reflect on each second's untold vibrancy. To make the moment of being stand still—that's how Virginia Woolf frequently thought about her quests in consciousness. What I seek is "a *willingness* instead of willfulness, an ability to take life on life's terms as opposed to putting up a big fight," as Lauren Slater expresses it in *Lying,* her astonishing memoir about the impossibility of telling the whole truth and nothing but the truth.

The huge evergreens in the circle of beauty, their boughs weighted down by heavy loads of snow and ice, lead me to wonder, do dead soles and frozen toes symbolize a sort of hibernation during this long January? The still dark trunks of the pines in front of the house extend their brown-barked limbs under layers of white heaps that pull my eyes toward the untrammeled snow on the rough meadow, only pockmarked here and there by slender trails of hoof-marks. The interwoven branches of the firs droop from the weight, bendable but not brittle. I want to be just as still and somehow pliable and permanent in each moment of being alive, to ponder how transient and yet how pregnant each instant feels. I sense myself entering into a new era of responsibility not exactly like the one our inaugurated president has in mind, for mine relates not to fiscal or peace or environmental concerns but rather to weaning myself from irascibility and ambition, learning not to lean too heavily or drearily on my beloved family and friends, finding resource and resonance in an inner life that might transport me without complaint or struggle out of the present with the speed of the scrawny deer who stop grazing, momentarily startled by my sight in the window, and then bound off in leaps of graceful flight.

After Sandra's visit and after the third chemotherapy on January 28, the drain takes on the explosive power of detonated dynamite, recalling to my mind the dynamite lodged in the limbs of Kahlo's Judas. A trip to consult about the now insistently throbbing and oozing wound on my bottom leads to an immediate hospitalization lasting more than two weeks. To deal with pain management and weight loss as well as dropping blood counts, I am admitted not, as before, to the brand-new Simon Center but to the dark and labyrinthine IU hospital in which the debulking occurred. During what turns into a ghastly seventeen days, I am isolated and immobilized in a private room where I am reduced to stupor, weakness in all my limbs, and throbbing stabs in my behind. Within the eerie neverland of morphine, with nurses and, less frequently, doctors coming and going, I remain attached by various tubes to a bed of pain for two weeks and three days. The nurses in this surgical unit, endowed with exemplary compassion and efficiency, attend to the dreadful bandages and irrigations of *two* drains coming out of my bottom and to a host of technologically sophisticated measures devised for pain and weight management.

How did one horrible drain morph into *two* even thicker and more unwieldy drains? The logic still eludes me. On the first night of a stay that far exceeded my imagination in its duration, I was sent back down to Interventional Radiology where I figured I could make a pitch for the drain's removal—or mine. I could not manage to exist with my flesh so afflicted. It had to be removed or I would remove myself to hospice. The radiologist addressed me on the gurney in the hall with an anguished admission: "The drain has not solved the problem. The drain will not solve the problem." Good, I thought, we finally agree. With Dr. Matei out of town, the radiologist, clearly distressed, wrestled with his need to make a decision for which I was unprepared. Dr. Agarwal says, "I will put in two larger drains so that the viscous stuff does not clog. They may feel uncomfortable, but they will help manage the situation. This is what I would recommend if you were my mother."

Am I old enough to be his mother, or do I just look old enough to be his mother? Anyone with a psychoanalytic bone in their body would dread being treated like someone's mother! Dr. Agarwal's logic sounds harebrained to me, and tears roll down my cheek. But he convinces Don that this is what should be done. As for me, prostrate on an uncomfortable gurney, stunned passivity has me in its thrall, or extreme fatigue, or depression, or pain, or sedation. Returning to consciousness in the basement labyrinth of halls means consciousness of the aching pulsations given off by two huge tubes emerging from my right buttock, attached now to two large bags: one fecal, one bloody. The pain radiates throughout my bottom and down my right leg.

Despite Dr. Agarwal's assumptions about my old age, what comes to my mind are the innocent maidens of Gothic fiction, for a gurney conveys me denuded and sheeted through crooked corridors, beds waylaid here and there, shapes hunched under white linen with tubes from every orifice, until I land back in my room where I will be tied up and then branded. In this passive grammar, I am being held captive, used and abused, and none of the hospital gowns tie up properly in the back or the front. Marilyn French, ordinarily a fierce fighter, experienced the same stunned compliance that envelops me: "enervation had turned me into a docile patient, helpless, caught, trapped in a system." The astonishingly courageous Reynolds Price records that the hospital "plunged" him "into degrees of pain and realistic depression that produced a dangerously passive state. In that psychic bog of helplessness, like most trapped sufferers, I was transfixed by the main sight in view—my undiminished physical pain."

A peripherally inserted central catheter, a PICC, is installed on my upper left arm to create two major IV outlets: morphine I can self-administer every six minutes and Total Parenteral Nutrition, "TPN" or liquid food sent directly into my veins. The PICC with its two IVs effectively chains me to the post by my bed, as do the blood transfusions. The setting reminds me of a passage in Sandra's book *Death's Door* in which she examines the differences between hospitals and the hotels, motels, or inns they try to mimic in their replications of home life:

> The hospital offers mostly stripped-down anonymous—in effect defamiliarized—versions of [the comforts of home]; mechanized beds that are and aren't like "real" beds; rolling tray "tables" that are and aren't ordinary tables; cubicle curtains that function as "walls" but aren't really walls; "gowns" that don't fasten in the usual ways; lights that never go out; "aprons" made of lead; hallways that don't seem to lead anywhere usable or familiar; "tables" on which people are placed like objects; examination "rooms" that turn out really to be machines; and so forth.

My room has the flimsy impermanence of a stage setting, especially under the dim lighting.

Penetrated by numerous devices, I am subjected to the pedagogy of pain—the doctrine that chastisement and suffering will bring about clarification or enlightenment. The word "pain" comes from the Latin *poena*, meaning penalty or punishment. I mull over Robert Browning's line in "Childe Roland," for I must be wicked to deserve such pain. The sadistic ambiance induces and sustains stupefaction, a swoon of limp submission. Never do I rebel, scream, or protest my confinement. Instead, my mind shuts down; my physical body, addled by morphine, shudders off. If no one comes to draw the blinds, they must stay open to a courtyard where any of the workmen can see me. I am given no real food—only Jell-O, tea, or popsicles. I am chastised in the hospital through a series of unnatural acts, but perpetrated by whom? Not by the nurses who pat my shoulder and sympathize with my suffering. Not by the lesser attendants who drop in periodically to ask, "Anything you need?" Maybe Beckett rather than Sade: no one to blame and the need to keep on going on. I can't go on, I do go on.

Each of the next eight hospital days and nights crawls through crippled time in fractured segments. At 4 a.m., when vitals are taken, I awake to pain in the drains because the morphine button has not been pushed for five hours. Making up for lost time, in the dark I watch the drain bags emptied, pushing the button and dozing until 7:30. From eight until ten, if strong enough, I am detached from the IVs and the bed so I can hobble to the bathroom sink to wash my upper body, brush my teeth, and put on a clean shirt and a cap since my bald head freezes without one. When I shuffle back to a newly made bed, the tray table must contain everything I need to have within reach: glasses, water, reading matter, and the iPhone for e-mail, my sole means of communication with the outside world. I become engrossed by Salmon Rushdie's *Midnight's Children* with its resonant refrain: "What can't be cured must be endured." But who knows how the morphine along with the clear liquid diet befuddles comprehension? When a *New Yorker* essayist on James Baldwin views King's death as a pivotal point in Baldwin's political evolution, I wonder (for a few seconds) why Baldwin cares about a king of England, and which one.

Since I have ruled out visits and the landline does not work, novels and magazines are a godsend until early afternoon when the bandages on my bottom must be removed, the leaking wounds cleaned, and new dressings applied to a large area now raw with irritation from so much taping. Will my skin start tearing or stripping off? As the day progresses, the throbbing pressure of the garden hoses in my bottom neither increases nor decreases, but the irrigation of the second tube spikes into torment. One caring nurse experiments with various methods of flushing—slow, fast, intermittent—but to no avail. I moan and whimper over what feels like the quintessence of physical affliction, so I inform my doctors that this pain cannot be touched by the morphine. My numerical response to the twice-daily catechism—"On a scale from one to ten, with ten being extreme pain, what's your level?"—creeps higher and higher. E-mail is my preferred mode of communication with physicians and anyone else outside my Clinique-colored room with its view of another wing of the hospital and its broken slats of window shades.

Pressing my feet against the footboard of the bed to remind me that they exist, I continue to lie flat on my back, the patches under bandages and near the wounds setting off high-pitched alarms that dull to audible roars. I lie perfectly still, dozing on and off, except to limp to the nearby commode which I can reach without being detached from the PICC lines. In this murky green sea, Don arrives two out of every three days with a T-shirt, a portable CD player, and once with yellow roses. He comments on the "anguish of rivers," prompting my appreciation of tragic ecological warnings and of his verbal facility, though weeks later he laughs, explaining that he was referring to a television announcer's lament over the troubles of a football player named Rivers. As the days pass, he sits in a corner of the room where I cannot see him, mumbles what I cannot hear, or garbles the medical information I impart. He supports the decision of the second drain because "I want you with me." In short, he suffers acutely—rattling around like a marble in a glass jar wherever he is—at home or in the hospital or in the car on the tedious highway between the two.

After an afternoon with Don or Salman Rushdie, some *Headline News* ends each day. On bad nights, amid the television sounds and coughs and groans from down the hall, I hear wretched voices— "Somebody help me. Help me!"—or a sustained clamoring of wailing grief. On better nights, there are the lurid melodramas of *Grey's Anatomy*. And when I close my eyes, beneath my eyelids I see the textures often found in Victorian crazy-quilts: furry velvets, ribbed chenille, filmy silks, latticed lace, shiny satins. Once or twice the objects on the wall opposite me—sink, paper towel dispenser, bulletin board—relocate to the ceiling above me. I pass out at 11 p.m. in my standard corpse pose.

The perverse Rube Goldberg bags, floor-level when I manage to stand up, dangle like filthy colostomy pouches bizarrely hung at too great a remove from the body. On early morning rounds, the doctors begin thinking aloud about colostomy as a surgical solution and alternative to the drains. Feces kept away from the bowel would enable the abscess and perforation to heal. An intense resident appears by my bedside and argues passionately, "You will get your life back." I hear the echoes of a Rilke lyric ("You must change your life"), but the nurses agree. Colostomies do not hurt after recovery from surgery, they can be managed and cleaned by the patient herself, they are often reversible, and they can be easily concealed.

Most crucial to me in my state of physical affliction: after recovery from surgery, people live painlessly and independently with so-called "ostomies." How many new words will I have to learn?

On the eighth day of my stay, a young resident casually asks if I would like the second drain removed, the one emitting blood and tormenting me at irrigations. I burst into tears of disbelief and ecstasy. A few minutes later, it lies stuffed in a garbage pail and I profusely thank her, for its irrigation had exceeded any level of suffering I had thought imaginable. Its removal as well as my grati-tude at its removal causes me to ponder the pedagogy of pain. I am pathetically grateful to the doctors for righting the wrong they had done. I am abject in appreciation that I have been returned to the original condition (the hurtful first drain) that brought me to the hospital in the first place. There is something rotten in this emotional dynamic—like caressing an attacker who stops running a razor blade across your neck. I am worshipping the doctors as beneficent deities and thanking them profusely for undoing the grievous harm that they and they alone inflicted. How can I be so stupidly fervent when they set in motion the evil to begin with?

During the next few days I would consult with a youthful bowel surgeon, Dr. Bruce Robb, who won me over by saying, "I hate drains. I hate what they do to patients," and also by using the Yiddish word *tuckhes* to refer to my miserably raw bottom. His idea was to strengthen me with PTN (what the nurses call "steak in a bag") and with injections and transfusions to boost blood counts for a surgery that even my oncologist now believes to be necessary. But what if the colostomy does not heal the infection? What if it is not reversible? What if the surgery only adds to my miserable bodily anguish? And hadn't I sworn *not* to engage in any procedures or surgeries except for the six rounds of chemotherapy prescribed for ovarian cancer? Slowly I am getting sucked into procedure after procedure, each with its ghastly physical repercussions and its train-load of drugs. Fuming at the flatulent assurances I remember from the *Johns Hopkins Patients' Guide to Ovarian Cancer*, I am aghast at the languages and treatment philosophies of the disease.

In a recovery room, Dr. Bruce Robb woke me with assurances that the operation had gone as well as possible. Sporting a surgical cap that hid his prematurely receding hairline, he radiated youthful ebullience about his success. He had performed not a colostomy but an ileostomy: bringing a loop of the small intestine up through the skin, folding it back like the turtleneck of a sweater or the top cuff of a sock, and stitching it in place on the abdomen. The stoma sprouts within a plastic pouch now sitting to the right of the belly button (reconstructed by two abdominal surgeries) and its nature makes possible a reversal of the operation, Dr. Robb assured me. To my relief, the drain in my bottom had been removed. There was a plastic tube attached to a drainage bulb coming out of the left side of my belly, but much smaller and flexible. The surgeon wants me to heal; the oncologist needs to resume chemotherapy: their com-promise consists in putting off the fourth session for two weeks. A few more days in the hospital would let a team of ostomy nurses teach me how to change and clean the pouch collecting the brown fluid emitting from the stoma. So very painful had been the drains that a temporary ileostomy at first seems like a reprieve, though its quite distinct horrors would become apparent in the days after my release from the hospital.

Did seventeen days flat on my back with feeding and narcotic
IVs explain the terrible backaches and muscular enervation I suffered upon my exultant arrival home? Had catheterization during
the intestinal surgery somehow harmed my bladder or induced an
infection, causing me to scream in anguish every time I urinated?
Physician assistants in Indianapolis keep on phoning in a series
of prescriptions for each and every ailment until my entire day
consists of pill-taking. Yet I try to assure myself that the pouch of
liquid poop may require emptying every few hours and replacement every five days, but it does not hurt, and I can manage its
care and that of the small drain on my stomach myself. Don has
only to anoint my bruised bottom. The burden has at least been
lifted from his perpetual ministrations. *Somewhat* lifted, for he
helps with the daily self-injection against clotting and of course
with the delivery of each meal and indeed of each pen, book, or
scarf located beyond my reach. Still, we are relieved to be home
and alone together.

Even the most degrading experiences are shared with Don. Yet
I understand how much secrecy surrounds the stoma, as did Gillian
Rose, who could not find one detailed account of a person living
with a colostomy. The budding intestine pulled outside the body
looks like a dark red knob and emits liquid waste (in the ileostomy) or denser feces (in the colostomy). In Rose's discussion of her
thwarted ambition to write about "shit" so as to "invent colostomy
ethnography," she described her stoma: "tight coils of concentric,
fresh, blood-red flesh, 25 millimeters (one inch) in diameter, pro-
trude a few millimeters from the centre left of my abdomen, just
below the waist." Mine, on the right, is smaller in diameter because
formed from the ileum, the last part of the small intestine. Without
elaborate nerve endings, the rust-red stoma on my belly sticks out, a

protrusion less than an inch long, less than an inch wide, about three inches to the right side of my belly button, and a bit lower.

There is a tiny hole at the stoma's center from which lique-fied crap drops intermittently. The word shit does not pertain to its languid eruptions which smell like a mixture of adult excrement and baby poop. It is a foul mouth with pursed lips, lips that press out to emit crap and then withdraw back in reticence. Since the word "stoma" means mouth and since the puckering protrusion involuntarily spews filth, an ileostomy might be considered the physical analogue of Tourette's syndrome. At erratic moments, this mini-Vesuvius spurts or burps out drops of brown fluid that descend down into the plastic bag in which it remains encased. Although the bag's contents often resemble nothing so much as chocolate pudding before it has set in the refrigerator, quickly I learn about indigestible foods—corn, nuts, seeds. The mass and heat of its brown liquid weigh against my groin until I sit down on the toilet and open the Velcro pleats at the bottom of the apparatus to let the contents drain out. Unless it just pours out, cleaning the pouch—no, it never looks clean—emptying the pouch resembles what movie milkmaids do to a cow's udder. I ease the brown gunk down toward the bottom end which I then clean with toilet paper and re-pleat. The ostomy nurses taught me to wipe inside the bottom pleats, before I pray that the Velcro will hold the end closed so no fluids escape the bag.

If out of sight means out of mind, in sight means in mind. An evacuation that ordinarily cannot be seen and that occurs once a day dribbles incessantly in full view through the transparent front of the bag. A normally invisible internal organ resides vulnerable and visible outside the body. What should be hidden has been outed like Judas's foul intestines after his bowels explode. Additionally, a once discrete and volitional act has become uncontrollable and continuous. I can feel belches of liquid when they emerge from the stoma and every trip to the toilet involves emptying the bag which, I hope, might become routine. Each time, though, I think that vets would not do this to a dog. No need to consult Julia Kristeva on the psychic power of my horror, but the truth of Freud's insight—"dirt is matter in the wrong place"—comes home to me. I am perpetually dirty, defecating incessantly from my belly.

When I drain the pouch right before taking Ambien and assuming the corpse pose, I can get five or so hours of continuous sleep. In one of the rare accounts of life after such surgery, Barbara R. Van Billiard explains that "coming home from the hospital with a colostomy was like coming home with a new baby": "It kept me up all night, it demanded the same sort of cleanups, and it took up just about all of my time. The only difference was it never did get to the point where it would sleep through the night." Unlike the relatively simple draining of the bag, changing the apparatus still requires the supervision of an incredibly patient home nurse. Kind and efficient, Kim Scherer shows me how to clean the stoma; how to cut out the template on a flat disk or flange to be glued to my belly and meant to encircle the stoma; where to squeeze the tube of adhesive paste or calking onto the edges of the disk-flange (to create a seal); how to secure it around the fleshly bump of the stoma to the belly and then snap the bag onto the disk, all the while the stoma may of course be spewing forth its drips of brown lava.

Diarrhea and constipation are no longer an issue. The same holds true for gas, although Barbara R. Van Billiard describes her distress at the loud blasts or high-pitched whistles her "round, pink 'rosebud' " emitted without warning. At unpredictable moments, what the British call wind puffs up the pouch which inflates like a half-blown balloon. Will its bulge of bilge show under my panties and trousers or, worse yet, cause leakage? Should the infection heal, Dr. Robb assures me, the operation can be reversed. But I dread an accident. What if the folded Velcro pleats at the bottom of the bag don't secure properly? What if the Tupperware contraption that locks the ring of the flange onto the ring on the bag gets unhinged? What if the seal breaks and the disk-flange separates from the skin on my abdomen? When the tiny staples from my belly button to my pubic bone are removed, will some of the pain—of standing upright, of walking—get mitigated? Why won't Dr. Robb's nurse practitioner remove the small drain on the left side of my belly? Which pants will fit over the drainage tube and ostomy bag?

When I refrain from speaking about the most recent operation, I realize that the taboo has taken hold and seek comfort in the fact that the ostomy pouch can be hidden under my pants, though the drainage tube-and-bulb requires a long cardigan, jacket, or vest. From a hint here or there in illness narratives, I suspect that anxieties about intestinal obstructions and revulsion against bowel operations run high among ovarian cancer patients, so high that they can abbreviate or contaminate a life, or so one can guess from circumspect, scattered phrases. In an afterword to Barbara Creaturo's memoir *Courage*, a doctor explains that he had "urged her to accept a simple but permanent colostomy" which would extend promising treatments, but she "opted instead for an aggressive surgical tour de force" and died a few months later. After a colostomy, another survivor who calls herself Kathy "felt as though life as I knew it had ended": "I detested myself." When Andrea King Collier's mother regained consciousness after a debulking and a colostomy, she said, "If I had known that they were going to cut this hole in me, I would have wished that they just let me die" and then "It's horrible. I'd rather be dead."

Given similar self-revulsion, why do I force myself to write about foul matters—because it does require overcoming a strong urge to hide experiences that I find appalling? Indeed, while many of my friends know that I am undergoing treatment for ovarian cancer, very few of them have been told about the intestinal disasters with which I daily contend. But self-censorship gnaws at me. In part, I dwell on Virginia Woolf's lament in "Professions for Women" that her generation was not yet able to tell the truth about the body. Presumably, I am too well educated to be ashamed by a physiological phenomenon beyond my control, but all the social mores surrounding evacuation and excretion conspire to make the ileostomy unspeakable and unspeakably anxiety-producing.

One day when the home nurse arrives we realize that Hollister, which manufactures the equipment, has sent the wrong materials. We are without proper supplies to change the apparatus. Then my angst erupts. I weep from frustration. Will this filthy pouch on my belly have to stay in place unchanged until a Fed-Ex arrives from the manufacturer or the Indianapolis hospital? Might it loosen and leak? Could Kim drive to the local hospital's supply office to see if it has the proper size in storage? In fact, she does run and finds the right equipment, but my tears and blessings upon her return tell me a great deal about the levels of fearfulness the ileostomy has raised and how distressed I am at the stoma's upkeep.

On a bovine or porcine belly, a tautening and then elongating red protrusion might be mistaken for a swollen teat or engorged nipple. Yet despite my growing antipathy to academic jargon, I cannot help but think that the stoma seems and feels like an anti-phallus.

Moist and concentrically circled, it looks like the thick last joint of a fat finger or the tip of a circumcised boy's penis. When it is doing its peristaltic spasms (to eject waste), this small spigot bears a resemblance to the head of a one-eyed snake or slug trying to worm its way out of my stomach. Should it be exposed to the air (for cleaning purposes), the stoma has no ups and downs; it just droops. It represents what everyone dreads and loathes: the nauseating phenomenon of a slick and slimy internal organ protruding from the skin and thus the grotesque abrogation of bodily containment or integrity. Flaccid, small, and floppy, such a stubby stump could not penetrate anything at all, but would get smooched upon contact. At least for the morbidly minded, a miniature organ not of proud pleasure but of shameful evacuation stirs up ideas of castration, of wanting to tie up loose ends. Actually, an ostomy literalizes the statement, I am at loose ends. Impossible not to picture how easily this bit of gristle could be snipped off. When the stoma appears as it usually does, enclosed and barely visible within the (generally dirty) pouch, it also figures lack of control and the powerlessness of a foul embodiment.

Two capitalized words—"NEW IMAGE"—are imprinted on the wrapper of each of the disks to be plastered on my belly. When I "go to the bathroom" to empty the bag, I must massage it downward to eject its contents. Then, in a parody of a man shaking the last droplets, I shake excess watery excrement off the Velcro end. Outside the bathroom and often when I am dressed, my right hand surreptitiously stretches down to check that the pouch extends through the right opening of my panties onto the top of my leg. I am especially sensitive to the tip of the bag lying on my thigh. Often, I pinch what the manufacturer terms "the lock 'n roll" end of the bag to strengthen the hold of the Velcro folds that keep the gunk held within. The gesture reminds me of nothing so much as the groping of lounging men—think of the baseball players who unconsciously touch themselves as if to reassure themselves that the equipment is still there or (Don explains) to adjust an aluminum cup that will protect against speeding baseballs. The dirty bag marks my inferiority, the inadequacy of my system in voiding itself normally and properly. In public bathrooms, I marvel at the efficiency of other inmates, for it takes time to clean inside the grimed innards of the plastic end. Scrupulous hand-washing is required afterward. On the rare occasions I go out of the house, I carry pocket-size tissues and hand sanitizer in my purse.

Besides taking up an inordinate amount of my attention, the prosthesis, an inorganic pouch hidden from view, signifies a grotesque lack of authenticity—or worse. For me, the nightmare of the lock 'n rolling NEW IMAGE is the annulment or cancellation of my body's autonomy. No longer intact, I cannot contain or control myself. According to researchers in artificial intelligence, one major marker of what constitutes life (or a living form) is autonomy. Without the apparatus manufactured by Hollister, I would be reduced to a dribbling, drooling mess. With it, I'm defective and dirty, a rank freak but a closeted freak since I zealously conceal and guard my secret stigma. Recalling the resonant photographs I have seen of women's mastectomy scars or of their breast reconstructions, I wonder, who would want to see a picture of a bag lady like me? In the instructional *Ostomy Educational Theatre* DVD, amber beads fill the pouch to represent excrement. It hardly helps that many of Hollister's other products are emblazoned with the copyrighted logo ADAPT, though I make sporadic efforts to admire the ingenuity of the equipment's designers and marketers.

My sense of hypocrisy in public places—of a hidden and

shameful secret—helps me understand the climactic scene in a 1994 novel by Donna McFarlane, who also imagines the stoma as an anti-phallus. The heroine of *Division of Surgery*, after suffering through many operations and five impacted or retracted stomas that resulted from inflammatory bowel disease, finally manages to establish an intimate relationship with a man to whom she wishes to reveal what only she and her surgeons have seen:

> "So this is me." I pointed down at my exposed red moving stump of intestine. "Sort of looks like the end of a penis, doesn't it?" [He] bent down and studied my stoma's flux. A little drop of shit filled the opening. "I can't control it. No muscle to contract around it." I closed my fist tight to illustrate. "So I have to work fast or I'll make a mess."

Although the relationship thrives, the heroine of *Division of Surgery* decides to have an abortion because she cannot abide the prospect of seeing the stoma protruding from "a belly swollen with nine months of pregnancy." She will always live with "lumps of stool" on her side, "bumps" under her clothes, a need to touch the bag on her abdomen "to check if it's full," and "worrying if the person next to [her] in a public washroom can hear the plastic."

In the breezy parlance of self-help books, I am "a new ileostomate," whom the more experienced remember with nostalgia:

> Looking back, do you remember the first feelings of something "alive" on your abdomen as you experienced the peristaltic action of the stoma? How about the feeling of warm stool draining into the disposable pouch, wondering if it was "in or out" of the pouch and looking to see? Did you carry a

sack full of supplies everywhere you went, afraid you would
break a seal? Do you remember, in your early post-op days,
holding your hand on your pouch or stoma when you walked?
Don't kid yourself, you did, too, and probably still do at times.

I do not sneer at the tone of gritty cheerfulness in advice books
because I have become aware that an ostomy must be a godsend to
the millions of people suffering from inflammatory bowel disease,
ulcerative colitis, Crohn's disease, and colon cancer.

One such sufferer, Sandra Benitez, embraces the altered "attitude" due "a new life, free of pain and anxiety and drug side-effects,"
an "attitude adjustment" after surgery that allows her to celebrate
"my little red stoma, sitting up there so perky and businesslike on
my tummy." The warm bag on her belly becomes "my own attached
rubber bottle." So the pouch won't be a "turnoff" during lovemak-
ing, she constructs "little mitts" for it out of "flannel fabric with cute
designs: hearts, polka dots, even some with Mickey Mouse faces."
Sandra Benitez concludes her memoir with a grateful letter to "my
little spout": "Thank you, thank you. You're an incredible helper.
I'm so glad I have you."

What an ingrate I am in comparison. Though I appreciate Dr.
Robb's skill as well as his respectful form of address—he takes care
to refer to me as "Dr. Gubar"—I have to struggle against feeling
betrayed by the cancer *and* by the well-intentioned doctors fighting
it. Not just the weight loss but also a floater in my left eye, hearing
problems in the right ear, aching holes in my buttock, cramps under

the small drain on the left side of my belly, the weight and heat of the bag against my right groin, and extreme exhaustion take up too much of my attention. Should I attribute my fatigue and soreness to the advanced cancer, the suboptimal debulking, the three rounds of chemotherapy, the radiologists' drains, or the ileostomy operation? Again I understand that this passage of weeks constitutes not a war against cancer but rather a fight to deal with the treatments of cancer, procedures and therapies devised not by sinister or nefarious scientists but by the most benevolent of doctors, each highly motivated to do his or her best but each diminishing me bit by bit.

"Looks like two bullet holes in your ass, Mom." So Molly declared as she smoothed a skin protectant over my bruised bottom while I used a towel to hide the bag from view. Leaving her family for a few days, she came alone to see if she could keep my weight from plummeting below 100 pounds, and what a wonder it was for me to watch her patient ministrations. My older daughter could not have been gentler during the hours she produced meatballs and spaghetti sauce as well as an infinity of blueberry muffins for the freezer. Convinced that I would be too weak to cook in the weeks to come, she preached the high fat content of Stouffer's mac and cheese, pizza bread, and chicken pot pie, without rebuking me for eating only a forkful of what was put on my plate. But I had read about "cancer cachexia" which sounded exactly like the effects of chemotherapy and surgery: nutritional depletion "characterized by weakness, poor appetite, alterations in metabolism, and wasting of muscle and other tissues."

For the most part, though, I tried again to cultivate stoicism. "What can't be cured must be endured." Even though Andrea King Collier's mother believed that she would "never be able to accept this awful, disgusting hole or the stupid bag I have to wear," in "about a week . . . Mother was ready to start taking care of herself and be in full control." I, too, could handle what was required of me, despite my bruised bottom with its dark smudges of degenerating skin, despite the fact that my feet felt tightly cellophaned and numb, despite the self-injections and pills, despite the weariness. As for yoga stretching, swimming, running, sex: the less said the better, though the ostomy books available on Amazon.com promise, "Yes, you can!" Thinking of Seneca, I tried to bend to the leash without going into boring or graphic details with the kids and friends, for, after all, I had been freed from physical anguish and from the horrors of the hospital. Tonglen, as well as all my diversions of knitting, quilting, reading, and writing, might soothe my spirits or at least anesthetize me. Reynolds Price, whose spinal cancer landed him in a wheelchair, has explained "a home truth that chronic-pain sufferers often forget—the fact that a thorough immersion in absorbing and, if possible, nonstop activity is far more narcotic than any drug." What works against pain might also work against revulsion.

Reynolds Price's "nonstop activity" is writing, but reading also involves immersion in an absorbing activity that can alter consciousness. Why do I contrast my divergent temperament and reactions to those of Sandra Benitez, for instance, when reading her account allows me to enter into her ways of knowing? Couldn't I supplement my response through hers—yes, even through an appreciation of her zany Mickey Mouse mitts? Isn't that why we read memoirs and novels—to glimpse other people's or characters' experiences not to supplant our own but to grapple with how our feelings might be or become different, how we might be or become beings other than who we are? What we might have gone through, what we may go through, and how others were there before us, finding a way. While reading, I am moved by cadences and vocabularies, values and contexts tangential to or beyond me, but somehow pertinent to how I might begin to apprehend myself and the world differently or how foreign worlds I never encountered or even imagined might catch my attention and sweep me up in their sustained asymmetries. Never have memoirs and novels meant more to me than during these difficult times.

Jan arriving with a milkshake; Mary phoning with department gossip; Jayne sending e-mail accounts of catching mice in her kitchen; Jo planting her chair just a few feet from where I recline, talking about the mind's obscurity confronting its own demise; Don bringing grilled cheese sandwiches to my study: all are welcome distractions, though I am beginning to resemble the skeleton on the top bunk of Kahlo's painting more than the fleshly woman below. One library book about Kahlo includes a black-and-white photograph of the artist seated next to her canopied bed, on which a cardboard skeleton actually lodges. I am dumbfounded by the painting again. I understand it to be more profoundly autobiographical than I had realized. Kahlo did not try to force death to depart, but instead slept with death—slept with Judas—nightly. Staring with sightless eyes directly at the viewer of *The Dream*, Kahlo's impassive Judas confronts us with life's ultimate betrayal, pain and death.

How curious that the living dreamer below—not the constructed folk figure above—is swaddled in the twelfth apostle's traditional color of gold. She shares the burden of his identity. Taken together, the dreamer and her cardboard twin witness the fact that they are embedded in narratives not of their own devising and inimical to their own well-being. Does Kahlo sleep with Judas every night, does she represent herself in bed with Judas and sharing his identity because people taken up with sickness or impairment (from disease or its treatments) become so self-absorbed, so diminished or debulked in their emotional capacities that they betray their own values as well as their intimates? It is also possible, of course, that Kahlo's sleeper envisions her own suicide or the destruction of the traitor-within-her who tricked her into betraying herself and whose explosive annihilation might secure her own demise.

Still, the painting is not titled "The Nightmare" but rather *The Dream* (or *The Sleep* or *The Bed*), which means that the sleeper might wake up released from or curiously refreshed by her proximity to death. She could awake to see her phantom is nothing but a flimsy papier-mâché construction, an artwork of her own devising that she can easily trash or stow in a corner of her closet. Or, like Kahlo herself, she might decide that sleeping every night with such a memento mori imprints on her consciousness the realization that we are all capable of tumbling into the misjudgments, sins, perversities, diseases, or sinister scenarios so often projected onto the lone figure of Judas. There is no betrayer other than ourselves, Kahlo seems intent on reminding me.

In bed at night, I sing the praises of the ostomy nurses—I refer to them as "angels" because they are so patient and knowledgeable and solicitous—who always mention the "excellence" of my stoma, the "good shape" of the skin around it. Apparently quite a few people suffer with retracting stomas that require constant tending or with skin breakdown under the glued-on appliance, so beamish Dr. Robb was quite justified in taking pride in his handiwork. Things could be worse, things are worse for other people, I admit to Don, before I add that things were far worse for me when I had to contend with the terrible pain of the drains. "Nobody had a more miserable bottom, Bear, no one in all of America." While clasping my hand, he recalls a grade-school joke that cracks me up, the one about the lady who backed into a propeller: "Dis-assed-her!" Then we shake with laughter, remembering an anesthesiologist who, as I was about to be wheeled into the operating room, declaimed, "Into the valley of death rode the six hundred!" The anesthesiologist had discovered that we taught English and exclaimed over the need for people to read more poetry so they could better understand life. He followed his first volley of recitation—apparently unaware that I had not been allowed foods or fluids for the previous fourteen hours—with "Water water everywhere, and not a drop to drink."

The fantasy of composing an irate letter to the interventional radiologists also nudges me out of self-pity. I would of course delete from my fantasy protest all the railings against the swinish radiological sadists that I have expressed in mental fugues of rage that sometimes spill out as irate words sputtered to nurses. My high-minded epistle simply advises Dr. Agarwal and his associates to confront their failures and then urges them to shut down their practice, indeed to oversee the demise of their discipline. They should go into a different line of work altogether. Only at the removal of time do I really take in Dr. Agarwal's piteous tale. The radiologist had sought Don out in the waiting area after what would be the last of his multiple procedures on my bottom. "It's only a temporary solution," he explained about the second drain, adding after a pause, "It was done to my mother." Tears welled up in his eyes as he wept over his mother's death. Don had told me the sorry story of Dr. Agarwal's grief in my hospital room and I asked about it again while we waited interminably in a darkened antechamber for Dr. Robb to perform the ileostomy. Without my glasses and dazed, I had then asked my dear husband to read the banner wrapped around the nearby nurses' station. In bold capital letters, the logo urged, "BE A FOUNTAIN, NOT A DRAIN!"

· 6 ·

A POSTHUMOUS EXISTENCE

URING THE PASSAGE of time punctuated by March 5,
March 26, and April 23, when I received the last three rounds
of Taxol and carboplatin, I teetered on the fearful edge of a precipice into which I fell. "No worst, there is none," Gerard Manley
Hopkins starts one of his "terrible sonnets" about the dark night
of the doubtful soul. A simple declarative sentence like "this is the
worst" would not convey the double negativity of a bleak psychological state beginning with "no" and ending with "none." Within
such a condition of incommunicable despondency, time accordions,
elongating into interminably prolonged durations or collapsing into
brittle brevity. The miserable depletion produced by accumulative
chemotherapy, probably inflected by the ordeal of the ileostomy,
stupefied me, mired me in the monotonous paralysis of Beckett's
nattering monologues about the "unworsenable worst": "Blanks
how long till somehow on? Again somehow on. All gone when
nohow on. Time gone when nohow on." I did not prize or hear the

sound of my own voice, though lines of the poets I had taught for four decades rattled in my head.

Against the backdrop of national economic disasters reminiscent of the Great Depression, the succession of my undifferentiated days accelerated, flying off the calendar as in old movies, but time also seemed to stand still in recursive stagnation. About the boredom of temporality under such circumstances, the heroine of *Wit* explains, "if you think eight months of cancer treatment is tedious for the *audience*, consider how it feels to play the part." To avoid the imitative fallacy—to refrain from producing dreary pages about a tiresome period during the midpoint of my first conscious year with ovarian cancer—I have collapsed into one chapter a period of three months in which I am eventually driven to consider my resemblance to zombies and golems, creatures who suffer what John Keats called "a posthumous existence." As the side effects of chemotherapy accumulate, they wring one overwhelming question out of me: how does my worthless life get lived without me? While I cease clinging so obstinately to the conviction that I need to keep on announcing to myself my own impending mortality, I realize that there might be worse conditions than mortality.

Paradoxically, each of the three cycles of profound lethargy always begins with a chemically induced high in which my spirits soar. Hail to thee, blithe dexamethasone, whatever thou art or wert! Before and after the fourth chemotherapy, as with all the others, these anti-nausea pills produce bursts of energy and attentiveness. Naturally, I had asked if I could take them throughout chemo, since my earlier proclivity to avoid medications had thoroughly eroded by this juncture. But no, Dr. Matei explained, this potent steroid can produce stomach disorders, diabetes, mood swings, hypertension, and acne or rashes (which I was developing on my face and arms). Still, how lovely that such a burst of energy coincided with a sleepover visit from my darling godchildren, who looked askance at how skinny I was, but then went on to recount or reenact their social studies projects on Roman games and Greek myths, their fascination with Harry Potter, their addiction to Game Boy or DS, their shouts of "Infinity and beyond" as they jumped off chairs and bounced on sofas, their delight at raiding the kitchen drawers and pantry shelves to present a loony assortment of desserts—chocolates, cookies, Pez, Twizzlers, individually wrapped charms, whatever they could scavenge (no matter how stale)—for whatever meal we were about to conclude.

After Cassie and Ben left and the magic pills petered out, I found myself for the first time feeling tired of being tired, exhausted with exhaustion, weary and wary. I was out of pain, so I tried to spend mornings at my study desk, writing or reading or paying my or my mother's bills, afternoons in the family room investigating books about ovarian disease, evenings with a novel or a movie. Every hour or two I ate some peanut butter on graham crackers and drank diluted cranberry juice or green tea. But the days began to feel stale and time weighed me down. Was I exhausted by even the steps upstairs because of the drains, the ileostomy operation, or the accumulative buildup of the chemotherapy? Or was I wasting away from all the waste to which I endlessly had to attend? Emptying the pouch, I like to think, will become fairly routine, every four hours or so; however, I awake to find myself clutching at its folded tip—a sure sign of my alarm that it will open and foul me, Don, and the bed.

Beyond trepidation and aversion, tedium makes me wonder whether it would be better to have taxing demands—a job to which I have to travel, a child to tend, something to take my mind off my own weakness, though I feel too feeble to initiate or sustain any physical exertion. Depleted, am I so empty of inner resources that I cannot keep myself mentally entertained? Maybe at the diagnosis I had leapt straight into thinking about hospice and dying to circumvent this dreary period in which I really do not know if the chemotherapy will or will not work or for how long, in which I have to be patient about not going among crowds of people who could transmit germs, in which I try to eat to bring up low blood counts, to offset anemia. Friends remain steadfast in their supportive communications, but each empty hour oppresses. A waiting game, and there are two more chemotherapies to get through. Might this be the onset of the fog of depression?

Yet my condition feels somewhat dissimilar to the weepy dejection I experienced when (many decades ago) my first husband refused all my pleas and decided to move out of the house on University Street. With thirteen-year-old Molly and nine-year-old Simone off at summer day camps, I sat listening to *Fidelio* over and over again, bemoaning my fate since no one in my family had ever gone through a divorce, and what would become of the children in a broken home? Miserable in my loneliness and unable then to confront the incompatibility my husband expertly analyzed, I staged coffee shop discussions and trial weekend sleepovers in futile efforts at reconciliation that left me hopeless about convincing him to patch up our differences. Pounds evaporated when sorrow and regret blighted my appetite, when insomnia at night turned me into a sleepwalker during the day. I plummeted into depression, but no, this sort of despondency—distressing as it may be—cannot be conflated with the impotence and incapacity generated by cumulative chemotherapy.

Chemotherapy does induce many of the symptoms related to depression, though the two phenomena have different etiologies. Like burgeoning states of depression, accumulative chemotherapy can spawn malaise, confusion, loss of appetite, failure of mental focus, an excruciating sense of joyless paralysis or worthlessness, memory loss, exhaustion, and insomnia. In times happily gone by, a depressed or repressed personality was thought to cause cancer probably because, as Sarah Gabriel sardonically puts it, "we don't like depressives, and we don't like the cancerous. Insisting that depressives get cancer is the perfect way of expressing our latent hostility for both in the guise of righteous wisdom." During times sadly still with some of us, "the slow erosion of the self" in depression feels "as insidious as any cancer": as Martha Manning observes, "like cancer, it is essentially a solitary experience. A room in hell with only your name on the door." The words pertain as well to cancer's treatment.

About the cause of his own entrapment in dejection, the novelist William Styron once argued that "chemical induced" depression arises "amid the neurotransmitters of the brain, probably as the result of systemic stress." In *Darkness Visible*, he sensed that his "thought processes were being engulfed by *a toxic and unnameable tide* that obliterated any enjoyable response to the living world" (emphasis mine). Here, at the origin, is where depression parts company with chemotherapy. Both feel like a "toxic tide," but the tide of depression remains "unnameable," whereas the cancer's arrives with labels like Taxol and carboplatin.

The cancer patient realizes that her symptoms have been "chemically induced" not mysteriously by physiology or the inexplicable decisions, fates, or temperaments of others, but systematically and therapeutically by the oncologist. This disjunction explains why depression sometimes leads people to suicidal thoughts and to suicide, whereas generally chemotherapy does not. Without a timetable, depressed people may become hopeless about the isolated "room in hell" they inhabit, regardless of the social situations they continue to face with relatives and friends clueless about their internal desolation. The person on chemo, however, knows exactly how many weeks or months her condition will last, and most of her acquaintances have been informed of the temporal brackets of her treatment. Okay, not "exactly," because some side effects linger indefinitely, but the general parameters are clear. Just as important, the cancer patient's impermanent condition often constitutes a radical break from her earlier identity.

The unnerving peculiarity of finding myself crouching on the bathroom floor clutching a hot water bottle or simply staring at a wall for minutes on end means that linearity, actions, and therefore narrative break down—I am not performing any meaningful deeds—so analogies take over. The spirit, according to Gerard Manley Hopkins's sonnet "No worst, there is none," confronts "cliffs of fall" that are so sheer and appalling that no one can bear contemplating them. Such a precipice may be visible only to the mind's eye, but those who cling for dear life apprehend their vertiginous fright: "Hold them cheap / May who ne'er hung there." Even though I remain physically in the house, chemo plunks my psyche down on such a terrifying ridge where dizziness deprives me of my "capacity for balance" and I quail, as does Andrew Solomon when he gets "close to the edge" of depression. Alone, isolated, I am petrified by my shocking fragility and vulnerability. A silly, compulsive act reveals how scared I am. I take my purse with me from room to room, even to the nightstand next to the bed, as if I might need my identification or insurance card at a moment's notice. With the nearby purse, and the thick woolen socks I now wear in bed, I will be equipped to flee imminent catastrophe.

Who, perched on a crag or hugging a rock face, exposed to torrential rain and wind, would dare to be tipsy? Is it fearfulness about my fragility and vulnerability that has terminated my drinking problem? While reeling from the medications after two abdominal surgeries, I lost an insatiable thirst for wine that had regulated my daily life from six in the evening until it landed me groggy in bed, an ingrown habit that now seems broken. I appear to have been shocked out of my addiction to alcohol not by a cure or a higher power but by the toxic tide of chemicals and by the necessity of cultivating the sort of wariness only possible in sobriety. The idea of being inebriated, like that of driving myself, alarms me, given the drain and the pouch and the absence of any reserves of energy. One sip of anything alcoholic just further weakens or dizzies me. Nevertheless, my expensive addiction to Nicorette thrives, maybe because it gives me a modicum of energy. Stranded at home, I peer at the abyss of emptiness below and above, hanging on by my slipping fingertips, bracing against the hostile elements, realizing my own limited powers of endurance, and chomping gum: "Nor does long our small / Durance deal with that steep or deep."

Composed as a response not to disease but to a spiritual crisis, Hopkins's psychic geography nevertheless captures the paralysis of chemo-time. Others have dealt exuberantly with the challenges of mountain climbing in stormy weather, whereas I—a gum-chewer buffeted by blasts of self-doubt—dig in my fingernails and breathlessly wait. Out there on that lonely edge, self-pity leads me to fret at menacing catastrophes I do not have the strength to survive. *The*

Ostomy Book insists, "A medical-alert emblem or an emergency card belongs with you at all times" with the warning "Do not remove ostomy pouch without doctor's orders." I do not have the ingenuity to laminate such a card or the fortitude to stand in line for money at the bank or for checkout at the supermarket. Hopkins conveys the self-loathing motivated by fearful weakness, the conviction that you are a creep or creeper on the ledge, a wretch shuddering at the precipice, drawn to a downward plunge, conscious only of anguished isolation. The single imaginable respite from the fierce gale of dread consists of loss of consciousness itself. Either you let go, shattering upon impact, or you resort to the good offices of Ambien: "Here! creep, / Wretch, under a comfort serves in a whirlwind: all / Life death does end and each day dies with sleep."

To what extent am I an anomaly, a weakling too feeble to hang on or clamber to safety? I have read about other women in chemotherapy who tour foreign countries, work, shop, and eat out at restaurants. The *Johns Hopkins Patients' Guide to Ovarian Cancer* states about chemotherapy, "Women can continue their normal daily activities during the treatment process." By way of goading myself, I consider the case of Joyce Wadler, who took dancing lessons and went to the gym three times a week during chemotherapy for breast cancer. The back cover of *No Time to Die: Living with Ovarian Cancer* informs readers that the fashion magazine editor Liz Tilberis "refused to let the disease get the better of her, continuing to participate fully in her life as a wife, mother, and career woman." In a photograph at the center of a commemorative "common threads" quilt crafted by Cynthia O'Dell and devoted to Harriette Grober, the cancer patient appears defiant, totally committed to her own survival on so-called maintenance therapy, with her arms crossed beneath a surgically marked chest and framed by the determined words "I will be on chemo for the rest of my life." Doris Brett used hypnosis to raise low platelet and white blood cell counts before her last two infusions of Taxol and carboplatin. Such images and accounts accentuate my lapses during a domestic hibernation that feels soulless, pointless.

Yet others have experienced in chemotherapy precisely the self-alienation that literalizes itself in, on, and through my hairless, emaciated body. During treatment for ovarian cancer, Chris Bledy remembers "lying on the floor alone, crying. My insides felt like creepy crawlers were taking over. I couldn't think straight." Juliet Wittman, because of a "seething" inside, feels "as if there's a witch's cauldron in my belly." To deal with the "pain and fear, fear and pain, alternating relentlessly," Kelly Corrigan describes taking "eighteen pills in twenty-four hours for everything from the well-known side effects like nausea and fatigue to the secret ones like runaway infections and tear-jerking constipation. Each side effect can be treated with medication, which usually has its own side effect." Vomiting and dry mouth, rashes and lip sores spiral revulsion at the flesh. With the addition of chest pains and tinnitus (a high-pitched ringing in the ears), Jackie Stacey admits, "the internality of my body was unbearable." No wonder that Arthur W. Frank found that his "deepest, even haunted, discussions" with other people in remission circled around "attempts to sort out whether chemotherapy is a form of torture."

"I found it extremely difficult to talk with my tongue stuck to the roof of my mouth," Maureen McCutcheon explains. "Some days, I felt like I had to pry it loose with my fingers." When Meredith Norton developed "a head-to-toe rash" as an allergic reaction to Taxol, she itched all over: "Knowing not to scratch, I sought relief by slapping myself. I slapped my arms and thighs, the harder, the better. I started using a wooden spoon, but it was leaving welt marks that actually intensified the itching as they disappeared" so then she lay on an "abrasive shag carpet" and writhed around "until the rug burns were more painful than the itching." Even when chemotherapy does not plague the body, it afflicts the psyche. As Treya Killam Wilber has explained, "Physically the chemo wasn't that bad. But . . . the bad part was that it felt like it was poisoning my soul, poisoning me not just physically but emotionally, psychologically, and spiritually. I just feel shot, totally out of control." *"I didn't know one could feel this badly and not die,"* Deborah Rose Sills once admitted.

A stick figure of disease and disgrace in a ridiculous-looking sleep cap, an extraterrestrial from the planet Chemo, I lather all appendages with Benadryl Itch-Stopping Gel and batten down, staring into space, seconds and then minutes ticking by. I gargle with the pink stuff in a bottle that surely cannot be nicknamed Mary's Magic Mixture. I blow my perpetually runny nose, rearranging the plastic bulb or tube of the drainage attachment, the panties and pants covering the ostomy contraption, unable to summon the willfulness or the willingness to engage with a single task. It is one thing to renounce willfulness, another to be robbed of willingness. That I am not my usually buoyant and easily entertained self weighs heavily on Don, who begins drooping, coughing, and stumbling, losing petals of conversational anecdotes like the decaying tulips my friend Dyan sent from Chicago.

Weakness of the body accompanies what I can only think of as the faltering of desire, a hesitancy that undermines dedication to anything or anyone. There is no pain (again, I tell myself this recurrently), just a discomfort around the various attachments. Diversions abound, but none catches my attention. Days disappear, but each hour crawls because I cannot get interested, excited, committed, or even vaguely attracted by any activity that comes to mind. Unable to concentrate on the writing of this manuscript, I force myself to produce what turns out to be such a sketchy draft that this chapter could not be composed during the time period it describes. Too unraveled, too devolved, I can neither talk nor write about my sense of being stalled, though I try to offset the lines of verse pulsing through my mind by counting my blessings. The sun is shining through the windows, affectionate colleagues e-mail, former graduate students send cards. But the flattening of any affect stultifies me. Curiosity, pleasure, suspense, focus sound like foreign words, as outlandish as Tonglen. There is only the waiting, the staring, the mute wondering if I can find the wherewithal to chop vegetables for a soup or stray down the driveway for the mail. Maybe I have to try to force myself more. It seems inconceivable.

The numbness of my paralyzed feet matches the numbness of my spirits. Even the news that colleagues are planning a reunion of my previous graduate students (in honor of my retirement in 2010) brings no pleasure or excitement, just listless watchfulness. I am oblivious to all past pursuits—in friendship, in books, in teaching, in marriage, in motherhood. Though I try to conceal my state of mind over e-mail and on the phone, nothing can capture my wayward attention. This is not me, I explain to myself. The chemicals drop me down to a barely sentient level of existence.

"How did her life live itself without her?" This sentence from a brilliant novel by Jonathan Safran Foer captures the oddity of experiencing oneself as a chemical receptacle. To pursue my career, I had always lectured myself that no momentary hesitancy or stoppage should be called a writing block. One must simply determine to go on writing, period. "Apply the seat of the pants to the seat of the chair": the mantra I learned from Sandra and recited to undergraduate and graduate students assured them that personal effort and the struggle to continue expression would win out with the reward of word following word in paragraphs and pages that reflected their thought processes and clarified themselves to themselves. But what to write about not wanting, not doing, not knowing how to get through minute by minute of this dull but fearful day, even though (thankfully) there is no pain (I try to concentrate on this), just discomfort. My source of being concealed in hiding, I have lost the spool of ebullience, the sense that I can buoy myself up with loving-kindness for those around me and learn from a process of reduction or diminution. Ennui, fatigue, and intimations of futility coalesce, dark clouds or heavy fogs weighing me down, now without the lightning that presages the relief of rain or at least some distracting thunder.

Authors of illness memoirs and mass-market books on cancer rarely elaborate upon the cumulative effects of chemotherapy, perhaps because treatments differ radically and change rapidly, but volumes like Ira Byock's *Dying Well* assure me that "people can become stronger and more whole as physical weakness becomes overwhelming and life itself wanes." Byock, an activist in hospice medicine, suggests that the journey toward "dying well" begins with two questions: "What would be left undone if I died today?" and "How can I live most fully in whatever time is left?" The second question sounds absurd in my condition, and the first must be rephrased in a more pedestrian way related to my ennui and isolation. What tasks might fill up my time now?

With nothing to feel but fearfulness about atrophied feeling, there must be things to do—no matter how banal. At many times in my life and in many of my friends' lives, making a list and checking it off can organize a day or a week of a difficult transitional period, so I itemize: contact contributors for an anthology of autobiographical essays by prominent feminist academics that I am editing; pay poetry permissions for *Judas*; confiscate more than thirty years of papers in my file cabinets; rid my closet of clothes not worn for years and bring them to Goodwill. Mental efforts must be made, too, about my decision not to undergo more treatments of the cancer so as to regain my un-drugged, un-debulked self and not to mull on or scheme to commit suicide. Parents who kill themselves make the act imaginable for their children, as I know all too well. I must close this destructive chain in the family by dying of ovarian cancer. Finding the thread to lead me through the labyrinth of lassitude and back to the inner pocket of mental ease that I experienced at the diagnosis seems an impossible task. The Greek word for thread is *mitosis*, I realize, a word that brings *metastasis* to my mind and then *malignancy*. When pressure builds against my backbone, intensifying into spasms, making sitting or lying down uncomfortable, I worry: is the cancer burgeoning or is the fluid in the abscess growing within me, pressing and causing pain?

On March 16, Dr. Robb's nurse practitioner phones. The infection in or on the bowel remains resistant to oral antibiotics. A PICC will be installed in my upper arm so antibiotics can be given through the veins, she tells me as I weep on the phone at the thought of another part of my body penetrated to cart yet another apparatus. Isn't it enough to have a drainage tube and bulb coming out of the left side of my belly, an ostomy bag plastered on the right? The very word "PICC" evokes my lengthy hospital confinement as well as picadors and the razor-sharp barbed sticks they heave to stab their bullfighters' dance partners. Now that books about Frida Kahlo stack up in my study, it also reminds me of the arrows she painted to depict her suffering. Attuned to the choreography of violence, Kahlo's *The Little Deer* distills her sense of being hunted down by murderous, weapon-wielding enemies. Elsewhere Kahlo painted blood transfusions and splints or casts and corsets to record her responses to the some thirty operations she endured, but on this canvas Kahlo emphasizes the pain of wounded flesh in a wounded landscape. If *The Dream* records serenity even in the overarching presence of death, *The Little Deer* mourns the physical anguish of life-in-death.

A windbreak near the ocean, consisting of two columns of trees, appears cut off to show only their gnarled and gashed trunks. Not darting but darted, the hybrid creature within it suffers a post-humous existence. Kahlo has painted her human head and face attached to the body of a deer shot by nine arrows whose points stick into the animal's flesh and whose shafts stick out of its body. At the place of each penetration, blood spurts down the porcupined hide. A creature of quick and graceful flight has been immobilized at the moment of stunned stasis before it falls dead to the ground. As if considering the satyr or Sagittarius, Kahlo understands herself to be divided between two species, human consciousness and animal body. One art critic associates the central figure of *The Little Deer* with Virgil's Dido, who, after being "struck by an arrow in Crete's forest," can only deal with her unrequited love for Aeneas by plunging a dagger into her chest and throwing herself into a pyre. To my eyes none of the arrows look self-inflicted. Also, Cupid's thrilling darts may relate to Kahlo's tangled infatuation with Diego Rivera, but they do not pertain to my situation or to

her decision to define herself as female (the human face) and male
(the roe's body).

The wounded stag in *The Spiritual Canticle* of St. John of the
Cross races in search of cool waters or to comfort a mate, but Kahlo's deer is transfixed far away from any companion and from the
lightning glinting over the distant sea. Like Keats, as envisioned by
Shelley, Kahlo has become a "herd-abandoned deer struck by the
hunter's dart." Like Yeats, she is "fastened to a dying animal" who
is herself. "The Aztec called deer tines 'flowers,' or *xochítl*, a name
[Kahlo] had long ago taken for herself." She is the dear little deer
with its branching crown of antlers. Also, the word "Carma"—
added to her signature on the bottom right of this canvas—suggests
that the artist meditates here not on the dangerous liaisons of desire

but rather on the physical misery of her unique incarnation. Like
many women in Greek mythology—Io who turns into a heifer, Kal-
listo into a bear, Daphne into a leaf—Kahlo's central figure cannot
control the boundaries of her body. Just as the female of the species
"swells, she shrinks, she leaks," she also "suffers metamorphoses"
and thus loses her "form in monstrosity." Kahlo's distinctive face
in this surrealistic self-portrait looks contemplative with its clear-
eyed gaze, but there are several indications that she cannot contain
multitudes.

The incongruous mind/body, human/animal, female/male
amalgam will self-destruct: animal fur appears to be creeping up
her neck, and antlers sprout beneath her well-combed, upswept
hair. At each impaled arrow, now a body attachment, leaking
blood weakens the deer. With its jagged and bifurcated branches
lopped off, the barren tree in the right foreground—a truncated
cross—hints at a botched crucifixion. A figure related to St. Sebas-
tian, often depicted tormented by the arrows shot at him, Kahlo's
stag or hart signifies her martyrdom, while her adamant gaze and
her closed mouth and even her earring and antlers and testicles
protest against it. Inland, the wounded deer pauses, poised as far
away from water as I am from health. A branch of peace beneath
the deer's hooves, mirroring the fragility of its new-grown antlers,
appears broken and wilted.

I manage to put off the insertion of the PICC for a few days, but
my spirits plummet. I feel as if I can feel the fistula or the pocket of
infectious fluid bulking beneath my tailbone. I resume oxycodone,
prescribed upon my last hospital release, and return to my to-do
list only when the daily and arduous medical regimen does not
take over.

THE DAILY MEDICAL REGIMEN

....

1. Remove one bomb of the antibiotic from the refrigerator upon waking.

2. Wrap the PICC (a semi-permanent intravenous line under the skin on my upper left arm) in Saran wrap, if there is sufficient strength to shower. The hand of my left arm, wrapped in Saran wrap, holds the small plastic bulb attached to the drain coming out of the left side of my belly, as I stand with my back to the water so the puncture hole of the drainage tubing and the ostomy bag don't get too drenched.

3. Change the wet bandage around the tube. Huddling under towels, crouching on my bed, I try to warm up afterward. Woolen pants, turtleneck (on the bottom of which the plastic drainage bulb can be clipped), a jacket or sweater, and a headscarf on my bald head remain the uniform.

4. Empty the filthy ileostomy contraption every few hours and replace the apparatus every five days.

5. Detach the drainage tube from the bulb and inject saline to irrigate twice.

6. Attach the PICC on my upper arm to the ball of antibiotic that travels through my veins to work against the infection. Before and after this infusion of about forty minutes, administer several flushes with saline and heparin syringes.

7. Drink juices, teas, and water constantly because of the fluid leaving my body through the stoma, as well as eat caloric food periodically.

....

At the start and end of each day, when I have to brush my teeth, wash my face, and put on or take off my pajamas, I am startled by my lack of pubic hair. It feels demeaning, as if I have been hurled back before puberty, to be forced to see—without the concealing cloud of black kinky hair—the girlish lips below looking so silly and vulnerable between my skinny thighs. On the bathroom counter, the "cranial prosthesis" sits neglected atop the box in which it was purchased at Wigs We Care. Bald, with no eyebrows or eyelashes, I smear various lotions on the rashes that turn my emaciated arms into dry and scratched appendages. In the mirror, I see the clear asymmetry of my hips around the long vertical scar on my belly. Little puckers of flesh tucked together around the scar make me look quilted by the sort of inept needlewoman who must hide extra fabric with a tightening line of stitches. This gothic doll-maker has supplied me with macabre accessories: a filthy bag hangs from one side of my stomach, a tube and bag from the other, while a white armband-type bandage encircles the PICC on my upper left arm. The shrunken frame with its meager but loose flesh—old-lady, wobbly, chicken-skinned flesh—brings to mind my emerging skeleton. Dem bones, dem bones, dem dry bones stuck out above my labia, topped by deflated breasts and a bald pate, recall the swaying dead-alive newsreel phantoms in my nightmare about the Chelmo of chemo. Doctored, I am a maundering wreck of the woman I had been.

Not a smidgen of that earlier sense of release, equanimity, loving-kindness endures during the week leading to the fifth chemotherapy and another CT. The day of the next-to-last chemo arrives in a springtime splendor to which I have been oblivious. The magnolias have already bloomed, the shapely pear trees are showing their white blossoms, and they will be followed by the haze of the redbuds, the floating petals of the dogwoods, and finally the glorious outburst of the beech by the side of the house, which puts forth tightly curled shoots that mystically open into tented leaves delicately hanging from the boughs of a huge trunk. Its trunk looks like a massive elephant's thigh.

What I see, though, is a slashed, gashed elephant's hide. I must gird myself to keep up the cheery chitchat that seems to be required during the taking of vitals (weight, blood pressure, temperature, pulse), the search for usable veins, the insertion of needles, the hooking up to plastic bags. Self-pity, in which Kahlo dared to wallow when she painted herself as a victim in *The Little Deer*, engulfs me. Her portrait configures my nauseated sense of surreal defilement and misery. An anomalous creature isolated from the human community, Kahlo's accursed hybrid labors under the doom assigned Judas: "Woe to that one," Jesus warns his disciples. "It would have been better for that one not to have been born." Like Judas, the little hart harbors a wretched conviction that it should have been aborted, for it will not be saved.

Who am I to complain about gagging down the Kool-Aid; squeezing in a meeting with Dr. Robb's nurse practitioner, after the consultation with Dr. Matei; a lower pelvic CT; a shorter infusion through the PICC so I need not endure the many sticks and resultant bruises on my hands and arms to find a usable vein; and then a drive home in bright sunshine, for once not shivering from the cold? Around suppertime, Dr. Robb's unexpectedly upbeat phone call, assuring me that the volume of the fluid in the abscess has decreased, means that the situation has improved and the drain coming out of my belly is properly positioned. The patient has to be patient, he advises, about what he poetically calls "the tincture of time"—or is that my invention? Chemo-brain—a term cancer survivors brought into currency that has recently received some scientific usage and credence—has rendered me uncertain of what I hear and what I think I hear.

Neither the medical good news nor the appearance of a few scattered reviews of *Judas* captures my wayward attention, for I am again "doing time": counting the days till the final chemotherapy, just trying to get through each day with distractions, now with growing awareness of chemo-brain. I find myself unable to follow magazine articles. I read a paragraph, then immediately forget it, and read it again. I check the page number to see if my incomprehension results from having skipped a page. This has happened to other people, specifically to a breast cancer survivor named Terri: "After three months I noticed that my comprehension abilities were almost gone. It would take me twenty minutes to read a paragraph in a book, and even then I didn't understand it and couldn't remember it. I couldn't think of words . . . I couldn't even think." With my flesh pierced and my innards oozing and now my mind dimming, the skeleton in Kahlo's *Dream* with its clean and dry bones takes on a sort of glamour. Atop leaky flesh, my head has become as hollow as his.

At the closing credits of wonderful movies, the specifics of the characters' names and dilemmas vanish from memory. As my attention drifts, I go into the bathroom explicitly for scissors, but notice the overflowing wastepaper basket, and by the time I empty it, there is no trace of the need for scissors on my mind. Although I jot down an appointment, say, or an idea for this book on a Post-it, later I stare at the illegible scrawl, unable to decode it. When at noon I decide to make lunch, I discover that I neglected to turn off the gas burner for a morning cup of tea. My cognitive impairment could be dangerous. I must keep track of things, maybe with my calendar, but at the moment it's lost. Attention and retention deficits are not produced by the raging delusions—directives to kill or be killed, for example—that plague schizophrenics but rather from the damper of a thickening envelope of hesitancy through which my tentative eyes peer, my halting voice echoes.

Losing confidence in myself, I read or say the word "right" for "left" or the word "lift" for "laughed" or "hanger" for "hunger" or "miscarriage" for "marriage," a dyslexic confusion that Elyn Saks terms "word salad" in which "one says [or reads] words that sound similar but have no real connection with one another." What I say is mis-said or goes unsaid so as not to be mis-said. I explain to Don that "my college friend Georgette is traveling by car from New York to visit us on New Year's Eve," when what I mean to say is the Fourth of July. I try to tell Mary and Andrew about the girls' renting a house for a family holiday near a beach in—"Bell Harbor?" I ask Don; no, "South Haven," he patiently reiterates for the umpteenth time. In Saks's approach to the onset of schizophrenia, she captures the incoherence of my interior state: "The 'me' becomes a haze, and the solid center from which one experiences reality breaks up like a bad radio signal."

As the toxins accrue in my body after five chemo sessions, there are diversions, but no real pleasures; lists of things-to-do but no keen gratification, and of course the daily medical regimen. Doctors Dizon and Abu-Rustum reassure readers with ovarian cancer, "You should be able to carry out most normal activities even while on chemotherapy . . . In fact, most studies show that some people feel better on treatment than they did when they were diagnosed." A president of the Society of Gynecologic Nurse Oncologists promises, "chemotherapy doesn't mean that you can't cook dinner or go out dancing or do all the things you like to do." Unable to carry out normal activities, I try to remind myself of my good fortune.

Barbara R. Van Billiard suffered "fecal vomiting" that usually ended with her fainting. Meredith Norton's chemotherapies caused aching bones, "as though my thighbone was being stretched lengthwise," as well as "freakish skin discoloration" and "stinging, burning cramp" in her hypersensitive hands. Jackie Stacey's "severe chest pains" prove that the chemotherapy has resulted in "lung damage." After "three drops of Taxol," Sue Skalinder "had an anaphylactic reaction—whole body heat flash followed by intense tingling, huge drop in blood pressure and whole body contractions inside and out. It took four hours to stabilize me so I could go home." An ovarian cancer patient named Patricia, whose chemotherapy proved ineffective against a tumor blocking her bowels, had to "have a stomach-drain into a bag" and eventually could not eat: "all I get is intravenous with saline to keep hydrated. And they're continuously draining my stomach because otherwise I throw up bile." My physical symptoms—feet and toes paralyzed, rashes, aching right hip—pale in comparison to the psychological ones. Despite Don's loving presence, he hardly chinks the armor of my parochial self-absorption. Better dead than leaden, I think when the phone rings.

"Susie, I had to wake up twice last night, and around 4 a.m. I had to go to the bathroom."

"Oh hi, Mom, did you get back to sleep?"

"They want me to get dressed. I had a tray brought in, and I want to stay in my housecoat. My belly is hurting and the pain pill didn't help."

"Take another, Mom. Maybe it would be good for you to try to get dressed for lunch?"

"Do you think Don could come to get my laundry? I just got the official notification of a big prize, and I want you to send a check to some of these charities."

"Ma, those prizes are a scam, I told you, and Don has his hands full with the paperwork for your taxes . . ."

"I know. I'm writing back to them, telling them why I can't give this year. I can't ask him for more folders."

"I'll get you some folders. And if you want to stay in your house-coat, tell the nurse that you'll take a tray for lunch too."

"*Colored* folders, Susie? That's what I need."

It is during the wait for the last chemotherapy that I plunge from the "cliffs of fall" into a posthumous existence. On the "cliffs of fall" I had felt terrified by my vulnerability in a threatening whirlwind of a world. I knew that I could not survive outside the protective shell of the house if I relied on my own desiccated powers. Virginia Woolf's ideal of autonomy—of going along with no arm to cling to—had evaporated in terms of my physical frailties, not to mention the medical regimen. Dependent upon Don and all the equipment Kim taught me to use, I was sheltered, but fearful about my own weakness. Now, though, the overwhelming depletion of my otiose psyche takes hold, for it seems as if my real life has disappeared. Vacuity and horror at my own vacuity stall time, expanding into an eternity each moment of crouching on the bathroom floor or staring at a wall, while constricting its uniqueness and significance.

Emily Dickinson's reanimated corpses evoke my state of non-being.
Consider the cadavers speaking in some of her opening lines: "'Twas
just this time, last year, I died"; "I heard a Fly buzz – when I died";
"My Life closed twice before its close –".

Emily Dickinson, projecting herself into or speaking as a dead
person, captures the life-in-death or the embalmed being of chemo-
time. I am neither alive (as Dickinson was when she wrote her verse)
nor dead (as many of her speakers seem to be):

> *To die – without the Dying*
> *And live – without the Life*
> *This is the hardest Miracle*
> *Prepounded to Belief.*

Without the experience of dying, it cannot be said that I have died
or am dead. But without the sense of living, I have no life. In these
lines the poet speaks in "a consciousness caught between registers,"
a phrase that could describe Kahlo's wounded deer. Such an ineffectual being contributes nil to the welfare of a world that would
not be lessened an iota by her disappearance. How to understand
the last two lines about a miracle quite distinct from the one experienced by Lazarus in the New Testament? Waiting for "the hardest
Miracle," a reprieve from an incurable cancer, I am pre- and re- or
pro-pounded by the capital letter Beliefs of medical authorities.

The authors of other illness narratives teach us to prize the value
of life, but I begin to comprehend the precious worth of death—
especially when considered in terms of the life-in-death conferred by
chemotherapy. Think of those mythic or fantastic creatures granted
eternal life without eternal health and youth: the Cumaean Sibyl, for
instance, or the Struldbruggs in the third book of *Gulliver's Travels*.

Immortal but decaying and dead to affection and curiosity, Swift's Struldbruggs may be exempt from physical termination but their unending devolution into querulous, envious, and impotent senility can only horrify Gulliver and the reader with "the dreadful Prospect of never dying." Death has departed from their world only to leave them miserably incapacitated in a never-dying but always degenerating afterlife. "What is truly horrible is not death but the irremissibility of existence" or "the facticity of being riveted to existence without an exit," as the philosopher Simon Critchley puts it more abstractly.

The breast cancer patient Sarah Gabriel best conveys my condition toward the end of accumulative chemotherapy. Her "complaint is that I don't exist any more. Everything that makes me *me* is gone. I can't read, interact with a friend, cook, do a basic act of care for my children, or get to the end of the street. 'This isn't me,' I explain. 'I can't live with not being me any more.' " The rub and the gall of realizing oneself no longer oneself: "The degradation. The nothingness of it." It is as if an invisible umbilical cord connecting me to the aura of my prior personality or temperament had somehow been severed.

Those who inhabit the space between the register of life and the register of death are humanlike but not-quite-human. In a 2008 movie that I cannot bring myself to watch, *Zombie Strippers*, a chemo-virus triggers the transformation of humans into zombies. This species has a long history, including book and movie versions of *Invasion of the Body Snatchers*, in which pod-people look like the exact physical replica of the town folk they replace but with one major difference. Pod-duplicates evince absolutely no emotion, except when they widen their mouths to emit a piercing scream (to disclose the appearance of a real human being). More outwardly normal and active than I am, the vacant pod-people exhibit a lack of responsiveness comparable to that of the golem of Jewish legend, a creature made of clay or mud. A clumsy and slow-witted humanoid who follows orders, the deactivated golem is me. When the first letter of the Hebrew word *emet* (which means "truth") is erased from the golem's forehead so as to read *met* (which means "dead"), the golem degenerates into the matter from which he was composed. Taken together, these legions of the undead constitute the genealogy of my chemo-ized state.

In southern Indiana, a euphemistic expression that I used to find jarring takes on new resonance. "She passed," someone murmurs to communicate a death. Not "she passed away" because apparently she might have passed "over" or "through" to some heavenly kingdom—with the mortal body putrefying, the spirit presumably soars—so a trace of piety clings to the phrase "she passed." A posthumous existence ghoulishly recasts this idea, for I have passed out of generosity and tenderness, of subjectivity itself, even though I am not physically relegated to the past. If the dead can live in Christian resurrection, in chemotherapy the living can reckon themselves dead. Are the dead living or the living dead in the first two stanzas of one of Dickinson's more gruesome poems from the grave?

> *Do People moulder equally,*
> *They bury, in the Grave?*
> *I do believe a Species*
> *As positively live*
>
> *As I, who testify it*
> *Deny that I — am dead —*
> *And fill my Lungs, for Witness —*
> *From Tanks — above my Head —*

Weighted down by gravity as if buried underground or underwater, I gasp in the alien element, fearful of the reliability of attached pipes to far-off tanks of air. Like Edgar Allan Poe's, Dickinson's quarrel with Christianity recalls the gruesome question about the corpse "planted" at the end of the first section of T. S. Eliot's *The Waste Land*: "Has it begun to sprout?"

As the weather warms, smells leach from the drainage bulb or the ostomy pouch, though luckily Don cannot discern them. In so-and-so-many days, I keep on counting, I will have my last chemotherapy. I just have to get through it. Then perhaps my head might clear, I might feel like my old self. In a book about "embracing life as a healthy survivor," Wendy Schlessel Harpham recapitulates trepidations about harsh cancer therapies that seem to use "a hammer to kill an ant on a glass window: You fear they will hamper or destroy your body's natural ability to fight your disease and, worse, hurt your body's ability to recover and function normally ever again." How, then, can she urge cancer survivors to live with cancer "as a chronic disease" that can be controlled with ongoing treatments? The goal is to get to a "partial remission" or to "stabilize or compensate for the abnormalities for long periods of time." One can be *healed* without being *cured*, apparently. Her cheerful view butts up against my determination *not* to prolong false hopes or debilitating procedures that rob me of my self. The so-called healing efforts have all produced grotesque side effects.

With one week and two days left till the last chemotherapy, I check off the days like a prisoner chalking them one by one on a cell wall, pay the taxes, e-mail the girls with smokescreen reassurances, fold the laundry, and sink into profounder ennui about my miserable failings. During occasional phone conversations with Molly or Simone—they are trying hard not to lean on me—I am appalled by my shackled self's inability to acknowledge or respond to their needs even verbally. In the grip of a ghastly fright at my maternal inadequacy, my tongue is stapled by the simulacra of implanted memories and affects. Although my girls face stressful circumstances of their own, I am horrified that I can offer them neither solutions nor consolations for their various dilemmas. All I can convey to them, and to Don, is a dumb determination not to communicate my compulsive concerns over the side effects of the chemo while millions of people face unemployment, soldiers and civilians die in faraway wars, and more children find themselves at risk in poverty here in the United States.

Nerves too often jolted by horrific procedures and treatments attend to consciousness, but attend as if stunned and inert. The house, which hides, protects, and shelters me, becomes my cage or tomb. Within it, I feel parts of my psyche atrophying. I'm inside a deep cave with a series of projected images on the walls, but a very limited perspective on the sky. I am less real than the Persian rugs on the floors or the bright oil canvases on the walls. They will outlive me, of course, but even now they contain more vibrancy than I do. Better for all that I am debarred from the university, for my conceited professionalism seems to have consisted of nothing but placating fussy colleagues in pointless meetings and bloviating in front of undergraduates better off elsewhere. Given the budget crunches and miserable job market in the humanities, too many of my graduate students will have to take jobs incommensurate with their training. For all our so-called activism, have feminists in the academy failed to ensure the future of our successors? The ceremonies of my truncated life have stiffened my heart so thoroughly that my experiences in school and, indeed, my experiences yesterday occurred centuries ago. No one's feet could be more mechanical than mine. Without shoes, they freeze. With shoes, if and when I can move my toes, only pins and needles remind me they exist. Stumbling, my mechanical feet take me from the study to the kitchen in a wooden way that robs every task of its previous and quite ordinary delights.

I cannot stand to stand. Chopping an onion or peeling a clove of garlic, for instance, exhausts me but also drives me to irritation with my own incompetence. Slipping around on the cutting board, the onion first gets gashed in the process of my removing its skins and then drops apart into ugly uneven bits, some of which fall on the floor. The thin peel around the garlic clings to my fingers until I am driven to knife off all but the core and wash away the slime on my sticky hands with water that ends up scalding me. Empty bird-feeders and piles of unopened mail remind me how inefficient, how inadequate I am. Stones no more feel contentment than I do. Literally, I am always freezing, huddling beneath a quilt which conceals a blasting heating pad, and blowing my dripping nose. There are exceptions to the rule that chemotherapy does not issue in suicidal impulses. Hospitalized for treatment of a deepening depression, Martha Manning describes another patient who "tells us how she took an overdose after rounds of cancer chemotherapy and reassures us that she cried continually for a week when she found out that she was going to have to live." One ovarian cancer patient has explained, "When they told me I was disease free, I cried for a year."

The questions about protocols and prognosis that I prepare in my head for my next meeting with Dr. Matei explain why there is no point writing extensively about the period after the fifth chemo, for they governed my psyche: how effective will the six rounds be and for how long? Waiting for the last of the toxic infusions, I know nothing about how my checkups will be scheduled, whether (or rather *when*) there will be a remission and its so-called durability.

Banished from myself, with rigor mortis settling on the rictus of a grin in any chance social encounter at the drugstore, I want nothing except that the chemo be over and normal awareness return. I have canceled my favorite spring holiday, Passover, and arranged for my mother to attend the synagogue's Seder. Neither the girls nor Jayne nor Jan nor Jon will arrive to participate with Mary Jo taking us through the Haggadah before an annual meal celebrating deliverance from bondage. This night is no different from any other night, from the night before or the next night or the one after that.

Perhaps because I have fallen from the brink into depression, the recurrence of pressure against my coccyx convinces me that the infection and the fluid and the perforation have never gone away or have returned. Regardless of the diagrams and discussions of usually rushed physicians, the abscess and hole remain hazy in my mind. Both their cause (the suboptimal debulking? the tumors?) and their shape and placement in my body elude my comprehension, but retain a sinister hold. On Easter, my friends Shehira and Judith join us to share one of the installments of *Little Dorrit* on PBS. The countdown has begun for them and for all our other friends. Just a handful of days before the last chemo, they exult, wanting to believe that this will be the promised end. But the fact that a brief lunch out with Mary leaves me shaking with cold and fatigue, my teeth chattering, should have served as a warning that my blood counts have plummeted. On the day I am supposed to receive my last chemo, Dr. Matei orders blood transfusions that delay the final session for another week. The next day, Dr. Robb puts me back on antibiotics through the PICC, for the status of the infection remains inconclusive. Taken abruptly off dexamethasone, I skulk home barely able to drag myself around.

So once again I begin counting the days to the last chemo, this time often huddled fully clothed on Molly's old bed. Either the debilitating buildup of toxins or the infection can be blamed for my return to painkillers and stupor. Unable to sit comfortably at my desk, I take refuge in a small space filled with sunshine. I tell myself that I can take a sunbath and lie down on my left hip, the only position that takes pressure off my coccyx. Shooting pains from my right hip down into my leg make no sense to me at all. I am dying without death; living without life. Inconsolable, I do nothing but lie there—slightly shifting my limbs, wandering in my mind, breathing rhythmically for short periods of time, concentrating on the books that I should but will not rearrange in Molly's jammed bookcases, letting the minutes slide by and get me closer to the last zap. In this late stage of chemo, I resemble those punch-down inflated plastic clown toys, except I don't pop right back up. You hit it, but it sort of flutters on the floor, before it slowly lists to the diagonal without achieving the full verticality of an upright position.

At a certain point, I imagine, a collar has been placed around its neck to drag this rubber inflation from room to room. Noosed by whom? By another diminished shred of myself that has determined to get through these sessions and has no pity for the recumbent rubbery bozo that nevertheless feels like the realer me. "Sometimes," an ovarian cancer patient admits, "you lose that desire to carry on and to keep going . . . but you just keep putting one foot in front of another." I seem to be lying down on the job these days.

At the April 16 meeting with Dr. Matei, when she delayed the last session for a week, I had brought only two words as questions: protocol and prognosis. About protocol, she explained that I would see her every three months for blood checks after the final chemo. About prognosis, she declared, the remission would probably last from three months to three years. When pressed about my case— the lowering CA-125 marker proved the chemo to be effective—she guessed about a year. Or at least I heard her guessing at a remission of one year. Later, when we compared mental notes, Don heard only three months to three years, so perhaps once again chemo-brain has invented what I thought I had been told. One healthy year of life: was this what all these toxins added up to? "To some extent," specialists agree about people with stage III or IV, "all chemotherapy for ovarian cancer is palliative," working to achieve "the best quality of life (QOL) and quantity of life possible from an almost always terminal diagnosis." Is one year of life worth it? Impossible to say, but it seems important to let the girls and my stepdaughters know the parameters of my future. Molly and Simone understandably respond with shock. I immediately follow up with e-mails assuring them that recurrence must not be interpreted as death. It takes quite a bit of time to "fall off the twig."

In responding to their responses, I doubt that I will ever become a Buddhist or what has been popularized as a Buddhist by mostly non-Asian translators. Judgment seems to be a default position. I was trained as the sort of literary critic who bases her ideas on affective reactions to texts, and there is no way I could reach detachment, which seems too closely aligned to the vacuity of chemotherapy. In health, attraction and revulsion and hilarity color my every mood. As much as I value the goal of attaining mind-fulness, loving-kindness, and compassion, I will never be able to achieve these states by emptying myself of narratives and emotions, desires and dreads. Such an emptied self would simply not be me (and of course according to Buddhist aspirations it is supposed to be not me). Some of the techniques of breathing and of meditating, of distancing oneself from oneself and thinking of the other can help with fearfulness and impatience. But I will always be a secular Jew, never a Buddhist. The "peace which comes from selflessness," Karen Armstrong explains, "is a condition that those of us who are still enmeshed in the cravings of egotism . . . cannot imagine."

If faith in new faiths floundered, I nevertheless found comfort in Don, who could find me weeping on Molly's bed ("Frederick, the summer will never come") and simply stroke my back while sitting companionably next to me. Or in the e-mail response to my report of Dr. Matei's prognosis from his daughter Julie, whose words I read and reread:

> You have not erred in sending this e-mail. The thing about the unvarnished truth the doctor told you is that it is so vague and in the end meaningless. Who CAN number the days, after all. What IS for sure is that the days ahead will be filled with love and that you have Donald, above all, close to you, as well as your daughters and friends and other family, so that there will CERTAINLY be happiness ahead, no matter what else happens. The prognosis for all of us is ultimately the same, and trying to guess at the future is futile, so trite as it sounds, focusing on the present, especially when your present there . . . is often so lovely, is key. I'm sorry you had this bad day and about the transfusion and that you have to go back to Indy again, but there are going to be better days ahead as well and you got through this one. I love you—Julie

I finally received the last dose of Taxol and carboplatin in a thoroughly unremarkable "infusion." The redbuds were in bloom, the white and pink dogwoods beginning to show, as Don and I drove home through temperatures climbing toward eighty. I had weathered the course, and only had to endure three or four weeks of its side effects before a more normal consciousness might (and I hoped would) arrive. Maybe my dead soles would reanimate, my hair grow back, as I decided to switch from stigmatizing scarves into a Paddington hat or baseball caps. In mid-May there would be a CT which would tell Dr. Robb if he had cured the infection and could reverse the ileostomy. But there would be no more chemo: this conviction would steady me on the tightrope I would shakily traverse back to ordinary existence.

People tend to celebrate the end of chemotherapy with a gesture that speaks, "Hence loathed melancholy": flowers and chocolates and cards arrive, visitors ask to call again, and jubilation resounds, though of course the side effects of the last poisons hang on. In lively phone conversations with Sandra, I try to repeat that ovarian cancer is treatable but not curable, a sentiment the author of *Death's Door* fully comprehends but tries to forestall. When I describe to Dr. Robb my need to reverse the ileostomy so it will not present a problem in hospice, he explains that stomas and ostomy bags are actually easier for caretakers of the dying, but quickly cautions me against "morbid thoughts."

Ironically, on a warm and sunny April 27, the last day of dexamethasone after my last chemo, I have my first mishap with the ostomy bag. Jo had taken me on a trip to May's Greenhouse to get sweet potato plants—she was calculating that the inexpensive plants would bring down the cost of her grocery bills—and I sat in the sun on her back porch while she put them in a large wooden bucket and then watered them, along with the perennials in her garden. Did the heat of the sun melt some of the adherent that glues the disk to my stomach? Only when I get home do I feel the slimy rivulets of shit coagulating under my jeans. Was the new sort of caulking not as effective as the last, somewhat different-looking tube of the glue encircling the stoma? Or had I somehow not snapped the bag properly to the disk, not plastered the disk properly to my belly?

In subsequent days, Jan arrives with memory foam for my desk chair. Jayne plants a bunchberry and a primrose near the kitchen door. Jo brings an elaborate foot massage contraption, Mary a striped scarf picked out by my godchildren. But I brood about my negligence in not packing supplies for my infrequent outings. Now I would fill a kit with the necessities—not inconsiderable—for such a change. For the thought of excretions fouling me and disgusting others sends shudders through me. Legend has it that a donkey defecated on the stage during a production of the opera *Cavalleria Rusticana*. "The eminent conductor, Sir Thomas Beecham, stopped the performance at this point by tapping on the rostrum; he then turned to the audience and announced, 'Ladies and gentlemen, a moment's reverent silence, please. We are in the presence of a superior being: a critic.' " Not my bald head, dead soles, scarecrow frame, or enervation, but a nightmare of waste arrests my attention. I must fear and avoid the heat of the sun. I should laminate a medical-alert card to keep with me at all times. Will I never be able to soak in a hot bathtub with a candle flickering on the nearby sink, Brahms's *Requiem* or Ray Charles resounding in my ears?

REMISSION

"THERE'S A TREE on fire and it's about to fall on your house." The hysterical voice on the iPhone issued from my only neighbor and interrupted a dinner Don and I were eating in Indianapolis on May 13, the day we consulted with Dr. Robb about that morning's CT. Lightning had struck one of the sixty-foot-tall pine trees which now burned at its core. Though water from the firemen's hoses was dousing flaming limbs, apparently the blazing interior of the trunk continued to consume the huge tree from within. Should it plummet into the circle of beauty, the length and width of the majestic pine might ignite other trees, or if it fell onto the house its weight could result in the destruction of the roof, our bedroom beneath it, and the dining room below. The resulting fires could catch and destroy the entire edifice.

What would be lost, I wondered as we made our way back to our hotel room. I pictured all the photographs and the quilts not yet given away and of course this manuscript-in-progress. The baby quilts are packed in the study closet, the bed-size quilts simply layered on beds, all inside the house. I had backed up drafted chapters of this book, but on a flash drive also inside the house. Needless to say, Don could not dawdle in Indianapolis while everything might go up in flames a mere one-hour drive away. After I sat down in a standard hotel room—with its king-size bed, picture window, the TV hidden in a cabinet on a chest of drawers—and reassured him that I would be fine alone and he should drive carefully through the passing storm, I heard the door slam, placed the iPhone next to the hotel phone on the nightstand, and attended to the moment when I first felt myself to be "in remission," a phrase Dr. Matei had used before my fifth and sixth chemotherapies and would probably reiterate tomorrow.

The actual experience first occurred a week earlier, on the floor of my study, when I laid out two fabrics for cutting. Soon it would be too hot to work on the quilt made from Don's striped shirts, which I had not touched in months, so I should have a piecing project for the good summer in which we have placed our hopes. Despite mouth sores and dead soles, the drainage tube-and-bulb and the ostomy bag, exhaustion and rashes, at this moment the fog of internal vacuity began to lift. In the hope that quotidian matters finally would start to eclipse medical decisions, I determined to pick the easiest pattern—bar stripes—with the most vibrant fabric in my stash: a few yards of a Liberty's tiny floral print and a few yards of a vibrant solid that picked up its royal blues. Starkly symmetrical in its verticality, bar stripes is a classic Amish design. I must have purchased the Liberty's fabric on a trip to visit my British cousins, the sons of my father's brother.

As I prop up a pillow and recline on the bed in the Indianapolis hotel room, two fears escalate. Would the blazing tree crush and consume the house? Would Don safely make his way back to

Bloomington on the rain-swept highway? We had asked Andrew to drive out to the house and keep me informed of what was happening until Don arrived. I wait to hear from Andrew and Don, recollecting anxious phone calls that went unanswered almost half a century ago, during a late afternoon stretching into the early evening of June 10, 1960. I dialed the shop again and again; again and again, the distant phone rang. Where could my father be? A highly conscientious man, he had worked upon his arrival in a Brooklyn war munitions factory. He skimped and saved until, the war over, he managed to rent a body-and-fender shop in a broken-down neighborhood not far from the slum in which we lived. Ruled by methodical plans and schedules, determined to provide for his impoverished family, he carried a black tin lunchbox crammed with four or more sandwiches—"they hardly fill my hollow tooth," he groused—so Mondays through Saturdays he could arrive at 6 a.m. and leave at 6 p.m. without starving. As I waited and waited at the end of the line, the phone in the shop rang and rang without being picked up, inconceivably kept on ringing. How he loved the battered Oldsmobiles and Chevrolets, as he banged away at dented fenders or applied putty and repainted them. The fall of GM would have been inconceivable to my father.

Neither the hotel phone nor the iPhone can ring yet with Don just wending his way out of the city, but I worry that the beer he drank will affect his efforts to negotiate huge wind gusts after a wearisome day of driving to Indianapolis and of interminable waiting that only eventuated in Dr. Robb "leaving as is" the drain and ostomy bags attached to my belly. Because tomorrow Dr. Matei will probably repeat reports of my remission, the fraught trek in a torrential downpour seems pointless. How difficult it must have been for my father, whose family owned real estate in Hamburg, to have left his parents and the property they had accumulated in Germany, to have plummeted into the ranks of manual laborers in America. Since my mother (with her baby son) escaped Germany a few months before him, she was never sure if or how my father bribed his way out or crossed the border to Holland.

They had left behind her deaf and blind grandmother, booted out of an old-age home, hauled off to Theresienstadt; uncle Edgar and his wife, Liese, deported and *vershollen* (missing without a trace). Only in 1943 did they learn about the deaths of my father's parents a year earlier. A Red Cross telegram and some sleuth work revealed that my father's mother resisted deportation by taking poison. A solicitous concierge brought her a sleep-inducing drug. "*Meine heissgeliebten Kinder,*" Elfriede's letter read to those who finally received it: "You cannot imagine how we were tormented. When I think of what they can do to you, then I think it is better to take one's Veronal and quietly go to sleep." Upon learning the news, her husband, in the hospital for an angina attack, turned his face to the wall. "Turned his face to the wall" became the repeated phrase to speak the sadness of the fate of my father's father as well as the dubious state of our knowledge of it.

Every night as a child, I glimpsed my father through the bedroom door, hunched over his desk, whispering German numbers as he paid bills or balanced the checkbook or calculated whether he could afford to purchase a window air conditioner for one room of the cramped apartment from which he would liberate us on Sunday trips to a beach or a park. But firemen expected payoffs at the shop so there was no way of knowing what would be demanded when by whom. Car trips were therefore planned and executed with dispatch bred by anticipation of dire mishaps—traffic jams, parking problems, expenses we could not afford, inexplicably malevolent

policemen, potential accidents—lending such outings the semblance of jailbreaks. Yet for all the paranoia and dread, he roared
with laughter at a joke until tears filled his eyes. Though he might
rage when I was "fresh" to my mother, the warm grasp of his palm
cradling my hand remains my most tactile memory of a man whose
relish of food, cars, an ocean swim and whose determination to keep
his family safe still amaze me, or so I reflect as I look down at the
hotel pad, on which I scribbled the phone numbers of the iPhone
and the hotel for Don so that he could let me know his whereabouts.

The atmosphere in my immigrant family's walk-up apartment in Flatbush was filtered through the pathos of watching my
exhausted mother earn money by sewing so many gloves that she
permanently scarred her hands. The dilapidated rooms reeked of
worry and distress—the shame of a German accent, of not knowing
American customs, of hideous canned vegetables and convertible
sofas, of infestations of worms or nits, of decrepit relatives bringing bits of personal rubbish as "presents" for the "smart" son, the
"silly" daughter. My mother, sympathizing with the problems of a
bereft cousin, crooned *"selbstverständlich"* into the phone, while my
father erupted to no one in particular but with inexplicable anger
and frustration, *"Donnerwetter noch einmal!"* Tension pulsed to the
frequency of the TV's flickering images of the McCarthy hearings,
since it could happen again, even here, and then they would have
to pack up and leave once more, or perhaps they would not be so
lucky this time. *"Alt und arm und krank und Jüde—ein vier fasch
Katastrophe,"* my father used to misquote Heine: "old and poor and
sick and Jewish—a fourfold catastrophe."

If only I could convince Don not to return tomorrow just to
hear Dr. Matei speak again about my remission, a state that feels
physically exactly like chemo. What else would be burnt to a cinder,

I wonder, trying to take my mind off my father inhaling the poisonous fumes and Don battling a lightning display now accompanied by distant thunder. As if on cue, the iPhone beeps and Andrew's voice assures me that the fir tree has been sawed at an angle so it will fall away from its adjacent twin pine and also from the house. The firemen will hack it into logs "for the elderly couple" in apparent need of such help. But, no, Don has not yet arrived, though Andrew will hang around a bit longer to greet him. Might he have had an accident on the road, I fret silently. It is surely too soon to worry.

My father would not have heard the phone in the shop, ringing from four and five until six and later, for he must have passed out in his car with the windows closed except for a crack to let in the carbon monoxide. At fifty-six years of age, he might have been brooding on his parents dead in Hamburg, or the illegal gold he had hidden in the hollow bottom of a hutch, or his wife's competency as she moved from hand-sewing to a clerical job, or his bright son's facility in science, or his daft daughter's flightiness, or some searing pangs he had hidden from everyone because disease costs money that he could not afford, and anyway what can doctors do? As a youth during Germany's interwar Great Depression, he had brought a basket of paper money to buy an apple at market; he left behind the family's fortune when he fled a decade later; he would not squander what he had put away this time. Or maybe he was in the vise of depression. Inside his filthy body-and-fender shop—littered with car lifts and girlie calendars, canisters of paint and putty—he must have slumped over the wheel of his automobile. Only decades later did I read the words in my mother's account: "Now I see the hose connected to the exhaust, leading through a nearly closed window back into the car."

What if Don sits slumped at the wheel somewhere, killed on

the road by a drunk driver or by some sort of stroke or heart attack that caused the car to crash into a ditch? I should have accompanied him, though how would that have helped? Just this afternoon, when I took off my cap to scratch my scalp, Don asked with his lizard grin, "Hair getting in your eyes?" All my feeble attention has been directed at determining not to pursue any medical interventions after the six rounds of chemo, instead of what dawns on me now—the terror that Don could die before me. The miserable word "predeceased" rattles me with dread of the waves upon waves of grief that inundate the soul longing for that one unique being gone and never to be recovered. How I sobbed when informed about "Dad's heart attack," how I twirled through miseries of regret and bewilderment, guilt and self-recrimination—hadn't I been a disappointment to him with my hectic dating and my spotty school record—after the funeral when I was informed about his determination not to be. My father had enrolled me in a business track at Erasmus Hall High School so I could learn typing. His highest hope for his boy-crazy, cigarette-smoking American girl—maybe she would land a secretarial job.

How could it never have penetrated my thick skull that a man seventeen years older than I might die before me? Not just the solipsism of the sick but the stolidity of Don's rooted presence in the world—so different from my uprooted and transplanted father's fragile hold on existence—blinded me to a disaster whose possibility now overwhelms me in terror. What I adore about Don is his relish in living, his confidence that he belongs in the world he inhabits. Unlike me, he never seems to feel the lure of not continuing, of wanting to stop. Unlike me, he would want, he would deserve "extraordinary measures." It would be my fault entirely should his life end on the damned highway he has been traversing monthly, sometimes weekly, sometimes daily for the past half a year. A man who does justice and loves mercy and walks humbly—he trekked south to teach in segregated schools; later in the sixties, he served as a buffer between protesting students and obdurate administrators; in the seventies and eighties, he devoted himself to untangling the legal cases of colleagues denied tenure or treated unjustly by deans and departmental chairs—he cannot be gone. The suppurating wound would be catastrophic. Panting with dread, I turn on all the lights in the room, realizing that I would end up flushed with death, aggrieved and bereaved beyond solace. By the time the phone rings, I am ecstatic even as I listen to Don's account of the ruin inflicted by the storm that demolished the giant evergreen.

Inside the house, the electricity has been zapped, the phones and television cable too, as well as the water heater and the computers. "Bear," I exclaim, "I want you to stay put." I can easily find a car service to drive me back to Bloomington tomorrow. But no, we should "get our money's worth out of the hotel." Don will use this flimsy excuse to return at daybreak and take a hot shower before we check out of our room for the meeting with Dr. Matei, whose confidences about her vacation plans inform us that during remission we are on a leash longer than we had expected. On our return home, in a variation on gothic accounts of the cursed ancestral mansion, the wreck of the circle of beauty confronts us. Unlike the cloven chestnut tree on the grounds of *Jane Eyre*'s Thornfield Hall, the pine has been hacked into a blackened stump, the long trunk chunked into huge cindered logs strewn across the grass. Sap will flow no more in boughs that served as the backdrop for Molly and Kieran's wedding. It is a time to mourn, I think. I determine that I will, but jubilation takes hold. On getting out of the car, I cannot resist a two-step of glee, despite the flopping of body attachments.

During the rest of May and June and most of July, Don negotiates with workers from Grimes Plumbing, Comcast, AT&T, and Duke Energy, while the down on my head starts to come in salt-and-pepper, the eyebrows and eyelashes black. Before and after a flood in the basement from a rusted-out water heater, Don listens to the convoluted tales of workmen who tell of lightning flitting this way and that throughout their houses until it lands (without exception) on a mother or mother-in-law, toppled over in shock but miraculously unharmed. Meanwhile I fix my attention on bankruptcies set off by villainous investment traders, piracy on the open seas, the violent stifling of dissent in Iran and China, rising casualties in the Afghanistan war, and ongoing genocide in Darfur, Sudan, and the Congo. In the circle of beauty, there is a soft empty spot, composed of wood chips and pine needles, where the stump has been removed.

The crew that comes to fill in the sink hole and level the patch of myrtle around the birdbath in the backyard cuts the cable line because the so-called locators had marked the front but not the back of the house, leading Don to spend many hours punching phone buttons in response to questions from automated recordings. I admonish myself to consider the guy in *The Diving Bell and the Butterfly*, almost totally paralyzed and only able to control one eyelid which he used to communicate through a complicated series of timed blinks. Plaster falls from the ceiling in rooms where the house itself appears to be sinking so Don obtains the name of a firm that can jack up that end of the structure. I consider tsunamis, earthquakes, mass murders, terrorist bombings, serial rapists, tornados, melting glaciers, and swine flu pandemics. In this admittedly quirky manner and now stepping in and out of rooms faintly scented by a basement reeking of the pee of cats long gone, we ease into an unusually beautiful Midwestern summer during which I frequently look up and observe, for example, the sky.

Imagine the glory of chartreuse finches and scarlet cardinals against dark and lighter greenery, circling hawks gliding up on high, a setting in which it would be impossible not to feel the elated heart buckle at a succession of small events full of affectionate adults and children, notwithstanding the dire headlines, for I am more incapable of assimilating them than ever before. I chide myself, but the dire headlines cannot spoil the rush of returning vitality. Instead, they fuel vibrancy by putting into perspective my puny personal complaints. In that influx of life, the digital camera rarely surfaces. Had I continued to keep the sort of albums stacked in my study closet, their pages full of pictures of every year of the girls' development, they would record a succession of tableaux vivants that in this modern world of today would make up one of those tedious PowerPoint presentations through which returning travelers drone. Sporting a baseball cap with the logo "Dewey" and a long shirt over my tee (to cover the drainage tube-and-bulb), I cannot possibly look anything but goofy, but I savor each of these miniature communions sprinkling the fine summer that Don and I have been granted within a historical epoch that seems teetering toward entropy.

At the farmers' market, tucked behind the courthouse square at the center of town, Jan receives a neighbor-of-the-year award in recognition of her community service. In front of a cluster of folk massed before a small bandstand, near stalls filled with green beans, tomatoes, peppers, potatoes, eggplants, and goat cheeses, she receives a plaque and speaks words blown away by the breeze that teases nearby bunches of basil and zinnias and sunflowers. I clap my hands, congratulating myself for staying upright on my dead feet and withstanding the aches shooting down my right hip, pains that might have been caused by the drains in my bottom, or maybe they register the onset of cancer having spread to the bone, or perhaps they just mean that like everybody else I have arthritis. When is an ache an ache, and not the sign of a recurrence or a metastasis? Close by, Jayne does not know that her ailing father will suffer a stroke in a few days and that she will bring him home from the hospital to his retirement cottage, where he will die peacefully with his beloved dog curled at his feet. Jayne looks at her watch.

Another photo would show Jo and me laughing, wiping our sticky fingers on paper toweling while determining to avoid ceremonies of idiocy. We are lunching at a new ribs joint in a strip mall on the west side of town where we recall our celebration at an Indy ribs stand a decade earlier, when a doctor informed Jo that she need not subject herself to chemotherapy. I am paying for this meal because of a lost bet that reflects my disillusionment with the medical establishment. I had not expected a response to the letter I had sent my GP explaining that I would want to be able to count on her help when my condition deteriorates. "Recently, I read a book by Marilyn Webb (entitled *The Good Death*) that urges patients to consult with their general practitioners," my letter stated. "One sentence especially struck me: 'Those with cancer can hope for a doctor knowledgeable and sophisticated enough to provide whatever high doses of narcotics are necessary to ease suffering, even if the treatment hastens death.' I would be grateful if you could be such a physician for me."

Even though my GP did not respond in person, her receptionist phoned to make an appointment. So the lunch is definitely on me, and I am recounting to Jo the two funerals I have just attended, both of which lead me to think that a graveside service is the way to go. The backdrops and liturgies of the Greek Orthodox Church and Beth Shalom could not have been starker in contrast, but they both give public grieving a bad name. At the first, the priest testified with some pride that the erudite scholar of Continental modernism we were mourning had promised on his deathbed "to unlearn" all the wisdom he had accrued that did not conform to Greek Orthodox doctrine. At the second, the rabbi had meandered through comments about the broken vessels of the world until he consulted his notes about the energetic woman we were burying and announced, "She was superglue." In the fifth grade, Jo confides with mordant mirth, she had prayed every day not for the demise but for the "happy death" of Joseph Stalin; in later years, it was Mao Zedong. In this manner, she grasped the political history of Communism.

A single snapshot could not convey the glee of my godchildren hosing down the pig, frog, and owl on the patio while above them in the screened-in back porch Mary and Andrew plan the Thai spring rolls and fish stew we will concoct for Dyan and Rick's upcoming visit. Observing the soaked stone animals and the just-as-soaked kids, I recall Dr. Robb's analogy. "Before it was like sewing together two wet pieces of toilet paper. This time it would be like sewing together two dry pieces of toilet paper." After yet another CT on June 12 and clear indications that the perforation had not healed, my surgeon ruled out a third abdominal surgery, leaving me two alternatives. I could do nothing and wait with the drainage bulb and ostomy in place or I could let him try to stitch up the hole through the rectum. What a grotesque idea. He might be successful, but the odds were bad—only a 10 or 20 percent chance of success.

"Even dry, it's tricky," I remember a thoughtful Dr. Robb remarking. The conversation on the porch turned to concerns about friends and colleagues. Would Jonathan suffer under the burdens of becoming the department chair? Was Judith still in India, Amanda and Andrea in Italy? When would Zeke and his parents return? I had put Dr. Robb off by expressing my wish to consult with Dr. Matei. I had not expected her to e-mail me—when does a physician *initiate* communication?—and then to make a phone date in which she explained that she had dreamed of me during her Romanian vacation. Perhaps I should get a second opinion—she recommends a surgeon at Memorial Sloan-Kettering—about the perforated colon so the ileostomy might be reversed. A still photograph could not convey the drenched children clamoring inside to clear the table for the brownies and ice cream while I look for appropriate bowls, treasuring a haunted Dr. Matei but realizing that my wayward thoughts must not eclipse my joy in Cassie and Ben. Did I know they were going to climb Mount Washington in a matter of weeks? That they would then go to a beach near Dewey?

I am profoundly moved by Dr. Matei's dreaming and grateful to her, for she has given me the gift of these moments and many others unpictured in which, wanting to complete a draft of this manuscript by the start of school, I am writing and revising at the only breakneck speed I ever attain, which is very slow indeed. Though glad that I am no longer bringing my purse to the nightstand or assuming the corpse pose or, in terms of earlier problems, drinking myself silly, I worry about operations to fix the perforation and reverse the ostomy. The doctors at Sloan-Kettering have a reputation for being quite aggressive. It is true, however, that I who deal with one oncologist and one bowel surgeon might profit from the opinion of the physician Dr. Matei proposes, a surgical colorectal oncologist. When I phone to make general inquiries, the secretary explains that an appointment for a second opinion requires a "doctor-to-doctor" phone conversation, so I e-mail Dr. Matei the number of the surgeon. But do I want to fly to New York and consult with him? Might I cave in to some draconian procedure that would only further harm me?

Who herself beginning knew, as John Milton would never have put it? How had a bad girl from Brooklyn become such a wimpy dolt with the doctors in Indianapolis? Even when I stopped partying and started studying way back then, the feminism that had rescued my life promoted an irreverent attitude toward the stultifying hierarchies of what I then called the Establishment. No matter how pliant and decorous I seem inside the medical machine, my private doubts about it have only deepened. Rereading a *Times* article from May 31 confirms my skepticism about the state of contemporary medicine. Entitled "Doubts on Ovarian Cancer Relapse Test," the story begins with what sounds like twisted humor to my ears. " 'For the first time, women can be reassured that there's no benefit to early detection of relapse from routine CA-125 testing,' said Dr. Gordon J. S. Rustin, director of medical oncology at Mount Vernon Hospital in Middlesex, England." Women with ovarian cancer can breathe a sigh of relief. Why bother with early detection since, as a 2009 source puts it, "recurrent disease cannot currently be cured"? Earlier treatment does not improve survival rates, I learn during my remission. In therapy sessions with terrified cancer patients, Martha Manning has discovered that "the end of chemotherapy is not the point when it is all over. In some ways it is the point at which things are just beginning."

Remission, I could tell, would always have an invisible question mark after it. No one can predict how long it will last or, for that matter, when it actually starts. Still physically weak from six months of treatment, in remission I experience the influx of all those emotions and obsessions, neurotic though they may be, that characterized the pulse of my existence before chemotherapy. Medical logistics are finally, if only intermittently, put on the back burner. But it would be a seesaw between the semblance of normal life and then its eclipse as concerns about either my *kishkes* or the cancer would rise to prominence. Should I consult the surgeon at Sloan-Kettering or simply put up with the drainage bulb and ostomy bag? For weeks I procrastinate about Dr. Matei's advice to seek a second opinion, all the while fearing that it would ruin my family reunion during the last week of July. But "a wise man learns from experience, a wiser man still learns from the experience of others," my father used to recite. Not being "a wiser man still," I could nevertheless remember the haste that had drawn me too quickly into acquiescence and grotesque interventions that backfired into tribulation. Remission means not having to rush to judgment. Uncomfortable, revolting, anxiety-producing, and time-consuming, the ostomy bag and drainage tube-and-bulb warp the quality of my life but, because they are hidden, no one else's, and they would make caretaking easier in hospice.

Remission is a word that signifies absolution. As Google will guess if you begin typing it, the term "remission of cancer" derives from and echoes "the remission of sins." Those who obtain the remission of sins through baptism or atonement enter God's kingdom. Remission signifies pardon, forgiveness, release, or deliverance from offenses or debts, punishment or guilt. On the "cliffs of fall" or in my posthumous existence, I might have taken offense at the parallelism since no wrongdoing causes ovarian cancer. Also in a remission of advanced ovarian cancer, it is impossible to consider the body purified or cleansed since it often harbors cancerous cells that will return. Not baptismal, I might have argued, remission brings a heightened sense of contingency, of being healthy-but-only-for-a-while, and therefore the anticipation of waiting for the other shoe to drop, for the fat lady to sing, for the cookie to crumble. A better term for my condition might be dormancy, for the cancer is not gone but dormant, and therefore being in remission does not make me a cancer survivor. But in my happier frame of mind, the idea of even a temporary reprieve—a diminution of disease and a relaxation from punitive therapies—weaves itself into the thread of resolute equanimity that appeared at the initial diagnosis.

Similarly the word "recurrence," always linked in cancer talk to remission, sounds better to my ears than "relapse" since the latter conjures up reversion, a lapse in judgment, and therefore personal responsibility. In a relapse, the word used by Dr. Gordon J. S. Rustin, one falls back into sin, backsliding and failing, whereas the occurrence of advanced ovarian cancer usually predicts that it will recur. Such are my musings when Dr. Matei informs me that she has phoned the surgeon at Sloan-Kettering daily, and he has not returned her calls. The gods have spoken, I happily decide. Choosing between the New York surgeon's second opinion and Dr. Robb's proposed transrectal stitching will have to wait until they return from their vacations, I from mine. One day in the week on Lake Michigan encapsulates the quintessence of the summer's delights, despite a public drubbing one hardly expects to attend family gatherings.

After a morning in which Jo, Molly, Kieran, and Elliot picked blueberries, we walked two blocks to the sandy beach with its shimmering wavelets catching the sunbeams so intensely that the water looked like a mica or diamond field glittering here and there against the backdrop of a lighthouse and maybe two or three sailboats in the distance. The owners of our rental house in South Haven have supplied a royal blue umbrella and apple green canvas chairs that Don and Simone set up so I can sit in the shade, listening to the lull of lapping and watching Kieran coaxing three-year-old Elliot to step into the water or build sandcastles by the shore. Tiny against the length of the shoreline, he braves his fears, clinging to his father's hand, as I savor the holiness of the heart's affection for the overlapping of our lives, for successiveness.

Viscerally, it seems to me, my spirits quicken, launched by Elliot's tie to one of his namesakes, Sandra's unforgettably vibrant and so long dead husband: how he loved opera, despised cilantro, could gaze with a basilisk stare under his impressively bushy eyebrows. My gaze shifts to Molly and Simone swimming or sunbathing in all their beauty and strength, when the iPhone rings. It is Jayne, exultant about being the first to tell me about "the raves" *Judas* has received in the middle of a long article in *The New Yorker*: "It's like when she gets to you, she's gotten to the real thing," Jayne laughs into the phone. I've pushed my paralyzed toes out beyond the umbrella's shade to feel the warmth of the sun. What a wonderful day, I rejoice. Not one of my earlier books had been mentioned in this prominent publication, not even *The Madwoman*.

If you read and remember (but why would you?) Joan Acocella's snide essay "Judas Reconsidered," in the August 3, 2009, issue of *The New Yorker*, you would know that I was headed for quite a tumble. Her trouncing of me—I am an "amateur" who spouts "shocking nonsense," a "Neo-Freudian" or "postmodern" justice-seeker—did spawn a host of pathetic revenge fantasies (not unlike the ones I entertained about the interventional radiologists). In an e-mail my ex-husband simply calls her a "Camille Paglia type." Actually what eventuates, though, intensifies the poignancy of the day because in the rental we cannot connect to the Internet so when the family makes its way back to the house, Simone starts to read aloud the "rave" on her Blackberry, as we lounge around the living room, but then she stalls. "I can't read this, Mom. You will be so hurt." And so while Jo takes over the recitation of Joan Acocella's bruising prose, I revel in Simone, who does not want my feelings hurt, who murmurs again, "Don't let this upset you." And then through the quirky corridors of conversation, Kieran and Molly begin sharing parental puzzles and professional concerns that draw us close together until midnight. Elated, as I often have been by intimacy with my younger colleagues and graduate students, I think that Crazy Jane, Yeats's bag lady, might be right in her conviction that "nothing can be sole or whole / That has not been rent."

Of course, all bittersweet idylls must end, mine with a whimper since upon my return home, the drainage tube-and-bulb started slipping out of my belly, emitting a foul smell, churning up pain and panic. While I morph from a skinheaded Aristotle into a grizzled Uncle Ben, I realize that remission isn't all it's cracked up to be. For me it means a renewed life punctuated by unforeseeable flurries of worried e-mails, returns to the hospital, discussions of new procedures, and (alas) perhaps the concession that such new procedures must be undertaken. The pattern becomes clearer. Though I will have patches of familiar pleasures and pangs, I will continue to have to deal with the damage done to my intestines, with the discomforting drainage tube-and-bulb and ileostomy. These calamities, I finally discover from the doctor who covers for a vacationing Dr. Robb, were produced *not* by the cancer but definitely by the debulking. "Very common problem in such surgeries," Dr. Robb's stand-in explains. As Barbara R. Van Billiard surmised in her memoir about ovarian cancer, "there are many conditions that can develop following extensive debulking surgery, some of which have perhaps never before been encountered." An ovarian cancer patient named Cheryl has described "massive complications" after her operation: "I had a bowel obstruction and then I got septic. I was in the hospital two weeks after my surgery and in ICU for five days." One textbook passage lists multiple complications related to bowel resections: "pelvic abscess formation, bowel obstruction, anastomotic stricture, and anastomotic leak."

Just as my cramped feet, my bruised bottom, and perhaps my aching right leg were damaged by the chemotherapy and drains, the perforation and abscess were caused by the bowel resection during the debulking back in November. The peculiar shock of this revelation bludgeoned me. It was the ruthless instruments, technologies, and formulas of the medical machine that had pierced and battered me. The ileostomy, which was performed to solve the problem of the perforation and abscess and which has failed thus far, might not be reversible, I realized: examples of loco-oncology or lo-*con*-ocology. I put the emphasis on the "con," though I remind myself to remain convinced that my surgeons did as well as they could and though my sustained admiration for my oncologist bespeaks a successful transference through an identification with her not as a parental authority but rather as the sort of junior colleague who knows way more than I ever did or do and who humors me nonetheless. Yes, the six chemotherapies were worth all the communal moments they have brought and will continue to bring about. Yet despite Dr.

Matei's tenacity (and despite Dr. Gordon J. S. Rustin's caveats), much damage has been done and in any case at some point the CA-125 marker will rise and the miseries caused by loconocology will finally be trumped by a devolution leading to "the anaesthetic from which none come round."

Those are Philip Larkin's words in "Aubade," his poem about waking in the dark to the dread of death and then to the impossibility of confronting its sheer negativity:

> —*no sight, no sound,*
> *No touch or taste or smell, nothing to think with,*
> *Nothing to love or link with,*
> *The anaesthetic from which none come round.*

The lines help me understand Epicurus's famous postulation, "Where I am, death is not; where death is, I am not." After death departs with us, we cease to exist. Epicurus lays the groundwork for Larkin's sad certainty that in death we have nothing to love or think with. Philosophers call this the no-subject objection to the badness of death. Death is not experienced as bad by me simply because in death "I" do not exist and therefore "I" cannot experience death or anything else. True, the death decreed by ovarian cancer deprives me of a longer life, but a longer life under some circumstances may not be better than a shorter life. Whereas medical efforts to prolong my life have damaged me, the prospect of a sooner dying need not harm what is left of my life. Indeed, it could be said to heighten the fewer moments that remain. Yet there can be no doubt that Larkin finds the prospect "Of dying, and being dead" horrific perhaps because as the dead we lose everything, including the capacity to know or judge death. Although Epicurus finds it consoling that we will not conceive the inconceivable, Larkin expresses bafflement at not being able to comprehend the incomprehensible.

Larkin cannot imagine a sufficient response to "the total emptiness for ever":

> *—Courage is no good:*
> *It means not scaring others. Being brave*
> *Lets no one off the grave.*
> *Death is no different whined at than withstood.*

Brilliant lines, I believe, but I quarrel with Larkin because "not scaring others" remains high on my list of priorities, specifically not scaring my daughters with a suicide. On the basis of personal experience, Andrew Solomon explains, "the pain of living when someone you love has annihilated himself can be almost intolerable." Solomon defends every person's right to die; however, the suicide of his mother, who took Seconal to avoid further medical responses to her advanced ovarian cancer, incited "the cataclysm" of his life. "If that story had been a little bit less tragic, then perhaps I would have gone through life with depressive tendencies but no breakdown." Betty Rollin's mother, also suffering from ovarian cancer, also escapes "the frequent eruptions and blockages of her bowels, her ongoing inability to digest food, and her pain" through the escape hatch or "door" of suicide. Though I sympathize with and intermittently envy Solomon's and Rollin's mothers, I do not want to trigger the breakdown of my daughters. Seneca notwithstanding, the person who wills herself dead fails to acknowledge responsibility for others, much as I failed to be responsive to the beloved people in my life during chemotherapy. My family has been riddled with too many suicides—so many that one fears a sort of contagion, with each suicide breeding another. While I will attempt to resist resorting to Seconal or its equivalent, this does not mean that I must struggle against cancer up to the very end.

American memoirists of illness narratives almost always affirm their commitment to fight the good fight. "I am convinced that the chances of surviving cancer are greatly increased by having a passionate desire to live—a raging, fighting spirit, and HOPE!" "Without hope, there is no fight to survive, and without a fight, there is no hope." All meditations on death should be avoided, according to Reynolds Price: "Never give death a serious hearing till its ripeness forces your final attention and dignified nod." American antipathy to discussions of mortality has recently stalled efforts to reform the health-care system. As I write, a proposal for patient-driven end-of-life consultations has been caricatured and attacked as an imposition of government-run "death panels" dedicated to euthanasia of the disabled and the elderly. Pointing to widespread opposition to any reconciliation with the inexorability of suffering and mortality, a number of commentators have claimed that Americans exhibit a national addiction to narratives of individualistic self-improvement and perseverance.

Many people take remission as a mission. If they can survive until death departs, they will live happily ever after, and of course I hope they do. Many also believe that hope for a cure *provides* a cure, or at least the proper environment for the return of health, and of course I hope it does. But our culture sometimes seems to collude in the idea that death can be cured. If we only eat the right foods or eat less, if we consult specialists or unconventional nonspecialists and down the proper combination of pills or herbs, if we travel to the countries where we can buy the proper organs or reprogram our embryos' genes or channel our energies properly or counteract our damaging patterns of behavior with psychological or physical exercises, we can cheat or beat death—so the suppositions go. We must battle on, it seems, until death departs from the human condition. According to Philippe Ariès, "the interdiction of death in order to preserve happiness was born in the United States around the beginning of the twentieth century." At the present time, many doctors fear that should they refrain from taking extreme measures to stave off death or should they employ humane measures to ease the suffering of the terminally ill, they will confront endless and costly lawsuits.

How can death be banned or revoked? "Death has superior forces," surgeon-writer Atul Gawande admits. "And in a war that you cannot win, you don't want a general who fights to the point of total annihilation"; rather you want someone who understands "that the damage is greatest if all you do is fight to the bitter end." Numerous books have confirmed Ariès's and Gawande's point that we are death-deprived not only by medical and mortuary businesses but also by much more generalized social prohibitions against acknowledging dying or mourning. Writing about her grief, Joan Didion realizes "how open we are to the persistent message that we can avert death. And to its punitive correlative, the message that if death catches us we have only ourselves to blame." "Mazel Tov!" is the subject heading of my childhood friend Evie's e-mail in which she congratulates me on averting death: "We received a fabulous letter from your mother giving us such wonderful news. Mazel Tov! You are now cancer-free!" How to explain my mother's persistent denial of my condition? Why does she think we keep on having to schlep back to Indianapolis?

On a bright day in late summer, Don and I attend one of the regular conferences about my mother's welfare scheduled by a social worker at the Health Pavilion. At a circular table situated in a windowed bump-out of the dining room, I ask a nurse about the advisability of taking my mother off two especially dangerous drugs, but otherwise it is a perfectly standard meeting. Yet afterward my mother heaves a sigh of relief as we wheel her back to her room. "That was easier than I feared," she murmurs. "I thought they were going to throw me out." Pointless to tell her we are spending her entire savings, thousands upon thousands of dollars, and the management would never consider letting such a gold mine go. "They must like me," she smiles. We heartily agree, "What's not to like?" But the incident wrenches, reminding me that my mother has never recovered from a series of calamities that must have left her reeling and rejected.

My mother's first memory, from the age of four, consists of hearing the gun that her mother used to kill herself. It will never be ascertained whether my maternal grandmother grieved over a relinquished lover or found her staid husband uncongenial, whether her nihilism resulted from self-recriminations over a lost concert career or postpartum depression or the so-called rest cure to which she had been subjected. That violent event must have haunted my mother decades later when she was the one who had to clean up the Brooklyn bathroom in which her father slit his wrists. My grandfather had served as a medic in the German army during World War I, but was not allowed to practice medicine after he fled the Third Reich, first to Palestine, then to the States. Later still, my mother was the one who found my father slumped over the wheel of his

car. Not death-deprived, she has been glutted with death—and by
a form of death that has always been difficult to grieve.

Such brutal, bruising events might have turned others depraved
or desperate. Instead, my mother toiled against them as best she
could, and in the process strengthened her remarkable and heroic
will to survive. *How We Survived* is the title she gave her memoir of
the family's history. Just last week she handed me with some pride
a green piece of construction paper bearing my name in glittery letters. Glued on it, a lacy and scalloped gold sheaf had been accordion-
pleated. A sticker with the lettering "I'm Your Biggest Fan" tacked
the base of the fan down with two purple streamers. She relishes
all such activities staged in her alien community—the other day she
exclaimed over the visit of two Chihuahuas trained to play poker. I
should be thankful, for her sake but also for mine, that the coping
strategies she adopted in order to endure the miseries she suffered
as a daughter and wife have secured her satisfaction in maternity
by suppressing realization of my condition. Her efforts to sustain
herself and her attachments drive home my greatest fear about my
own demise. In my absence, who would cherish Molly and Simone
with my ferocity and unconditional adoration of who they are, no
matter what they do or become? Who would be their biggest fan?

Fear of agony and psychosis in the dying process, of depleting
the energies of Don, of surviving him without anyone upon whom
I would want to depend for caretaking permeates my consciousness
as well. Because I have found no factual first-person accounts of
dying from ovarian cancer, I do not know where the cancer might
migrate and how symptoms will present themselves. I do not understand how long it takes to die from ovarian cancer or which organs
or capacities are the first to go. If I manage to stay the course—not
to do bone marrow transfers or stem cell replacements or whatever

expensive and snarky "therapies" physicians might advise—what exactly will I experience after my year or so of remission? Given my secular background, doubtfulness about what happens *after* death takes less hold of my imagination than doubtfulness about what will actually happen *during* my dying and *at* my death. Perhaps one cannot approach the idea of one's own death until it ripens.

The sentence *"I am going to die"* remains quite distinct from the sentence *"I am dying."* Still, I can imagine how I will probably end up: wasting away, unable first to eat and then to drink, metastases in my bowels or bladder or liver, the bone or the brain, in a hospital bed, a problem with swallowing, mottled skin, dry mouth, my bodily temperature changing as blood starts to pool and my jaw juts out, my breathing laborious. Richard Powers's novel about ovarian cancer concludes with its heroine swallowed by grinding agony: "Soon enough, she loses whole afternoons to sharp crescents of black. The pain digests her." Jaundiced and catheterized, Gail Godwin's frail character feels the "thrumming" of pain, "Thrumming at me from below: 'Do-o-on't forget, M-a-a-gda . . . you belong to me-e-e.'" During the last conscious moments of dying from ovarian cancer, Jessica Queller's mother looks terrified, "her mouth frozen in a permanent O": "Every breath she took was like drowning. The thick, heavy, gurgling sound of her gasping breaths will forever haunt me." A caretaker, Andrea King Collier relied on hospice and used pain patches as well as morphine, but her mother's "pain was a wild thing, out of control." From books in my study, I know that delirium, hallucinations, depression, shortness of breath, and excruciating pain inflict their toll on a large percentage of terminally ill people, even those receiving palliative care. In part, this occurs because of anxiety about assisted suicide.

But is it assisted suicide if an oncologist accepts my decision

not to endure a second or third line of treatment? Is it assisted suicide if my caregivers refuse to supply feeding tubes or if a general
practitioner writes a prescription for Seconal? Is it assisted suicide
if a hospice worker sets up a morphine drip that a spouse presses
once and then several times again? How to quantify intention and
responsibility for a death definitively caused by advanced ovarian cancer and by a request for the alleviation of suffering from a
dying person? The terminally ill must quail at placing burdensome
guilt on caretakers. In the context of those coping with a future
of terminal pain, we need another term, perhaps "assisted death,"
to help caretakers do what (in an office consultation) my general
practitioner avoided discussing, namely to "ease suffering, even if
the treatment hastens death": not PAS (physician-assisted suicide)
but PAD (physician-assisted death). Palliative sedation, increasingly
accepted by medical authorities, alleviates agony even if it accelerates
the dying process. As in childbirth, I speculate to Jo, in dying we
may need a doula.

It is a weird sort of comfort to recite, "Being brave / Lets no one off
the grave." Just as important, there are different forms of bravery.
I want to strengthen my commitment not to the sanctity of life in
general over and against death but to the integrity of my previous
life before cancer and its demeaning treatments. I want to fight to
defend at least a shred of my autonomy against the brute bodily
degeneration and mental confusion of a miserably extended existence. If I respect the values that imbued my personal trajectory, I
must avoid the degradations and dependencies of pointless suffering.

"Death has dominion," Ronald Dworkin explains, "because it is not only the start of nothing but the end of everything, and how we think and talk about dying—the emphasis we put on dying with 'dignity'—shows how important it is that life ends *appropriately*, that death keeps faith with the way we want to have lived."

Although many people believe that fighting cancer depends upon hope, that surrender to disease constitutes quitting and hopelessness, I can count the myriad ways I continue to hope in a decidedly hopeless situation. These hopes spring not only from the pronoun "I" of Epicurus, but also from all the other pronouns. I hope that I will die without prolonged physical pain, that I won't end up in a hospital with doctors needlessly extending my existence but at home and sufficiently sedated, that Don and the rest of our family and friends will survive me, that the girls and Kieran will prosper knowing they have been the boon of my life, that Sandra receives all the poetry awards she deserves, that Jo manages to manage her own aging and dying with the dignity she has evinced throughout her living, that Elliot and my other dear grandson, Jack, thrive and evolve, that researchers find early detection tools and cures for ovarian cancer and that its treatments cease subjecting women to misery. And these are just my hopes in the puny realm of the personal, for who does not yearn for social justice and peace and the preservation of the earth?

Whereas hope springs eternal from the probable or at least the possible, I have a bouquet of improbable wishes too. At my death-bed, I wish that someone would find a way to administer a wee overdose while a slow movement of one of Beethoven's late quartets is sounding in my ears. In other words, I wish to experience a tranquil dying without whining about or withstanding death. "Like birth," my treasured collaborator Sandra warns in *Death's Door*, "death is surely by its nature undignified." True, but with the help of hospice at home I wish to avoid being cut, drained, wired, monitored, intubated, and ventilated within the artificial life support systems of an ICU. "To die 'naturally' is to find a way to have a graceful death when the prognosis is terminal and further treatments are of questionable value. It is not a rejection of medical science, but rather an attempt to use the sophistication of modern medicine to treat—in a different, better way—those who are seriously ill or near death." I wish to die without having placed my faith in macrobiotic diets or crystals. I very much hope and wish that the newest breakthrough drugs in the treatment of ovarian cancer, which (I am convinced) will not be available during my lifetime, will help generations of women to come. Happily, I have not put my family and friends through the roller coaster that eventuates from faith in complete recovery. Now it is my wish not to put them through the witnessing of further medical miseries that would make our lives a living hell.

I think of finding closure for this narrative by imagining myself lighting a candle, filling the tub with hot water, playing Brahms's *Requiem* or Ray Charles on the CD, and soaking with my bag of poop, my bulb of gunk, as happy as the proverbial clam. But such a scene goes beyond even the improbability of wishes. To an avuncular visitor who says, "I want to commend you on your attitude toward your impending situation," I fantasize a non-Buddhist response, "At least I have a life to lose, loser." Such spiteful bravado, however, seems equally unlikely. Also, I have lost much of my life. The life I have left to lose remains a shadowy semblance of my existence before cancer, only partially discerned through this writing. On the mantel, I find a Valentine's card with a picture of one black, one white standard poodle sitting on the red upholstery of a limousine's backseat. Under the inside print message, "We belong together," appears the penned script "Love Love Love Susan" with a heart drawn next to my name—a sign I would never use in a handwriting I cannot recognize. It takes quite a while for me to realize that during my prolonged hospitalization I must have asked Jayne to send Don a card on my behalf.

Yet at least I know now that I am not going to laminate some damned ostomy alert card. Who in the world (except a doctor or nurse) would want to or know how to remove the tube emerging out of one side of my belly, the pouch on the other? And I am driving again, after a mechanic diagnosed the problem with the power steering: moss had grown up around the engine and jammed the belt. A rolling car apparently gathers no moss, I realize as I also understand that seatbelts represent a challenge to those with ostomies. Since probably I will be able to begin teaching in September, perhaps I should take Don's advice and end this account with me walking into the classroom, back where I was before it started. For I plan to teach one more graduate course before retirement, when I am "gone but not forgotten," a fate far better than that accorded faculty who drift on after retirement, as Don puts it, "forgotten but not gone."

Already drafted, the syllabus of the fall graduate class is a twofer: a survey of women's literature in the twentieth century as well as feminist approaches to it. Will my students know the particulars of what my avuncular visitor called my "impending situation"? I have tactfully deleted *Wit* from a syllabus that reflects my sense of the social revolution in which I have been lucky enough to participate. Dr. Matei stands as a tribute to it, as do innumerable female judges and soldiers, computer scientists and day-care workers, firefighters and law enforcement agents, pastors and porn stars, as do Alice and Kyeong-Hee, Rod and Tricia, Helene and Matt, Ferda and

Ashley, Amy and Todd, and all those other former and current
graduate students whose pedagogy will keep gender and sexuality
studies alive in future classrooms. The revolution that feminism has
effected—possibly the most momentous and radical transformation
of modern times—remains ongoing, of course, but it has profoundly
altered every aspect of our ways of being and, I believe, for the better. It has made possible lives unimaginable to our fathers and our
fathers' fathers, to our mothers and our mothers' mothers.

But I realize that this will be my last class, one in which too
much of my attention will be expended on not mourning the end
of my teaching career and on passing as a physically normal person,
so maybe I should close with the simpler pleasures of, say, a twilight
vigil on a pleasant August evening, calm and free. I move a plastic
chair from the back porch to the front of the house. The towering
pine widowed in the circle of beauty displays damage where its
long limbs were intertwined with the burning fir. The fading light
brings out its mottled and knobbed trunk with its single stroke
of ash. Many branches had to be chopped off the side of the tree
facing me. On the fir's far side and at the lowest level, its widest
limbs extend downward, brushing the ground like a shaggy grass
skirt. Amid the din of the crickets and frogs, its losses underscore
mine. Still surviving, the ragged fir has been mutilated by the fire
but also by time. The bedraggled remains of its spindly horizontal
branches slope downward, bristling with tough needles on shoots
that hang perpendicular to the ground as if pulled by gravity, like
the sad sagging flesh on aging arms. Narrowing to a tender top that
I can barely glimpse, it droops majestically against the darkening
sky and the bright gold of a lone leaf glittering here and there on
nearby bushes.

I step through the thick growth of the rough grass and the

adjacent padded patch of soft woodchips to measure the lowest wingspan, which turns out to be forty-four times the length of my foot. Its roots must be yet more massive below the ground. When I return to the front door, as the bottom of the tree disappears in the darkness and the cicadas' chirps build in a crescendo with the frogs' croakings, I pray to the tree for acquiescence in what the future holds, thinking of the end of Rilke's *Duino Elegies*:

> Once *for each thing. Just once; no more. And we too,*
> *just once. And never again. But to have been*
> *this once, completely, even if only once:*
> *to have been at one with the earth, seems beyond undoing.*

What I cherish is being here fleetingly on this specific and minuscule bit of the globe, realizing I will exist only once in my idiosyncrasy, no more and never again. Yet may not the deepening of my heart seem rooted and beyond undoing to those I have loved? And hasn't another fiber twined around the thread of equanimity that broke in chemotherapy, a filament braided with my earlier treasuring of life—a newborn appreciation of the value of death: not a chosen but a decreed death? Rending me is an insight rendered by Mark Doty: "death's deep in the structure of things, and *we* didn't put it there." The vision of dying as a disarmed surrender imbued Rilke with the conviction that "We need, in love, to practice only this: / letting each other go," a difficult discipline because of the uniqueness of each living creature.

Rilke's perspective on the fall of an irreplaceable existence conjures up barely conceivable moments after the scenes of anguish painted by Frida Kahlo—when, for example, the shelved skeleton and then the sleeper in *The Dream* turn over and out of their bed into the buoyant atmosphere surrounding it or when the stricken deer drops, relinquishing suffering and melding its antlers with the broken branch of peace on the pliant earth of the windbreak. As gravity exerts its sway, they may bow down not in a terrified plunge from the slippery "cliffs of fall," but in a willing descent into alien elements that are not ourselves but that we will become or that will become us. On the canvas, though, the figures of *The Dream* and *The Little Deer* eternally levitate above the earth, as they convey the pulse of a creator fully absorbed in making a singular and fleeting moment of consciousness permanent. Kahlo's paintings have meant a great deal to me, but they turn out to be quite small in their physical dimensions: no, I reconsider, not "but"—*and*. And they are quite small.

Scale is important. *The Dream* is approximately 29 inches by less than 38 inches, about the size of a movie poster; *The Little Deer* is about the size of a sheet of construction paper—not quite 9 inches by not quite 12 inches. I wish I could see the originals, not just their replications on the Web or in books. I probably never will. In an age of reiterated mechanical reproductions, their singular and diminutive materiality gets lost. As I try to imagine how concentrated these images must be in their contracted dimensions, I realize that Kahlo was not making a big deal about her suffering, despite her self-absorption. She was bewildered by her anguish, open to exploring it, and somehow minimalizing it by attending to it with tenderness. Through their visual and literary lines, Rilke and Kahlo seem to attain a sense of personal equanimity by entertaining the secular import of Thomas Browne's assertion that "there is something in us, that can be without us, and will be after us." Unlike Browne, I cannot believe that the released "something in us" will be a personal soul liberated from physical embodiment. But Rilke's and Kahlo's arrested and arresting images—existing without them and after them—enable me to translate Browne's faith into a vocabulary of secular trust in our continuance through the thoughts, feelings, and works of others.

A reader of Rilke, Gillian Rose may have gleaned from his verse an insight into the tender growth a crisis can inaugurate as the sick and the sound learn how to anticipate farewells:

> A crisis of illness, bereavement, separation, natural disaster, could be the opportunity to make contact with deeper levels of the terrors of the soul, to loose and to bind, to bind and to loose. A soul which is not bound is as mad as one with cemented boundaries. To grow in love-ability is to accept the boundaries of oneself and others, while remaining vulnerable, woundable, around the bounds. Acknowledgement of conditionality is the only unconditionality of human love.

The vulnerable boundaries of the self must be pierced by thin threads like the stitches that stretch and tighten between each piece of a patchwork, lending it elasticity, or between the backing, the batting, and the top, or between the binding and the body of a quilt. Absent to the eye here but present there, the invisible and visible threads that attach us one to the other augur the conditionality of scrappy human love, as well as what Alice Walker has called its "everyday use." Some but surely not all of the connecting stitches fray or unravel after our deaths. Yet frayed or unraveled edges continue to testify to our tattered selves, as do the more durable bonds that tie us together.

Tucked into the curiously Midwestern comfort of the massive continent stretching out beyond to the far distant north and south, east and west, I want to stay as intensely alive as possible until the end. When I begin dying more rapidly, I want to trust that successive generations will cultivate the careful loving-kindness that might shape more humane arts and crafts of living and dying, for we are all in remission from the terminal condition known as mortality. Before I begin dying more rapidly, I treasure the remains of the day and look again at the quilt I began to assemble when remission started. The bar stripe bit of piecing looks too regimented to my eye, its alternating floral and royal blue pattern constricted and predictable. I will take a clue from the quilters of Gee's Bend and cut free-form strips of bolder or black paneling to set it off, maybe with a border of irregular Chinese coins. Within its limits, accepting its limits, there are real possibilities. To adopt a line Don remembers from an old Billy Wilder movie, "the situation is hopeless but not serious."

·8·

LOCONOCOLOGY

WHEN REMISSION BECOMES an intermission, even the most transcendent moments-of-being threaten to pass out of consciousness. Though I had planned on ending this account with the previous chapter, events accelerated at a fast pace, prompting me to keep up with them, for how else could I be true to the pathological persistence of ovarian cancer and to the debilitating effects of its treatments? Something more, albeit rushed and addled, is owed my friend Ilinca and all the other women who have had to contend with this disease. It would be misleading, in other words, to end on a note of serenity. I need to quicken the narrative so as to conclude if not with a grisly nugget followed by a rousing peroration, then at least with some sort of "take-home": the two or three sound bites audiences want to take away from a presentation. "So what, who cares?" we teachers pester student-writers or, more tactfully, "What's at stake and for whom?"

After a recuperative summer, an academic year sailed by, filled with the revitalized delights of teaching, reading, writing, and loving that had been lost to me earlier. Miraculously, the dread and dank fogs, the cliffs and tombs of chemo-time simply evaporated. Yet then, like Kafka's Joseph K. in *The Trial*, who returns again and again to inexplicable scenes of torture, I would find myself returning, *consenting* to return to chemotherapy after exactly the period of remission my oncologist had predicted. Worse still, I am currently facing a third abdominal surgery. How could this happen? Why did my months of resolve—to accept with tranquility my transitory existence ("*just once*. And never again")—evaporate so quickly? Does the crash of recurrence bring in its wake more intense realizations of mortality ("just once. *And never again*") that wash away acquiescence? Given my initial equanimity about mortality, my deepening pessimism about medical protocols, and my commitment to hospice care, can I blame my turnabout on the importunate urgings of doctors, family, and friends?

No. In my case, it is not or not only the importunate urgings of some of my doctors, relatives, and friends but also my own instincts that propel me toward further treatments that can retard but not stop the spread of cancer. Indeed, my doctors disagree about what course I should take, as do my relatives and friends. I doubt that I fully understand my own outlook, but I suspect that it illuminates end-of-life issues and what exactly we mean by the period we call "end of life," a demarcation that appears to recede as I approach it. The closer I get to the close of my existence the more distant it becomes. Increasingly, I have to admit, my reactions and desires seem tangled, contradictory, inchoate. My "take-home" or "so what?" will therefore consist not of advice based on insights I have garnered while coping with ovarian cancer but rather of a list of treatment liabilities that can only be changed by people much more knowledgeable about the disease than I will ever be.

Even before recurrence, during the revitalized year of remission, my state of being elicited a number of social interactions that perplexed me. "I just broke my leg and lost my job and my best friend, but it's nothing compared to what you're going through" or "I'm dealing with problems; but, thank God, not yours" were hardly the responses I sought out in chance encounters, but I nodded, smiling. It was more upsetting when a dear friend exclaimed about her sick sister, "If she has to live with a shit bag, she'd be better off dead"— a mindless remark registering her ignorance of my condition and the cost of my dissembling. "I've had what you've had, and you'll be fine" is another distracting if not deeply distressing sentence, this cheerio launched in a drugstore by an acquaintance I hardly knew. She was referring to breast cancer, which has begun to be drained of the stigma attached to it for centuries, although cancer discrimination still exists.

Coming out of the claustrophobic tunnel of chemotherapy can make anyone hypersensitive to exposure, so my first efforts at social resurfacing started out infrequent. It took a concerted effort to redirect my energies into preparing for and teaching the some twenty-five mostly first-year students in my fall graduate class, for I felt the urgent need to bear witness to the alphabet soup of MOAS, PEG, QOL, BRCA, NG, TFI, PICC, PTN, PAS, and NED ("no evidence of disease"). But soon I became engaged with the class and aware of the weird shift in perspective remission brings about, for now my outer life looks and feels entirely normal: I attend lectures and poetry readings, read and respond to my colleagues' writings-in-progress, churn out letters of recommendation, vote at various committee meetings, and start dismantling my office to make room for its next occupant. Despite the ostomy and drain, I am fine and fully functioning. The equipment works, after all, and takes less of my attention and time.

I have learned something not about hopefulness but about engagement from Elizabeth Edwards's response to the information that breast cancer had metastasized in her bones. She understood that the disease would kill her, but refused to let that realization take over every minute of her remaining days. The "noisy truths" had to sit at the children's table, she explained: "Those truths are ill-behaved, they don't know when to speak and when to be silent, and so they have to sit at the children's table in the next room. I go and sit with them periodically . . . I let them yell at me about death for a few minutes so that I don't yell at me about death all the time." At odd moments after leaving the "noisy truths" that yell at me about the incurability of ovarian cancer, I find myself murmuring "thank you, thank you" to the powers that be—for my not being hooked up in a hospital bed, for an especially stimulating class discussion, for the clarity of the stars at night, for my daughters' well-being and affection. As so many cancer patients and survivors have attested, grappling with the disease does enhance appreciation for the brevity and preciousness of existence. Don and I are worrying about the grandchildren: this, too, seems like normal life. On some days, it is hard to convince myself that I am not being paranoid when I think that there is something inside me that I can neither feel nor see and that this something is still out to murder me.

Happily I am grateful that I have outstanding doctors. Many patients complain that, like the proverbial elephant defined only by his trunk or his feet or his ivory tusk, they have been divided into parts by specialists whose sole concern is this or that particular organ or operation. The breast cancer patient Joyce Wadler, for instance, wants "a contractor—or at least a place where we could get all the specialists in one room." Given my ignorance of science and a sort of bewildering dull-headedness that makes it impossible for me to take in my doctors' words while they are speaking them, I sometimes do think, wouldn't it be nice if Dr. Robb could actually meet Dr. Matei? Maybe only the parents or children of doctors receive the sort of care that takes into consideration the whole person. Yet it is nevertheless the case that I was not neglected or mistreated. On the contrary, I have been given state-of-the-art treatment by deft physicians wishing to do their very best for a colleague on a different campus but at their own institution of higher education.

Their alacrity was phenomenal. If I e-mailed a worry or query, even on a Saturday night, Dr. Matei in particular promptly responded. Despite my qualms, I have no complaints about medical lapses, insensitivity, or misplaced priorities. Dr. Robb, dealing with the intestinal abscess but ever aware that ovarian cancer would cause my death, was an exception to the rule that most surgeons, emphasizing how few minutes they can afford to spend on one case, focus their attention on the single procedure for which they are responsible. How often Dr. Robb, cautioning me against a third abdominal operation, took out a pen and paper to show me where the abscess and perforation reside in my body, even though he must have sensed that the diagram would not sink in, could not be comprehended by me or by Don. A perforation I could visualize, but despite all the problems the abscess had caused, I never fashioned a template for it, a way to envision it. And the word "fistula" continued to repel me. Yet I admired the evident integrity of a surgeon advising me against surgery that could be dangerous.

So when I find myself mulling over what I now call loco-oncology or lo-*con*-ocology, I am not directing any criticism toward my physicians. Despite their best efforts, however, each procedure undertaken against the havoc wreaked by cancer—debulking, draining, bagging, poisoning—has produced its own woeful consequences on the psyche and the body. Medical interventions designed to control the cancer often backfire, I have learned, and hurt some other aspect of treatment or the patient. When oncology morphs into loconocology, a mishmash of counter-canceling measures ensues, though their consequences should not be conflated with iatrogenic complications. The etymology of iatrogenesis—"brought forth by a healer"—underscores the ironic malevolence of unintentional but incapacitating and sometimes mortal harm delivered by those dedicated to doing no harm. Hospital infections, medication errors, botched surgeries, improperly recorded bodily responses: all fall under the rubric of iatrogenic effects.

By the term loconocology, I mean to underscore *not* inadvertent mistakes or errors but rather the double binds into which current protocols put medical practitioners of cancer and their patients. Physicians fully realize that standard treatments trigger destructive effects, but there is no alternative available to them. Battling ovarian cancer in her forties, Barbara Creaturo received chemotherapy that "ravaged her bone marrow." Cheryl Cushine's partner was treated for an ovarian cancer recurrence with Doxil, which "may lead to cardiac toxicity and congestive heart failure" and which did "absolutely nothing to control the tumors." The breast cancer patient Gail Konop Baker takes Tamoxifen while convinced that it increases her "risk of uterine cancer; cataracts; stroke; pulmonary embolism; not to mention fatigue, bloating, and weight gain; insomnia and mood swings; hot flashes and night sweats." The response to Susan Sontag's breast cancer produced another virulent form of cancer that killed her. The debulking operation to which I had to be subjected in November 2008 created the abscess and perforation that ominously ruled my existence in 2009 and 2010. For the rest of my life, I need to cope with the ills caused by the drains, the ileostomy, and the chemotherapy, all of which have undoubtedly extended my life, all of which shocked me either because I was not given sufficient information or because I had not been able to assimilate whatever information I had been given.

Only months after the diagnosis did I fully understand the prognosis established at the debulking. Had Dr. Stehman refrained from going into details that might be discouraging or was his language simply incomprehensible to me? Because of the perfunctory nature of the postoperative phone call, at an early meeting Dr. Matei had Xeroxed the pathology report and surgical narrative which I handed over to Jo, who eventually obtained a translation for a layman from a pathologist at a different hospital, a friend of hers. This belated but reader-friendly summary of the initial findings in November clarified my situation. "Doesn't look good," the first words of the translation state. "There are malignant cancer cells in the lymph system that drains into the veins, and from there through the heart, and to almost anywhere in the system." The prognosis is "poor" because tumor cells are "present at the margins of resections." A "caking" of the omentum means "very thick metastatic tumor cells." "Carcinomatosis" proves that the tumor is spreading through the abdominal cavity. Since tumor cells produce fluid, the surgeons removed four liters and therefore one has "to suspect some infection." Worse still, "they spilled some bowel contents in the abdomen during surgery" so again one has "to suspect an infection." Jo's pathologist friend supported my decision not to pursue extensive treatments after the standard six chemotherapies which I had already completed.

Despite this gloomy prognosis, the CA-125 blood test that I started taking three months after the end of chemotherapy and kept on taking every three months during remission worried me. Not reliable for early detection, its results also do not necessarily mark the need to resume treatment. Yet it causes consternation. My thoughts inevitably gyrate and swivel. *It will go up. Of course it will, since it was so low. Just 5. It can't go down so it must go up. Up how far? Maybe it will just stay the same. It would be a relief if it would go up. I could prepare for what's to come. But please, please, please, let it just stay the same so they won't try to talk me into starting chemo again right away and I could take a trip, visit my cousins abroad. Maybe it will stay the same, since I doubt it can go down. Up or down this time, what difference? It will ultimately go up. But there is a difference. Let it stay the same this time, is all I ask. But it won't stay the same. It will go down or up. It can't go down so it will go up—I'll have to deal with it. I won't tell anyone.*

Whereas my dumb interior monologues during the days before a blood test reflect my desire for a longer life, indeterminacy can also bring out loopy yearnings for getting the whole damned *megillah* over with. Worn out by past treatments and current upkeep that seem like "a dress rehearsal of . . . mortality," at times I simply want to get on with the last act of the show. This sort of psychotic reaction surfaced on September 8, 2009, when I braved heightened airport security (especially daunting for someone with an ostomy) to pilgrimage to the Mecca of cancer treatment in New York— MSK, as it is called by initiates. After a physical exam, Dr. Weiser dismissed the viability of Dr. Robb's proposed transrectal repair. A more extensive abdominal operation could remove the damaged part of the colon and resection it, though "there are no guarantees" and the operation is "associated with significant morbidity." Simone, usually impassive in public settings, blanched as the surgeon discussed life-threatening complications. As for me, I could not bear the thought that Don would have to be transplanted to New York City for an extended stay that would surely exhaust him.

So one aspect of loconocology involves having to choose between Dr. Robb's transrectal repair procedure which probably would not work and Dr. Weiser's major operation which could (but might not) work but which could (but might not) lead to death. Needless to say, I want to reverse the ileostomy, but do I want to die doing it? Actually, do I want to die just *trying* to do it, for Dr. Weiser's surgery would not reverse the ileostomy but only possibly make possible its later reversal in yet another operation. Gormlessly dense about the state of my body and about medical science, I take no solace in the idea that the choice is mine and mine alone. But there's another kicker as well. The drainage tube coming out of my belly actually keeps the hole from closing, Dr. Weiser determined. It has to be pulled back a few inches to see if (highly unlikely) healing might occur. What was positioned to help healing retards healing, indeed ensures the impossibility of healing.

Such examples of double or triple whammies seem typical of medical responses to the complications of advanced ovarian cancer. Patients are consistently offered decisions or choices with implications they cannot fully comprehend and with consequences they rationally dread. More than half a year after the last chemotherapy, my feet were still dead and I could not stand up for more than a few minutes without aches and fatigue setting in. After I determined not to proceed with Dr. Weiser at Memorial Sloan-Kettering, there were too many miserable tests and bungled procedures to recount—CTs, colonoscopies, Gastrografin enemas, surgical attempts at transrectal repair—all of which indicated that there were *two* perforations in my colon and the ileostomy probably could not be reversed. Though the drain-and-bulb was eventually removed, I hit a low point after one of these procedures when a technician forgot to inform and then caution me about the buckets of water squirted up into me. In a fancy, glass-ceiling atrium lobby, lined with potted plants and crowded with people getting coffee or lining up for registration, I stood stock still in shock as a torrent of filth flooded out of me onto the parquet floor. That image flailed me in the following days until it was nudged aside by an entirely new and bleakly comic suspicion. Could it be possible that the reputation of going to the bathroom the usual way has been highly exaggerated?

The news of a recurrence came on May 14, 2010, one year after the conclusion of chemotherapy and at the close of my first semester of retirement. I realized it immediately because Dr. Matei phoned me with the CA-125 results, instead of e-mailing. As I answered the iPhone, during a workshop I was attending in order to become a hospice volunteer, I knew the news was bad. Surely now was the time to switch my participation from volunteer to client or patient. After recurrence, events speed up. Disappointments can become keener, options more fraught, the stakes higher. And previous decisions—no matter how judiciously or passionately based—often get overturned. Why and how did my adamant resolve not to undergo further medical interventions against the cancer dissolve, even though it became obvious to me that none would effectively retrieve my life?

The CA-125 number relayed to me in May 2010 had soared.

Rather than stick to my resolution never to submit to the torment
of toxins again, I listened to my oncologist's plan about my enlist-
ing in a new trial. It was as if I had been split into two separate
creatures. With incredulity, my revitalized self urged the diseased
person I had been pronounced to be to undertake another round of
treatments that would haul me back to torpor. I was taking care of
a pathetic and profoundly uninteresting patient with whom I had
little in common but about whom I felt a high degree of responsibility. While Dr. Matei explained the trial, I wondered if this sick
personage should try a new medicine being tested, even though,
unfortunately, the drug's test would include a second line of the so-
called gold standard treatment for the recurrence of ovarian cancer,
namely carboplatin and paclitaxel. To get into this study, a CT
must show visible evidence of disease. Should I hope that it will?
Should I be pleased that it does? Despite my antipathies, I agreed
to follow in the steps of many others and signed up, in my case for
a research trial to be administered to approximately one hundred
participants around the world, half of whom would receive the
experimental drug.

Why, instead of accepting my fate, did I consent to yet another
trial involving precisely the chemicals that had made my existence a
life-in-death? The question makes me ponder not only the psychology of the ill but also the rules of hospice, which enrolls people who
have relinquished curative for comfort care. The first-rate hospice
in my community accepts terminally ill patients with end-stage disease; that is, with less than a six-month prognosis. I do not resemble
enrolled hospice patients, depleted people who suffer multiple ailments, who cannot take care of themselves, and whose caretakers
need help from trained professionals with access to powerful anxiety
and pain management medications. After my one-year remission

and recurrence, I am not yet "hospice appropriate"; that is, "someone with very advanced, terminal illness." While I can clean and dress myself, shop for food, cook, entertain friends, and advise graduate dissertators over e-mail, I am on the road to terminal but not there yet. But if I stop treatment, I will quickly and painfully totter farther down that road, for the returning cancer will immediately encroach on any number of internal organs. If I stop treatment, I will start dying.

Hospice administrators tend to consider chemotherapy curative, although most oncologists would consider it palliative with respect to ovarian cancer since it extends life without eradicating the disease; it keeps the cancer at bay without eliminating it. Perhaps curative and palliative caregiving establish a spectrum, rather than the polarity hospice posits. If the six-month prognosis and the repudiation of all but palliative care could be made more flexible, people like me might profit from the services and conversations hospice provides. Since I am not yet "ready" for hospice, I confront miserable options. Either I undergo the standard response to a recurrence of ovarian cancer, the second cycle of chemo with or without the new drug, or I allow malevolently invasive cancer cells to wreak havoc within my body. It might be useful to consult a palliative care physician, but to my knowledge there are none in my vicinity.

The lure of doing something to advance science, coupled with the ardent hope of my daughters that I would receive a miracle pill, propelled me back into a treatment I loathed. My oncologist's optimism surely played a part in this decision as well, but so did my dread of advancing cancer. Again, friends and family rejoiced, for research on this experimental drug looks quite promising. Fifty percent of the participants in the trial receive the new drug, odds that sound good compared to the mortality rates of advanced ovarian cancer. And it is not a blind trial: you know if you are getting it in pill form. A flip of a coin determines who will receive the pill and who will not: actually a computer places half of the guinea pigs on "arm A" with the experimental drug, while those on both "arms" receive the standard chemicals. The hope is that the arms will move into a position like the hands of a clock at three or six o'clock with those on arm A profiting from the innovative medication and those on arm B not.

At the start of July 2010, we are in the car driving home from signing on the dotted line when the oncologist's assistant e-mails: "You have been randomized to Arm B of the study." I have been relegated to the control group. That night, upon waking in the dark around 3 a.m., I ask, "Bear, where is the manual for that sick baby?" "I brought it back to the library," Don responds with a caress, assuming that I am talking in my sleep. The dream had involved our inability to find passages in the usual baby books about the condition afflicting the infant put in our charge: she had hyphens or equal signs spreading all over her body, hyphens or equal signs on her arms and legs, her chest and belly and groin, hyphens or equal signs running all over her back.

No pill, just poison for me. I have been randomized. I have been randomized not "by" but "to." I have been randomized to the wrong arm. Will I stay the course of another six treatments? I am free to drop out of the trial at any point. Given the cumulative effects of chemotherapy, would staying the course be a sign of mental health or illness? Without the clinical medicine, the remission promised by a second round of standard chemo consists of about six months, Dr. Matei explains as she fulminates at our bad luck. Should I now enter the state where ovarian cancer "goes into remission for a while, and then returns, is re-treated, goes back into remission, and so on"?

Confiding her hesitancy about the side effects of Taxol, she frets, "We can't get the new drug in another venue, since it has not yet been brought before the FDA." I am falling in love with my oncologist because she wants to extend my life without destroying my being, even when the ferocious grasp of this lethal disease tightens it claws and now cramped Arm B constricts me and contracts my future.

Much to my own surprise, even though I am relegated to the control group *not* receiving the new drug, I subject myself to the second round of chemotherapy. The thought of allowing the cancer to colonize my kidneys, intestines, and liver horrifies me, for I may be living a reclusive life in retirement, but it is a life filled with the usual pleasures of reading, writing, and loving. I can put up with the fatigue, hair and weight loss, vacuity, etc. Yet on August 11, a night of fever brings what I can only call the revelation of the illuminated books, images so real that I wake Don to say, "This is not a dream, but a vision," before dropping off and back into it again. When I open each volume, it shivers and then shines with colors pouring out of each letter, around each margin. Some are the sort of jewel-encrusted tomes raised up in church processions, while others display their thick deckle-edged pages between the glossy covers of paperbacks sprouting back and front flaps. I am gulping lemonade and astonished by what intense colors the illuminated, illuminating books bring into being. Simply by opening them up to any one page, I am dazzled by thick magentas and parrot greens and carrot oranges beaming out. In the morning Dr. Matei, who cannot trust a fever of 104 degrees to pass, insists that I go directly to the Bloomington ER. Within weeks, it becomes clear that the Taxol and carboplatin trigger infections in the abscess, causing fevers but also inexpressible levels of agony that cannot be alleviated by the strongest medications.

Just as I was thrown out of the first trial, I am thrown out of the second, again because of infections produced by the abscess in my pelvis. And an again anguished Dr. Matei—committed to decreasing or dropping Taxol but maintaining carboplatin—now starts agitating for an abdominal operation to remove the abscess, for it has kept her hands tied. Alas, the carboplatin by itself also activates raging infections that disable me with so much misery that neither hydrocodone nor OxyContin alleviate my suffering. Infected fluids in the pelvic abscess had found a way to pool under the bruised skin on my aching bottom. How? Everyone has heard of an infected toe or a sinus infection, but an infected *tush*? Would I need a tushectomy? The idea might be funny, if the experience were not so horribly painful.

Just as the debulking operation produced the perforation and abscess, the radiologists' drains had formed a weakened channel of cells, a sort of riverbed meandering from the internal abscess near my coccyx to the center of my right buttock. Again I am bludgeoned, stunned that the instruments, technologies, and formulas of the medical machine have so damaged me. Because fluids from infections in the fistula travel to form excruciating deposits on my behind, a stent has to be installed and padding must be placed into my panties to absorb discharge. At hospital appointments, I am so incapacitated that I must use a wheelchair to get from the drop-off door to the doctors' waiting rooms.

With sophisticated technology at their disposal, my physicians prefer ordering tests, rather than actually looking at the skin or touching the area around the dripping, swollen wound on my bottom. Who can blame them? Actually, it is worse for me when they do look, for I must kneel down on a sort of prayer board, and then place my stomach on a tabletop that is tilted to raise my bottom up for inspection: truly one of the most humiliating ways of being examined, up there with (or above) gynecological stirrups. Trips for innumerable CTs and blood transfusions and injections of Neulasta wear me down. The details are boring, profoundly boring, but I am in hell. For the first time in my life, I must miss the dissertation defense of one of my graduate students.

Afflicted by recurrent infections during the second round of chemo, I rely on the ever-helpful Dr. Robb, who attempts to ease my suffering through a series of arcane operations to drain the abscess. The conveyor belt of the medical machine cranks into overdrive, though every intervention takes meticulous and time-consuming maneuverings. Throughout August and September while I careen from fevers to hospitalizations, various stents—invisible, unlike the drains of the interventional radiologists—are positioned in various parts of my anatomy while I am "put out" by anesthesia. In addition to the ongoing doses of carboplatin, daily and sometimes twice-daily infusions of powerful antibiotics must be administered so a PICC is installed and maintained again. Will I die of septicemia instead of ovarian cancer? As I receive the daily and sometimes twice-daily doses of antibiotics in the windowless outpatient oncology room of Bloomington Hospital, I realize that people in my condition confront too many technicians, too many procedures, often at odds with one another and generally requiring larger and larger amounts of attention from a patient quite isolated from the specialists who have put them in place. Faxing and phoning for directives on when or where to put in, maintain, or take out a PICC, for example, can take up all of one's day. Thank goodness for kind receptionists who serve as conduits between me and overwhelmed physicians.

The strand of acquiescence to which I had clung at the diagnosis and which had frayed during my first round of chemotherapy breaks again. In October 2010, I am confronted by a Catch-22 explained

by a team of physicians summoned by Dr. Matei, including a gynecologic and oncologic surgeon who summarizes their perspective:
"You are between a rock and a hard place." Distressed and clearly
committed to a surgical solution, Dr. Matei exclaims more than
once, "You are my worst-doing patient!" Not her worst patient—her
fondness for me could not be more palpable—but her "worst-doing
patient." She has older, feebler women with more advanced, chemo-
resistant cancers who are not struggling, as I have, with an abscess
that keeps on becoming infected. Her frustration and concern are
apparent. It must be removed.

Either I have a third abdominal surgery that comes with its
own complications or I suffer from infections preventing future
therapies that would extend my life. The chemo which controls the
cancer triggers dangerous infections; a lengthy abdominal operation
to remove the abscess risks post-surgical miseries of the sort covered
by the phrase "mortality and morbidity." Between a rock and a hard
place, to what could I cling? Even when the infection is controlled,
I still feel aches in my pelvis and down my right leg. If such pressure means not that the abscess but that the cancer has progressed,
an operation of this magnitude would be an expensive waste of my
surgeon's skills and my spirits. While I knit or read or accompany
Don on errands, revulsion at the thought of another operation takes
hold again. How can I submit myself to further horrors when I look
and feel ensconced in my (albeit limited) life?

And the doctors in whom I have placed my trust do not agree
with each other. Dr. Robb wonders whether a six-hour operation
makes sense, given the time frame of an ovarian cancer that has
gone through one recurrence and two cycles of chemotherapy. Not
a specialist in my illness, he nevertheless worries, is Dr. Matei being
realistic or overly idealistic in her proactive stance? But Dr. Matei

throws up her hands in frustration at the conservative approach Dr.
Robb and I share. "I'll take full responsibility," she all but shouts.
"You need to get this abscess out of your body so I can treat you,"
she insists. She will make the phone call to get me on the surgical
waiting list herself. Her passion and determination, which remind
me of my collaborator's in her youthful heyday, convince Dr. Robb
to reverse his earlier decision and undertake the abdominal surgery. But how is it different from Dr. Weiser's dangerous proposal
at MSK and why won't it still present the treacherous difficulty of
sewing together two pieces of toilet paper? Like Simone and Molly,
I cannot answer these questions. We listen to an iPhone recording
of Dr. Robb's description of the operation over and over again, but
without real comprehension.

The imperatives of heightened pain play a part in convincing
me, for even toward the end of the second round of chemo, when
the infection seems somewhat under control, the aches in my pelvis
and leg continue to make sitting and standing extremely uncomfortable. Perhaps I am swayed by Dr. Matei because I have become too
diminished, too debulked to resist her judgment. Have two years
of dealing with my miserable physical state so circumscribed my
outlook that I can only imagine a future of perpetual machinations
dealing with my body? Maybe chemo has addled my brain? Yet the
removal of the abscess might enable me to live a more normal life
during the six months of the second remission. Six months, the predicted length of the second remission, would bring me to May 2011, I
keep on reminding myself at the end of chemotherapy in November
2010. But does the ratio between the time of recuperation from a
third abdominal surgery and the time I have left to live make sense?

Will post-surgical miseries rob me of the quality of the time I
have left? Will Dr. Robb "repair the fistula," as one nurse puts it,

or remove it entirely? Might not a resection result in another leak
or abscess? In cutting out part of my perforated colon, might my
surgeon need to exchange the ileostomy for a colostomy? Would a
colostomy be worse than an ileostomy? Yet there is also a possibility
that this operation might make possible a reversal of the ileostomy
(in yet another, later operation). But such are the vagaries of the
human psyche that the thought of defecating the way everyone else
does now fills me with fear. A perfectly strange fact about us human
beings is that we adjust even to what initially repels. An ostomy,
after all, is a negligible bother compared to the wretched wreckage
in which, on which many people agonize. Would a reversal return
me to the bowel fiascos of earlier times? Does it make sense in
terms of the likelihood of a quick recurrence of the cancer? Should
I reverse the ileostomy when I will end up in hospice in the long
(or short) run?

Pain turns out to be the ultimate taskmaster, nudging me toward
a third abdominal surgery. To celebrate Thanksgiving and the end
of the chemotherapy that was triggering the infections, I had both
the PICC in my arm and the stent in my buttocks removed. What
a holiday; I am free at last. Then just before Christmas, after a mild
sore throat, fluids start to accrue under the dark spots on my behind
again and again result in anguish. After a few days of incapacitating misery, a gush of bloody pus spurts out of the center of the right
cheek of my bottom. Don does not bat an eye when I emerge from
the bathroom with this information. We are no longer easily shocked
or frightened. Yet it is at this moment that I think: call me putrefac-
tion, a misbegotten abomination. And then King Lear's rant against
women comes to me: "there's hell, there's darkness, / There is the
sulphurous pit—burning, scalding, / Stench, consumption; fie, fie,
fie! pah, pah!" I am being histrionic, I know, ridiculously so; my

excuse is that I'm mumbling to myself. I spend Christmas with pain meds and experimenting with cutout baby diapers and menstrual pads stuck in my panties to absorb the ever-oozing infected fluids. In this case, chemotherapy cannot be blamed. Any slight cold or cough, it seems, might turn me into an engorged and then gushing freak, visited with continual leakage, unending seepage, the dampening pads, the agonizing aches, not to mention the carting around of excrement, the filthy bag. Perhaps Dr. Matei is right: the abscess must come out, but it will require one week in the hospital and six weeks of recuperation.

Counting on my fingers, I think, how greedy for existence we are, even the posthumous condition conferred by chemo or the fragile physical state conferred by surgery, for what else have we ever known? And what would it mean to relinquish Don, and my daughters, and friends, and yes Dr. Matei in an exit that I can only, and barely, comprehend as equivalent to some passage before my entrance into the world. I am torn between a furious determination not to linger, to be brief, and yet the need to continue wincing and singing with the poets on the age-old anvil of sorrow and grief.

Despite all my highfalutin ideals about the fine life I had been granted and my reasonableness about accepting its foreseeable close, every decision I have made thus far suggests that I might undergo this lengthy operation, for the devils you know (even surgeries with miserable complications) may seem less frightful than the dying you can never comprehend until it has inexorably descended upon you along with death itself, which remains a baffling unknowable. No matter how rationally I embrace the reality of my imminent demise, submitting *now* (maybe later, but *now*?) to the inevitable degeneration of dying and an inconceivable death remains anathema to me.

Even for those of us dedicated to acknowledging our own demise, it is difficult to negotiate a vertiginous divide. Theoretically we may understand that an acceptance of death will ease or enhance the dying process, but viscerally many of us cling to the existence we have been granted and to the people and places we cherish in that existence, for what else can we comprehend? Dread of physical suffering and terror of not-being, of the unimaginable empty state, tether and gall us. The discrepancy between my initial acceptance of mortality and my dogged pursuance of medical interventions has humbled me. Despite all my high-minded acquiescence, I remain uncertain about timing: will it always feel precipitous to arrive at the terminal?

Pointing out the contradictions, dilemmas, and confusions of *un*successful available treatments does not solve any of the problems, of course. Nor do I mean to whine, except maybe a little. But all those memoirs assuring readers that cancer teaches us to appreciate the preciousness of the present moment, that treatment is a journey with a spiritual pot of gold at its end ring hollow in terms of technologies and protocols that salvage ovarian cancer patients' lives by stunning, hurting, or harming us. By way of summary, then, I ask, what does medical knowledge do to or for women dealing with ovarian cancer? Many of us manage to appreciate the preciousness of the present moment and find a spiritual pot of gold at the end of treatment *not because but in spite of* medical interventions, for the state of contemporary approaches to ovarian cancer is a scandal.

"If there is no cure, I still want to correct a few things": the first line of Jason Shinder's last poem in his posthumous volume *Stupid Hope* can stand as a sort of epigraph to the list that follows.

Though there is no cure for me, there are still a few things that I cannot correct but that I very much want corrected. Today's scientists of cancer pride themselves on astonishing breakthroughs in their understanding of oncogenes and tumor suppressor genes, of decapitated and translocated chromosomes, but such pioneering research has had little or no impact on patient care: "the new science on the one hand and old medicine on the other." Here is my probably insufficient list of the cockamamie conundrums confronted by people treated for ovarian cancer by the old medicine. Each item may look like an abstraction, but the 200,000 women annually diagnosed worldwide suffer its consequences not in any abstract way but existentially, individually, miserably.

—Women are told to heed the early symptoms of ovarian cancer, but many have no symptoms. If others do manage to be alerted by early and muted or misunderstood signs, their suspicions cannot be allayed or confirmed because there is no reliable test or screening technique for early detection.

—Although evidence exists that over time the CA-125 test (administered with abdominal and vaginal ultrasound) can furnish a pattern that would allow women to discover ovarian cancer at its onset, these tests have not yet become part of the standard annual checkup of women with a history of ovarian cancer in their families.

—Anesthetized women who are subjected to debulking are in no position to decide that they would prefer not to, that they would rather not risk the high rate of postoperative complication, that living without a major body organ or impaired body organs might not be their choice.

—50 to 70 percent of debulking operations are suboptimal, leaving visible evidence of cancer that increases the risks of a recurrence.

—Debulking, which rarely eradicates cancer, often damages the organs surgeons try to repair after the destruction wrought by advanced cancer.

—Toxic chemicals infused into a woman so as to prolong her life may make her life intolerable, either physically or psychologically or both.

—Chemotherapy does not save most women with ovarian cancer from recurrence and death.

—Medications for the side effects of chemotherapy often produce deleterious side effects.

—Procedures (such as drains) and surgeries (such as ileostomies) to deal with mishaps after debulking or the ravages of cancer may be ineffective or injurious, either physically or psychologically or both.

—By lowering resistance to infection, ongoing chemotherapy can render procedures and surgeries (dealing with mishaps after debulking or the ravages of cancer) ineffective or injurious to the patient.

—Because of sophisticated blood screening, younger
women can discover if they have a genetic mutation that
would put them at high risk for gynecologic cancers; however, the only deterrent currently offered by physicians
consists of mutilation, early menopause, and infertility.

With such knowledge, I have to ask, who needs knowledge?
Though this question sounds like a joke to my ears, the punch line
of a Jewish joke maybe about Eve leaving the Garden of Eden, it
does not come easily from a person who has spent her entire life
in school. And it is meant more theoretically than practically or
pragmatically because I would urge American women to use whatever medical interventions exist to detect ovarian cancer as early
as possible and then to deal with it, should the day come when
every citizen will be adequately covered by health insurance. This
important promise, made while Barack Obama campaigned for the
presidency, was stereotyped and stymied by innumerable pundits
and politicians during the first year of my treatment. It was motivated, candidate Obama explained in a speech in Santa Barbara,
by the recollection that his mother "wasn't sure whether insurance
was going to cover the medical expenses." He remembered "being
heartbroken seeing her struggle through the paperwork and the
medical bills and the insurance forms."

Stanley Ann Dunham died of ovarian or uterine cancer on
November 7, 1995, thirteen years before her son's historic election
and my lamentable diagnosis. A single mother, she collected Java-
nese batik textiles, completed a doctoral dissertation in anthropol-
ogy, and helped build a microfinance program in Indonesia. She
placed her faith in what her son has called "needlepoint virtues"
until she died at fifty-two years of age. The first physician whom

Ann Dunham consulted concluded that she was suffering from indigestion, as do most doctors confronted by patients with ovarian cancer, as did mine. According to a letter sent to me by her mentor, Alice G. Dewey, "Eventually she was told by a doctor that she had problems with her appendix and so she had it removed. This of course did not help and finally she took the advice of friends and returned to Hawaii for a diagnosis." After treatment and a recurrence, when Ann Dunham's mother insisted that she consult the physicians at Sloan-Kettering, "Their diagnosis was that Hawaii had been treating Ann for the wrong cancer," but "by then it was pretty much too late."

In contrast to the evolution of breast cancer treatments over the past few decades, there has been little substantial progress in medical approaches to ovarian cancer. Advocates seeking to increase research for ovarian cancer should not compete against but instead join forces with breast cancer activists because, as Susan Love has put it about government funding, "We don't want a bigger piece of the pie—we want a bigger pie. Our government spends too much money defending the country and not enough defending people's lives."

On a more personal level, then, I am glad that I received my transient wish for a good summer and for a year of remission and now for another indeterminate period of a second remission, which I owe to the exertions of dedicated doctors and nurses. They, like me and like so many women with ovarian cancer, long for the public attention and political advocacy that will generate money for critically necessary research to invent screening devices for early detection and less frightful protocols of treatment as well as the most desirable of goals—methods of prevention. Given all that physicians, nurses, family, and friends have done for me, I do not want to

be averse to the surprise of an extended life. I have no way of knowing what may have happened to me if and when the time comes to
correct the proofs of this book, if and when it appears in print.

Perhaps the upcoming operation will enhance my second
remission. On ovarian cancer Internet sites, women who have
been through two, three, even four and more recurrences seek
and share information on further protocols. Not the testimonials,
composed retrospectively and often by relatives, but the brief and
urgent updates and questions about choices related to drugs or side
effects or trials, composed by patients in the midst of coping with
the unpredictable course of the disease and its treatments, amaze
me. As I study the posts on Ovarian@Listserv.Acor.org, I suspect
that I do not have their authors' resources of strength. Every day I
am stirred by their exceptionally detailed knowledge of available
options and by their careful courtesy to one another. And every
day there is a moment when I still find myself saying "thank you,
thank you" to the powers that be—for the listserv itself, for a less
hectic, more solicitous phone call from my brother, for the sight of
a beautiful bird or sunset, for the growing sweetness in my increasingly befuddled mother. And I owe these moments, as well, to my
physicians.

But the discouraging statistics and my misfortunes have taken a
toll. At MSK one oncologist (to whom Dr. Weiser sent me) cheerily
exclaimed upon our introduction, "The fact that you had a suboptimal debulking does not make you a suboptimal person!" Unspoken,
my first outraged reaction ("I've never considered myself a suboptimal person!") quickly tripped into the also unspoken but gloomier
conviction, "Yes, I have become a suboptimal person."

Only after Christmas, as the new year approached, was the
threat of becoming or being a suboptimal person seared into my

psyche by a question posed by my friend Mary and then answered first by her and then by Don: "What is your fondest memory of 2010?" she asked. Stumped, I could only think of the recurrence, the series of infections accompanying the second round of chemotherapy, the various hospitalizations, and the interminable quest for absorptive pads. Mary, who had worked hard to organize a reunion of my former graduate students in April, listed that event as a highlight of her year, which it was for me, too, so why had it faded so quickly from view? Some forty former students, now administrators and professors and high school teachers and editors, converged on Bloomington from as far away as New York and Florida, Italy and Brussels, Canada and California, bringing in tow a partner or a parent or a gaggle of kids or a new publication or photos of their own prized students. In a series of panel discussions on the future of gender and sexuality studies, or during coffee breaks, or at the sumptuous evening dinner, they crackled with intellectual excitement about future intellectual work that needs to be done and cackled over shared memories of their erstwhile adventures with me while they were preparing for doctoral exams or drafting their dissertations.

As I realized how the blinders of disease and its treatment had constricted my memory, Don recalled his sense of my best moment in 2010—an enchanted get-together in June with my British cousins when all of our children finally met in Hampstead to connect during a convivial evening that, I hoped, would ensure the ongoing future of our relatedness. What might it have meant to my father that his brother's sons and I—remnants of a family fractured by the Holocaust—managed to join our offspring together with such incredulous delight? How could I have forgotten these two marvelous experiences—one before and one after the recurrence—which would never have happened without a cadre of helpers? Have the arduous requirements of daily tending to the injured body subsumed all other realities? Would my future, like my past, be eclipsed or debulked by an obsession with medical procedures that activates a sort of soul murder, a morally and spiritually reprehensible solipsism?

At home, while Simone and Molly schedule coordinated plane trips to cover my caretaking during and after the next surgery, I ponder the treatment choices I will have to make as well as my struggle to relinquish a manuscript that has kept me company through all these hard times. Actually, it did more than keep me company. The personal narratives I found and then quoted, the memoirs and essays I consulted, bonded me to other individuals who have struggled with illness and buoyed me up in the conviction that this sort of witnessing supports numerous volunteers organizing for progress against dread diseases. Reading and writing about cancer cast a lifeline between me and people whose honesty about mortal encounters mitigated my fearful loneliness and thereby steadied me. The words of Corinne Boyer, a Canadian woman who died of ovarian cancer a decade ago, complement the patchwork of sentiments expressed by many of the others I studied: "Is this my protest against what is happening to me? No—it is a protest about what is happening to all women. Or, more exactly, what is not happening for them. I am reconciled for myself, and anticipate the entirely spiritual life that awaits me. What I was not reconciled to—nor should anyone be—is the injustice to women in allocating such a paltry medical research budget to illnesses that are specific to women."

Nurtured not only by memoirs and testimonials but also by the novels, plays, films, poems, and paintings on which I have mused throughout these chapters and by ongoing intimacy with family and friends accustomed to my perpetual reversals, I now dwell in the duration of "until," where the variable weather, rarely dull, offers intermittent prospects beyond me muttering "I" to myself. As the days grow shorter, I realize that this book is what I wanted to complete before any more medical interventions, consequences, and decisions have to be confronted. Two years and one month after diagnosis, it is finished, and Don can begin editing, as he has edited all of my writing, and I delight in the prospect of our ensuing conversations. So this is, after all, a happy ending, the happiest ending I can now imagine. In response to a worry that no one could slog through these pages without becoming mired in my misfortunes, I comfort myself with the knowledge that they implicitly contain and sustain a hymn to second loves, to the patient sensitivity and inventive responsiveness some of us are lucky enough to encounter in later life. For surely the mystic gaits of going along in tandem or side by side cure the spirit, blessing even an ingrate like me with a surplus of wonder for which I am and will be eternally thankful.

—December 2010

SOURCE NOTES

1. DIAGNOSIS

(2) "will be quite comfortable": Ritu Salani and Robert E. Bristow, *Johns Hopkins Patients' Guide to Ovarian Cancer* (Sudbury, MA: Jones and Bartlett, 2011), 8.

(2) "Long-term survival rates": Adam Rosenthal, Usha Menon, and Ian Jacobs, "Ovarian Cancer Screening," in *Cancer of the Ovary*, edited by Rodney Reznek (Cambridge: Cambridge University Press, 2007), 47.

(2) "People with ovarian cancer": Richard Powers, *Gain* (New York: Farrar Straus & Giroux, 1998), 76.

(3) "My treatment": Margaret Edson, *Wit*, in *The Norton Anthology of Literature by Women*, edited by Sandra M. Gilbert and Susan Gubar, vol. 2 (New York: Norton, 2007), 1472.

(6) "I don't care": Chris Bledy, *Beating Ovarian Cancer: How to Overcome the Odds and Reclaim Your Life* (New York: Aviva, 2008), 25.

(7) "A diagnosis": Juliet Wittman, *Breast Cancer Journal: A Century of Petals* (Golden, CO: Fulcrum, 1993), 39.

(8) "extinction was unimaginable": David Rieff, *Swimming in a Sea of Death* (New York: Simon & Schuster, 2008), 155, 156.

(9) "obliterative": Joan Didion, *The Year of Magical Thinking* (New York: Knopf, 2005), 188.

(10) "*I did it . . . loss*": Ibid., 160, 188.

(13)t "Ovarian cancer": Lois M. Ramondetta, Margaret M. Fields, and Michael J. Fisch, "Supportive Care," in *Ovarian Cancer*, edited by Robert C. Bast, Jr., and Maurie Markman (London: Remedica, 2009), 185.

(13) "insidious": Patricia Jasen, "From the 'Silent Killer' to the 'Whispering Disease': Ovarian Cancer and the Uses of Metaphor," *Medical History* 53 (2009): 489.

(13) "Like the kiss": Jackie Stacey, *Teratologies: A Cultural Study of Cancer* (London: Routledge, 1997), 80.

(14) "Few ovarian cancer activists": Agala Miron, *Ovarian Cancer Journeys: Survivors Share Their Stories to Help Others* (New York: iUniverse, 2004), 9.

(14) "kills more women": Bledy, *Beating Ovarian Cancer*, 43.

(14) "If *cancer*": William H. Parker with Rachel L. Parker, *A Gynecologist's Second Opinion: The Questions and Answers You Need to Take Charge of Your Health*, revised edition (New York: Plume, 2003), 275.

(15) "Ovarian cancer . . . recurrence": Mary L. Disis, MD, and Saul Rivkin, MD, "Future Directions in the Management of Ovarian Cancer," *Current Topics in Ovarian Cancer* 17, no. 4 (August 2003): 1075–76.

(15) "Of the 22,210": Virginia R. Martin and Carol Cherry, "Ovarian Cancer," in *Nursing Care of Women with Cancer*, edited by Karen Hassey Dow (St. Louis: Mosby Elsevier, 2006), 96.

(15) "the overall median": Bledy, *Beating Ovarian Cancer*, 43.

(15) "the majority of": Bryan T. Hennessy et al., Introduction to *Ovarian Cancer*, edited by Robert C. Bast, MD, and Maurie Markman, MD (London: Remedica, 2009), 2.

(16) "women with ovarian cancer": Barbara Goff et al., "Ovarian Carcinoma Diagnosis: Results of a National Ovarian Cancer Survey," *Cancer* 29 (2000): 2072–73.

(16) "All the symptoms": Miron, *Ovarian Cancer Journeys*, 4.

(16) "No warning signs": Powers, *Gain*, 76.

(16) "I am so attuned": Gillian Rose, *Love's Work* (London: Chatto & Windus, 1995), 79.

(17) "I looked like": Gilda Radner, *It's Always Something* (New York: Simon & Schuster, 1989), 66.

(17) "*ovarian cancer*": Arlan F. Fuller, Jr., Introduction to *Warnings, Sighs & Whispers: True Stories That Could Save Lives*, edited by Maureen Ryberg (Bloomington, IN: First Books Library, 2003), 5.

(17) "How could Gilda Radner": Radner, *It's Always Something*, 101–2.

(17) Many women . . . elevated levels: Peter E. Schwartz, "Current Diagnosis and Treatment Modalities for Ovarian Cancer," in *Ovarian Cancer*, edited by M. Sharon Stack and David A. Fishman (Boston: Kluwer Academic, 2002), 100.

(18) "Is there no end": Barbara Creaturo, *Courage: The Testimony of a Cancer Patient* (New York: Pantheon, 1991), 130.

(18) "torture": Ibid., 55.

(18) "poor reproductive performance": Jasen, "From the 'Silent Killer' to the 'Whispering Disease,'" 501.

(19) "render the gene": Joi L. Morris and Ora K. Gordon, *Positive Results: Making the Best Decisions When You're at High Risk for Breast or Ovarian Cancer* (Amherst, NY: Prometheus, 2010), 45.

(19) Cancer geneticists agree: Lori d'Agincourt-Canning, "Experiences of Genetic Risk: Disclosure and the Gendering of Responsibility," *Bioethics* 15, no. 3 (2001): 234.

(19) "a cancer pre-vivor": Kristine Conner and Lauren Langford, *Ovarian Cancer: Your Guide to Taking Control* (Sebastopol, CA: O'Reilly, 2003), 41.

(19) "Jewish people": Dina Roth Port, *Previvors: Facing the Breast Cancer Gene and Making Life-Changing Decisions* (New York: Avery, 2010), 31.

(19) "the worried well": G. Thomas Couser, *Vulnerable Subjects: Ethics and Life Writing* (Ithaca, NY: Cornell University Press, 2004), 188.

(19) "psychological distress": Port, *Previvors*, 50.

(19) "would always be ill . . . mutant": Marsha Gessen, *Blood Matters: From Inherited Illness to Designer Babies, How the World and I Found Ourselves in the Future of the Gene* (New York: Harcourt, 2008), 74, 72.

(19) "facile reclassification": Kelly E. Happe, "Heredity, Gender and the Discourse of Ovarian Cancer," *New Genetics and Society* 25, no. 2 (August 2006): 182.

(20) "in the form of": Sarah Gabriel, *Eating Pomegranates: A Memoir of Mothers, Daughters and Genes* (London: Cape, 2009), 25.

(20) "curse . . . within them": Diane Tropea Greene, *Apron Strings: Inheriting Courage, Wisdom and . . . Breast Cancer* (Highland City, FL: Rainbow Books, 2007), 44, 124.

(20) "*time bombs*": Amy Boesky, *What We Have: A Family's Inspiring Story About Love, Loss, and Survival* (New York: Gotham Books, 2010), 27.

(20) "African-American men . . . think": Andrea King Collier, *Still with Me: A Daughter's Journey of Love and Loss* (New York: Simon & Schuster, 2003), 124, 244.

(20) "cancer dynasties": Gessen, *Blood Matters*, 8.

(20) "While breast cancers": Barbara Katz Rothman, *Genetic Maps and Human Imaginations: The Limits of Science in Understanding Who We Are* (New York: Norton, 1998), 151.

(21) Joanna Rudnick, *In the Family*, producer Gordon Quinn, co-producer Beth Iams (2008).

(21) "lowers the odds": Port, *Previvors*, 117.

(21) "the 40 percent risk": Gessen, *Blood Matters*, 190.

(21) "risk of heart disease": Ibid., 82.

(21) "Ovarian-type cancers": Mary Briody Mahowald, *Genes, Women, Equality* (New York: Oxford University Press, 2000), 198.

(22) "gene therapy-based vaccine": Jeri Freedman, *Ovarian Cancer: Current and Emerging Trends in Detection and Treatment* (New York: Rosen, 2009), 52.

(22) "the use of contrast agents": Port, *Previvors*, 227.

(22) emerging treatments: Schwartz, "Current Diagnosis," 112–13.

(23) "miracle of medicine . . . have it": Jennie Nash, *The Victoria's Secret Catalog Never Stops Coming, and Other Lessons I Learned from Breast Cancer* (New York: Scribner, 2001), 71, 89.

(23) "breast cancer's poor . . . unspeakable": Gessen, *Blood Matters*, 75.

(23) "You hear": Kathryn Carter and Laurie Elit, eds., *Bearing Witness: Living with Ovarian Cancer* (Waterloo, ON: Wilfrid Laurier University Press, 2009), 74.

(23) "the paucity": Diane Sims Roth, *An Ovarian Cancer Companion* (Burnstown, ON: General Store, 2003), 145.

(23) "For the average person": Ryberg, *Warnings, Sighs & Whispers*, 303.

(24) "positive thinking": Barbara R. Van Billiard, *A Feather in My Wig: Ovarian Cancer: Cured* (Portsmouth, NH: Peter E. Randall, 1998), 58.

(25) "*I carry death*": Audre Lorde, *The Cancer Journals* (Argyle, NY: Spinsters Ink, 1980), 13.

(25) "It isn't a very nice exit": Carter and Elit, *Bearing Witness*, 9.

(27) "Where I am": Recast from Epicurus, "Letter to Menoeceus," in *Facing Death: Epicurus and His Critics* by James Warren (Oxford: Clarendon Press, 2004), 19.

(27) "there is something": Thomas Browne, *Religio Medici*, 1643 (Menston, UK: Scholar Press, 1970), 84.

(27) "the psychological 'undeadness' ": Nancy Mairs, *A Troubled Guest: Life and Death Stories* (Boston: Beacon, 2001), 59, 76–77.

(28) "the goal must be": Hester Hill Schnipper, *After Breast Cancer: A Common-Sense Guide to Life After Treatment* (New York: Bantam, 2003), 14.

(28) "Anyone diagnosed": Don S. Dizon, MD, and Nadeem R. Abu-Rustum, MD, *100 Questions and Answers About Ovarian Cancer*, 2nd edition (Sudbury, MA: Jones & Bartlett, 2006), 126.

(28) "if she dies": Powers, *Gain*, 317.

(29) "the rose-tinted spectacles": Simon Critchley, *Very Little . . . Almost Nothing: Death, Philosophy, Literature* (London: Routledge, 1997), 27.

(29) "surrender," "conspiring": Reynolds Price, *A Whole New Life* (New York: Atheneum, 1994), 68.

(29) *Surviving Ovarian Cancer* (DVD), provided by the Ovarian Cancer Research Fund, 1999.

(29) " 'clarity' . . . morality": Quoted in "Jason Shinder: The Lure of Death," by Melanie Thernstrom, *New York Times Magazine* (December 28, 2008): 58.

(30) "the person": Marie de Hennezel, *Intimate Death: How the Dying Teach Us How to Live*, translated by Carol Brown Janeway (New York: Knopf, 1997), 26.

(30) "Almost everyone": Sherwin B. Nuland, *How We Die: Reflections on Life's Final Chapter* (New York: Vintage, 1995), 233.

2. OVARIANA

(36) "dull and gray . . . hope": Natalie Angier, *Woman: An Intimate Geography* (Boston: Houghton Mifflin, 1999), 162.

(36) "no almond": Ibid., 164.

(37) "inferior": Thomas Laqueur, *Making Sex: Body and Gender from the Greeks to Freud* (Cambridge: Harvard University Press, 1990), 158.

(37) "the male testes": Ibid., 4.

(37) "The vagina": Angier, *Woman*, 84.

(37) "the woman's semen": Joan Cadden, *Meanings of Sex Difference in the Middle Ages: Medicine, Science, and Culture* (Cambridge: Cambridge University Press, 1993), 118.

(37) "Galen concurred": Eve Keller, *Generating Bodies and Gendered Selves: The Rhetoric of Reproduction in Early Modern England* (Seattle: University of Washington Press, 2007), 107.

(37) "the male seed stamped": Katharine Park, *Secrets of Women: Gender, Generation, and the Origins of Human Dissection* (New York: Zone Books, 2006), 142.

(37) "the egg's self-regulation": Keller, *Generating Bodies*, 116.

(38) Johannes van Horne: Matthew Cobb, *Generation: The Seventeenth-Century Scientists Who Unraveled the Secrets of Sex, Life, and Growth* (New York: Bloomsbury, 2006), 99.

(38) "provided the first": Ibid., 187.

(38) "to the credibility": Clara Pinto-Correia, *The Ovary of Eve: Egg and Sperm and Preformation* (Chicago: University of Chicago Press, 1997), 43.

(38) "all living beings": Ibid., 3.

(38) "held that God": Ibid., 13.

(38) "as perfect as eggs": Ibid., 273.

(38) "attributed uterine fury": Kathleen A. Wellman, "Physicians and Philosophes: Physiology and Sexual Morality in the French Enlightenment," *Eighteenth-Century Studies* 35, no. 2 (Winter 2002): 269.

(39) Before the introduction . . . confused: Jacques Roger, *The Life Sciences in Eighteenth-Century French Thought*, edited by Keith R. Benson, translated by Robert Ellrich (Stanford: Stanford University Press, 1997), 369.

(39) Ephraim McDowell: Ann Dally, *Women Under the Knife: A History of Surgery* (New York: Routledge, 1991), 16.

(39) "Normal ovariotomy": Martha Stoddard Holmes, "Pink Ribbons and Public Private Parts: On Not Imagining Ovarian Cancer," *Literature and Medicine* 25, no. 2 (Fall 2006): 492.

(40) "a disease . . . *vulva*": Lisa Loomer, *The Waiting Room* (New York: Dramatists Play Service: 1998), 13–15.

(40) "Leeching . . . treatment": Edward John Tilt, *A Handbook of Uterine Therapeutics and of Diseases of Women*, 3rd edition (London: John Churchill & Sons, 1868), 247–48.

(40) "Of all the organs": Ibid., 5.

(41) "Virchow": Dally, *Women Under the Knife*, 84.

(41) "it is only": Thomas Laqueur, "Orgasm, Generation, and the Politics of Reproductive Biology," in *The Making of the Modern Body: Sexuality and Society in the Nineteenth Century*, edited by Catherine Gallagher and Thomas Laqueur (Berkeley: University of California Press, 1987), 27.

(41) "The monthly activity": Henry Maudsley quoted in Vieda Skultans, ed., *Madness and Morals: Ideas on Insanity in the Nineteenth Century* (London: Routledge & Kegan Paul, 1975), 230–31.

(41) "the mania . . . lucidity": Ibid., 213.

(41) "the irritation . . . lust": Maudsley quoted in Skultans, 234–35.

(41) "faulty . . . source": Ben Barker-Benfield, "Sexual Surgery in Late-Nineteenth-Century America," *International Journal of Health Services* 5, no. 2 (1975): 283.

(41) "came largely": Dally, *Women Under the Knife*, 132.

(41) "the bowels": Ibid., 140.

(42) "not in response . . . symptoms": Deborah Kuhn McGregor, *From Midwives to Medicine: The Birth of American Gynecology* (New Brunswick, NJ: Rutgers University Press, 1998), 186.

(42) "Insanity is not": Dally, *Women Under the Knife*, 151.

(42) "One estimate": Barker-Benfield, "Sexual Surgery," 286.

(42) "the great increase": Ornella Moscucci, *The Science of Woman: Gynaecology and Gender in England, 1800–1929* (Cambridge: Cambridge University Press, 1990), 158.

(42) "the menstruation . . . impossible": Mary Putnam Jacobi, *The Question of Rest: Women During Menstruation* (New York: Putnam, 1877), 72.

(43) "at or just after": Laqueur, *Making Sex*, 212–13.

(43) "the long compressed lips": T. Spencer Wells, *Diseases of the Ovaries: Their Diagnosis and Treatment*, vol. 1 (London: John Churchill, 1865), 308.

(43) "These facts": Havelock Ellis, *Man and Woman: A Study of Human Secondary Sexual Characteristics* (London: Walter Scott, 1894), 256.

(44) "the menace": Ornella Moscucci and Aileen Clarke, "Prophylactic Oophorectomy: A Historical Perspective," *Public Health Past and Present* 61 (2006): 183.

(44) "between 1945": Michael J. O'Dowd and Elliot E. Philipp, *The History of Obstetrics and Gynaecology* (New York: Parthenon, 1994), 583.

(44) "The prognosis": Wilfred Shaw, "Ovarian Tumours," in *Recent Advances in Obstetrics and Gynecology*, edited by Aleck W. Bourne and Leslie H. Williams, 6th edition (Philadelphia: Blakiston, 1946), 295.

(44) W. H. Auden, "Miss Gee," in *Selected Poems*, edited by Edward Mendelson (New York: Vintage, 1979), 55–58.

(46) "It's hard": Sandra M. Gilbert, *Death's Door: Modern Dying and the Ways We Grieve* (New York: Norton, 2006), 196.

(46) "dangling . . . muscles": Coral Lansbury, "Gynaecology, Pornography, and the Antivivisection Movement," *Victorian Studies* 28, no. 3 (Spring 1985): 419.

(46) "growing . . . effects": Jasen, "From the 'Silent Killer' to the 'Whispering Disease,'" 496.

(46) "murderous . . . ovary": Thomas Mann, *The Black Swan* (Berkeley: University of California Press, 1990), 138.

(47) "Nature's revenge": Camille Paglia quoted in Rose, *Love's Work*, 77.

(47) "continuous or 'incessant'": Jasen, "From the 'Silent Killer' to the 'Whispering Disease,'" 490.

(48) "ruthlessly denied . . . seeks": Edson, *Wit*, 1477.

(48) "If you become . . . find it": Ibid., 1485.

(48) "Patients": Susan Sontag, *Illness as Metaphor* (New York: Farrar, Straus, & Giroux, 1978), 57.

(51) "because of": Albert Auster and Leonard Quart, *Thirtysomething: Television, Women, Men, and Work* (Lanham, MD: Lexington Books, 2008), 27.

(52) "was absolutely overwhelmed": Carter and Elit, *Bearing Witness*, 24.

(52) "recognizing . . . week": Ibid., 20.

(53) "was concerned": Roth, *An Ovarian Cancer Companion*, 36.

(53) "I was thirty-seven": Ibid., 121.

(53) Patients' stories: Miron, *Ovarian Cancer Journeys*, 12, 2, 25, 41, 44, 47.

(53) "My key message": Ryberg, *Warnings, Sighs & Whispers*, 88.

(53) "One thing": Ibid., 220.

(55) routine hysterectomies: Angier, *Woman*, 113.

(56) "It's not": Jasen, "From the 'Silent Killer' to the 'Whispering Disease,' " 408.

3. THE MOTHER OF ALL SURGERIES

(60) "proportion of . . . unknown": Janos Balega and John H. Shepherd, "Surgical Management of Patients with Epithelial Ovarian Cancer," in *Cancer of the Ovary*, edited by Rodney Reznek (Cambridge: Cambridge University Press, 2007), 72.

(61) "ovarian . . . cancer": Ramondetta, Fields, and Fisch, "Supportive Care," 185.

(61) "I was aware": Holmes, "Pink Ribbons and Public Private Parts," 476.

(63) "a disease . . . hard-to-visualize": Ibid., 482.

(63) "ovarian charts . . . noses": Annie Smith, *Bearing Up with Cancer: Life and Living With* . . . (Toronto: Second Story Press, 2004), 45.

(63) "With the patient's body": Sontag, *Illness as Metaphor*, 64.

(64) William Blake, "The Sick Rose," in *William Blake: Songs of Innocence and of Experience*, edited by Robert N. Essick (San Marino, CA: Huntington Library, 2008), 121.

(65) "the invisible agents . . . 'life' ": Ibid., 121–22.

(65) "imagined . . . spot": Lynette Walker, *Mother, Breast Cancer and Selfhood: A Memoir* (Victoria, BC: Trafford, 2002), 4.

(65) "this internal . . . within": Siddhartha Mukherjee, *The Emperor of All Maladies: A Biography of Cancer* (New York: Scribner, 2010), 182.

(65) "pathological . . . vessels": Ibid., 391.

(65) "feeding the cancer": F. J. Montz and Robert E. Bristow with Paula J. Anastasia, *A Guide to Survivorship for Women with Ovarian Cancer* (Baltimore: Johns Hopkins University Press, 2005), 29.

(65) "Let me not": Alicia Ostriker, "Scenes from a Mastectomy," in *Living on the Margins: Women Writers on Breast Cancer*, edited by Hilda Raz (New York: Persea, 1999), 181.

(65) "the cancer is eating": Martha Manning, *Undercurrents: A Life Beneath the Surface* (San Francisco: HarperSanFrancisco, 1994), 171.

(66) "Being eaten away": Arthur Kleinman, *The Illness Narratives: Suffering, Healing, and the Human Condition* (New York: Basic Books, 1988), 148.

(66) "I know": Jessica Queller, *Pretty Is What Changes: Impossible Choices, the Breast Cancer Gene, and How I Defied My Destiny* (New York: Spiegel & Grau, 2008), 213.

(66) "*lethal eel*": Price, *A Whole New Life*, 29.

(66) "cancer hosts": Ibid., 36.

(66) "embryo . . . once": Anne Sexton, "The Operation," in *Selected Poems of Anne Sexton*, edited by Diane Wood Middlebrook and Diana Hume George (Boston: Houghton Mifflin, 1988), 52–55.

(66) "monstrous birth": Stacey, *Teratologies*, 62.

(66) "germ cell": Ibid., 60.

(67) "fragments . . . teeth": Margaret Atwood, "Hairball," *Wilderness Tips* (New York: Anchor, 1989), 42.

(67) "flesh . . . herself": Ibid., 54.

(67) "This gift": Maxine Bailey and Sharon M. Lewis, *Sistahs* (Toronto: Playwrights Canada Press, 1998), 48.

(67) "Cancer was the crab": Rothman, *Genetic Maps and Human Imaginations*, 131.

(67) "never takes": Christina Middlebrook, *Seeing the Crab: A Memoir of Dying* (New York: Basic Books, 1996), 14.

(67) "cells . . . twin": Price, *A Whole New Life*, 28, 56.

(67) "berserk . . . adolescents": Nuland, *How We Die*, 207–8.

(68) "a crowd . . . doppelgänger": Meredith Norton, *Lopsided: How Having Breast Cancer Can Be Really Distracting* (New York: Viking, 2008), 119.

(68) "This image . . . organism": Mukherjee, *The Emperor of All Maladies*, 38.

(68) "are more perfect": Ibid., 6.

(68) "an enigmatic": Ibid., 39.

(68) "trying to lasso": Diane Lane Chambers, *Hearing the Stream: A Survivor's Journey into the Sisterhood of Breast Cancer* (Conifer, CO: Ellexa, 2009), 140.

(68) "refer . . . home": Doris Brett, *Eating the Underworld: A Memoir in Three Voices* (Sydney: Vintage, 2001), 260.

(68) "gargoyle": Gail Godwin, *The Good Husband* (New York: Ballantine, 1994), 9, 75.

(68) "a panther . . . assassin": Katherine Russell Rich, *The Red Devil: To Hell with Cancer—and Back* (New York: Crown, 1999), 81.

(69) "a lump . . . chaos": Lorrie Moore, "People Like That Are the Only People Here: Canonical Babbling in Peed Onk," in *The Granta Book of the American Short Story*, vol. 2, edited by Richard Ford (London: Granta, 2007), 539.

(69) H.D., "The Master," in *The Norton Anthology of Literature by Women*, 296.

(71) "all the machinery . . . origin": Nan Shin (Nancy Amphoux), *Diary of a Zen Nun* (New York: Dutton, 1986), 47.

(71) "I'm an empty shell": Ryberg, *Warnings, Sighs & Whispers*, 271.

(71) "They had gutted me . . . murderer": Smith, *Bearing Up with Cancer*, 51, 53.

(71) "It was a billboard": Collier, *Still with Me*, 55.

(74) "a little obituary": Gail Godwin, *The Good Husband*, 167.

(76) Ava Vanyo, *Sarah's Rain* (Lulu Publishing at www.lulu.com, 2005).

(77) "It forces": Anatole Broyard, *Intoxicated by My Illness, and Other Writings on Life and Death*, edited by Alexandra Broyard (New York: Fawcett Columbine, 1992), 24.

(78) "stories are antibodies": Ibid., 20.

(78) "Ovarian cancer treatment": Martin and Cherry, "Ovarian Cancer," 109.

(80) "Most patients": Disis and Rivkin, "Future Directions," 1076.

(81) John McCrae, "In Flanders Fields," 1915, in *In Flanders Fields and Other Poems* (New York: Knickerbocker, 1919), 3.

(82) "pseudosocial conduct": Oliver Sacks, *An Anthropologist on Mars: Seven Paradoxical Tales* (New York: Picador, 1995), 193.

(84) "draw a circle": Kathlyn Conway, *Ordinary Life: A Memoir of Illness* (Ann Arbor: University of Michigan Press, 2007), 3.

(84) "Treated . . . feel": Ibid., 59.

(85) "Cancer means . . . happen": Joy Erlichman Miller and Monica Vest Wheeler with Diane Cullinan Oberhelman, *Cancer: Here's How You Can Help Me Cope and Survive* (Peoria, IL: FB Press, 2005), 14–15.

(86) "quite comfortable": Salani and Bristow, *Johns Hopkins Patients' Guide*, 8.

(87) "it takes . . . lumps": Susan Love, Afterword to Joyce Wadler, *My Breast: One Woman's Cancer Story* (Reading, MA: Addison-Wesley, 1992), 173.

(87) "Once it gets going": Collier, *Still with Me*, 36.

4. STARTING "INFUSION"

(95) "there is absolutely nothing": Montz, *A Guide to Survivorship*, 29.

(95) "Approximately . . . survived": Conner and Langford, *Ovarian Cancer*, 342.

(96) "you've probably": Ibid., 377.

(98) "misery . . . rotisserie": Marilyn French, *A Season in Hell: A Memoir* (New York: Knopf, 1998), 255.

(98) "the punishment": Wittman, *Breast Cancer Journal*, 53.

(98) "Used in another context": Rich, *The Red Devil*, 91.

(98) "I expected": Betty Rollin, *Last Wish* (New York: Wings, 1985), 91.

(98) "chemotherapy fits": Arthur W. Frank, *The Wounded Storyteller: Body, Illness, and Ethics* (Chicago: University of Chicago Press, 1995), 173.

(98) "transforms . . . death": Jean Améry, *At the Mind's Limits: Contemplations by a Survivor on Auschwitz and Its Realities*, translated by Sidney Rosenfeld and Stella P. Rosenfeld (Bloomington: Indiana University Press, 1980), 33, 40.

(99) "the created world": Elaine Scarry, *The Body in Pain: The Making and Unmaking of the World* (New York: Oxford University Press, 1985), 30.

(99) "I was crazy": Deborah Hobler Kahane, *No Less a Woman: Ten Women Shatter the Myths About Breast Cancer* (New York: Prentice Hall, 1990), 27.

(99) "if the tumor": Terry Tempest Williams, *Refuge: An Unnatural History of Family and Place* (New York: Vintage, 1992), 29.

(99) "I told myself": Ibid., 39.

(99) "would have . . . poisoning": Ryberg, *Warnings, Sighs & Whispers*, 148.

(100) "capacity . . . cells": Mukherjee, *The Emperor of All Maladies*, 90.

(100) "in war": Scarry, *The Body in Pain*, 21.

(102) "being on chemotherapy": Sandra Butler and Barbara Rosenblum, *Cancer in Two Voices*, expanded edition (Duluth, MN: Spinsters Ink, 1991), 99.

(102) "never absorbed . . . harm": French, *A Season in Hell*, 36, 60.

(102) "between 50–80%": Katharine E. Kieser and Helen Steed, "Ovarian Cancer," in *Women and Cancer*, edited by Laurie Elit (New York: Nova Biomedical, 2007), 140.

(103) "the bizarre . . . alive": Arthur W. Frank, *At the Will of the Body: Reflections on Illness* (Boston: Houghton Mifflin, 1991), 79.

(103) "goes into remission": Montz, *A Guide to Survivorship*, 2.

(103) "With the bone marrow": Liz Tilberis, *No Time to Die: Living with Ovarian Cancer* (New York: Avon, 1998), 263.

(104) *"treatment is really"*: Lois M. Ramondetta and Deborah Rose Sills, *The Light Within: The Extraordinary Friendship of a Doctor and Patient Brought Together by Cancer* (New York: Morrow, 2008), 202.

(107) "I look at Mother . . . with them": Williams, *Refuge*, 97, 173.

(107) "Who can contemplate . . . order": Mairs, *A Troubled Guest*, 104.

(107) "No worst": Gerard Manley Hopkins, "No worst, there is none," in *The Oxford Anthology of English Poetry*, edited by John Wain, vol. 2 (Oxford: Oxford University Press, 1990), 536.

(108) "Made of stone": Peter Cameron, *Someday This Pain Will Be Useful to You* (New York: Farrar, Straus & Giroux, 2007), 153.

(112) "machines . . . truth": Butler and Rosenblum, *Cancer in Two Voices*, 51.

(113) "The patience": Havi Carel, *Illness: The Art of Living* (Stocksfield, UK: Acumen, 2008), 85.

(115) "wisdom lay": Primo Levi, *Survival in Auschwitz: The New Assault on Humanity*, 1958, translated by Stuart Woolf (New York: Collier, 1961), 106.

(115) "Cancer is not . . . disease": Mukherjee, *The Emperor of All Maladies*, 398.

(116) "There is a virgin forest": Virginia Woolf, "On Being Ill," in *The Moment and Other Essays* (London: Hogarth Press, 1947), 18.

(116) "no arm to cling to": Woolf, *A Room of One's Own* (New York: Harcourt, 2005), 112.

(117) "We float": Woolf, "On Being Ill," 18.

(117) "Fortune gives": Alain de Botton, *The Consolations of Philosophy* (New York: Vintage, 2001), 91.

(118) "No yoke . . . tighter": L. Annaeus Seneca, *Minor Dialogues: Together with the Dialogue on Clemency*, translated by Aubrey Stewart (London: George Bell & Sons, 1889), 134.

(119) "to catch . . . completely": Pema Chödrön, *The Places That Scare You: A Guide to Fearlessness in Difficult Times* (Boston: Shambhala, 2007), 46.

(119) "a life-threatening injury": Ira Byock, Foreword to Joan Halifax, *Being with Dying: Cultivating Compassion and Fearlessness in the Presence of Death* (Boston: Shambhala, 2008), xi.

(120) "I look": Williams, *Refuge*, 97.

(120) "Disease may score": Rollin, *Last Wish*, 129.

(120) "One of the cruelest": Brett, *Eating the Underworld*, 67.

(121) "The physical world . . . territory": Carel, *Illness*, 14, 38, 52.

(122) "raises ideas": F. Gonzalez-Crussi, *Carrying the Heart: Exploring the Worlds Within Us* (New York: Kaplan, 2009), 45.

(122) "the hard stool . . . spools": See Sidney Shrager, *Scatology in Modern Drama* (New York: Irvington, 1982), 64.

(122) "temple built": Simone de Beauvoir, *The Second Sex*, translated by H. M. Parshley (New York: Vintage, 1989), 167.

(122) "If men but saw": Gonzalez-Crussi, *Carrying the Heart*, 92.

(123) seeping, secreting viscosity: Elizabeth Grosz, *Volatile Bodies: Towards a Corporeal Feminism* (Bloomington: Indiana University Press, 1994), 203.

(123) "accusations of dirtiness": Laura Kipnis, *The Female Thing: Dirt, Sex, Envy, Vulnerability* (New York: Pantheon, 2006), 84.

(123) "Who will write": Dominique Laporte, *History of Shit*, translated by Nadia Benabid and Rodolphe el-Khoury (Cambridge, MA: MIT Press, 2000), 102.

(123) "when written": Roland Barthes quoted in ibid., 10.

(124) "between feces and urine": Beauvoir, *The Second Sex*, 167.

(124) "the taboo": Lawrence Kubie, "The Fantasy of Dirt," *Psychoanalytic Quarterly* VI (1937): 396.

(124) "Love has pitched": William Butler Yeats, "Crazy Jane Talks with the Bishop," in *The Collected Poems of W.B. Yeats* (New York: Macmillan, 1956), 254–55.

(124) "Like death": Mark Doty, *Heaven's Coast: A Memoir* (New York: HarperCollins, 1996), 233.

(126) "falling headlong": Acts 1:18.

(126) "Her skeleton": Gannit Ankori, *Imagining Her Selves: Frida Kahlo's Poetics of Identity and Fragmentation* (Westwood, CT: Greenwood, 2002), 191.

5. DRAINED AND BAGGED

(129) "employing . . . knowledge": Mary K. DeShazer, *Fractured Borders: Reading Women's Cancer Literature* (Ann Arbor: University of Michigan Press, 2005), 50.

(138) "when we encounter pain": Chödrön, *The Places That Scare You*, 88.

(139) *"integrate death"*: Lorde, *The Cancer Journals*, 13.

(139) *"we are living and dying"*: Deborah Cumming, *Recovering from Mortality: Essays from a Cancer Limbo Time* (Charlotte, NC: Novello Festival Press, 2005), 12.

(139) *"deeper sources"*: Lorde, *The Cancer Journals*, 11.

(139) "the sense": Pema Chödrön, *When Things Fall Apart: Heart Advice for Difficult Times* (Boston: Shambhala, 2007), 93.

(140) "exchanging oneself . . . practice:" Chödrön, *The Places That Scare You*, 70, 76.

(140) *"Tonglen"*: de Hennezel, *Intimate Death*, 137.

(140) "one of the great": Joan Halifax, *Being with Dying: Cultivating Compassion and Fearlessness in the Presence of Death* (Boston: Shambhala, 2008), 88.

(140) "an inner haven": Karen Armstrong, *Buddha* (New York: Penguin, 2004), 86.

(140) "when I thought": Barbara Kingsolver, *The Bean Trees* (New York: Harper Perennial, 1991), 160.

(142) "a *willingness*": Lauren Slater, *Lying* (New York: Penguin, 2000), 53.

(144) "enervation had turned": French, *A Season in Hell*, 110.

(145) "plunged . . . pain": Price, *A Whole New Life*, 112.

(145) "The hospital": Gilbert, *Death's Door*, 182.

(146) "What can't be cured": Salman Rushdie, *Midnight's Children* (New York: Random House, 2006), 159.

(148) "You must change your life": Rainer Maria Rilke, "Archaic Torso of Apollo," in *Ahead of Parting: The Selected Poetry and Prose of Rainer Maria Rilke*, edited and translated by Stephen Mitchell (New York: Modern Library, 1995), 67.

(151) "shit . . . waist": Rose, *Love's Work*, 87.

(153) "dirt is matter": Sigmund Freud, "Character and Anal Eroticism," 1908, in *The Freud Reader*, edited by Peter Gay, translated by James Strachey (New York: Norton, 1989), 296.

(153) "coming home . . . night": Van Billiard, *A Feather in My Wig*, 79–80.

(153) "round, pink": Ibid., 84.

(154) "urged her . . . tour de force": Creaturo, *Courage*, 254.

(154) "felt . . . myself": Miron, *Ovarian Cancer Journeys*, 42.

(154) "If I had known . . . dead": Collier, *Still with Me*, 55.

(155) lament: Virginia Woolf, "Professions for Women," in *The Norton Anthology of Literature by Women*, 244–47.

(158) "'So this is me'": Donna McFarlane, *Division of Surgery* (Toronto: Women's Press, 1994), 208.

(158) "a belly swollen": Ibid.

(158) "lumps . . . plastic": Ibid., 33.

(158) "Looking back": Jane Walker quoted in Barbara Dorr Mullen and Kerry Anne McGinn, *The Ostomy Book*, 3rd edition (Boulder: Bull, 1992), 119–20.

(159) "attitude . . . tummy": Sandra Benitez, *Bag Lady: A Memoir* (Edina, MN: Benitez, 2005), 165, 144, 157, 165.

(159) "my own attached": Ibid., 150.

(159) "turnoff . . . faces": Ibid., 166.

(159) "Thank you": Ibid., 214.

(160) "characterized by weakness": Nuland, *How We Die*, 217.

(160) "What can't": Rushdie, *Midnight's Children*, 159.

(160) "never be able . . . control": Collier, *Still with Me*, 56–57.

(161) "a home truth": Price, *A Whole New Life*, 12.

(162) photograph of Kahlo: Sarah M. Lowe, *Frida Kahlo* (New York: Universe, 1991), 98.

6. A POSTHUMOUS EXISTENCE

(165) "No worst": Hopkins, "No worst, there is none."

(165) "unworsenable worst": Samuel Beckett, *Worstward Ho* (New York: Grove Press, 1983), 33.

(165) "Blanks how long": Ibid., 32.

(166) "if you think": Edson, *Wit*, 1467.

(166) "a posthumous existence": John Keats, letter to Charles Brown, November 30, 1820, in *Selected Letters of John Keats*, edited by Grant F. Scott, revised edition (Cambridge, MA: Harvard University Press, 2002), 485–86.

(169) "we don't like": Gabriel, *Eating Pomegranates*, 214.

(169) "the slow erosion . . . door": Manning, *Undercurrents*, 107.

(169) "chemical induced . . . systemic stress": William Styron, *Darkness Visible: A Memoir of Madness* (New York: Random House, 1990), 47.

(169) "thought processes": Ibid., 16.

(170) "close to the edge": Andrew Solomon, *The Noonday Demon: An Atlas of Depression* (New York: Scribner, 2001), 28.

(172) "A medical-alert emblem": Mullen and McGinn, *The Ostomy Book*, 271.

(172) "Women can continue": Salani and Bristow, *Johns Hopkins Patients' Guide*, 5.

(172) commemorative quilt: Chambers, *Hearing the Stream*, 158.

(173) hypnosis: Brett, *Eating the Underworld*, 272.

(173) "lying on the floor": Bledy, *Beating Ovarian Cancer*, 14.

(173) "seething . . . belly": Wittman, *Breast Cancer Journal*, 54.

(173) "pain and fear . . . side effect": Kelly Corrigan, *Middle Place* (New York: Hyperion, 2008), 104.

(173) "the internality": Stacey, *Teratologies*, 184.

(173) "deepest . . . torture": Frank, *The Wounded Storyteller*, 173.

(173) "Some days": Maureen McCutcheon, *Where Have My Eyebrows Gone? One Woman's Personal Experiences with Chemotherapy* (Albany: Delmar/Thomson Learning, 2002), 79.

(173) "a head-to-toe rash . . . itching": Norton, *Lopsided*, 78–79.

(174) "Physically the chemo": Ken Wilber, *Grace and Grit: Spirituality and Healing in the Life and Death of Treya Killam Wilber* (Boston: Shambhala, 1991), 208.

(174) "*I didn't know*": Ramondetta and Sills, *The Light Within*, 5.

(175) "How did her life": Jonathan Safran Foer, *Everything Is Illuminated* (New York: Olive, 2008), 182.

(176) "people can become stronger": Ira Byock, *Dying Well: Peace and Possibilities at the End of Life* (New York: Riverhead, 1998), xiv.

(176) two questions: Ibid., 34.

(178) "struck by an arrow": Helga Prignitz-Poda, *Frida Kahlo: The Painter and Her Work* (New York: Schirmer/Mosel and Distributed Art Publishers, 2004), 234.

(179) "herd-abandoned deer": Percy Bysshe Shelley, "Adonais," in *The Norton Anthology of English Literature*, vol. 2 (New York: Norton, 1962), 718–31, line 297.

(179) "fastened to a dying animal": William Butler Yeats, "Sailing to Byzantium," in *The Collected Poems of W.B. Yeats* (New York: Macmillan, 1956), 191.

(179) "The Aztec": Lowe, *Frida Kahlo*, 102.

(180) "swells . . . monstrosity": Anne Carson, "Putting Her in Her Place: Woman, Dirt, and Desire," in *Before Sexuality: The Construction of Erotic Experience in the Ancient Greek World*, edited by David M. Halperin, John J. Winkler, and Froma I. Zeitlin (Princeton: Princeton University Press, 1990), 154.

(183) "Woe to that one": Mark 14:21.

(183) "It would have been better": Matthew 26:24.

(184) Chemo-brain: Ellen Clegg, *Chemobrain: How Cancer Therapies Can Affect Your Mind* (Amherst, NY: Prometheus, 2009), 52.

(184) "After three months": Kahane, *No Less a Woman*, 91.

(185) "word salad": Elyn R. Saks, *The Center Cannot Hold* (New York: Hyperion, 2007), 124.

(185) "The 'me' ": Ibid., 13.

(185) "You should be able": Dizon and Abu-Rustum, *100 Questions and Answers*, 77.

(186) "chemotherapy doesn't mean": Conner and Langford, *Ovarian Cancer*, 184.

(186) "fecal vomiting": Van Billiard, *A Feather in My Wig*, 22.

(186) "as though . . . cramp": Norton, *Lopsided*, 173, 175.

(186) "severe . . . damage": Stacey, *Teratologies*, 182.

(186) "three drops of Taxol": Roth, *An Ovarian Cancer Companion*, 44.

(186) "all I get": Carter and Elit, *Bearing Witness*, 56–57.

(188) " 'Twas just this time": *The Poems of Emily Dickinson: Variorum Edition*, edited by R. W. Franklin, 3 vols. (Cambridge, MA: Belknap Press, 1998), 344.

(188) "I heard a Fly": Ibid., 591.

(188) "My Life closed": Ibid., 1773.

(188) "To die – without the Dying": Ibid., 1027.

(188) "a consciousness": Diana Fuss, "Corpse Poem," *Critical Inquiry* 30 (Autumn 2003): 12.

(189) "the dreadful Prospect": Swift, *Gulliver's Travels*, edited by Christopher Fox (New York: St. Martin's Press, Bedford Books, 1995), 198.

(189) "What is truly horrible . . . exit": Critchley, *Very Little*, 60.

(189) "complaint . . . nothingness of it": Gabriel, *Eating Pomegranates*, 240.

(190) golem: Byron L. Sherwin, *Golems Among Us: How a Legend Can Help Us Navigate the Biotech Century* (Chicago: Ivan R. Dee, 2004), 32.

(190) "Do People moulder equally": *The Poems of Emily Dickinson*, 390.

(191) "Has it begun": T. S. Eliot, *The Waste Land and Other Poems* (New York: Harvest Books, 1934).

(191) "embracing life . . . ever again": Wendy Schlessel Harpham, MD, *Happiness in a Storm: Facing Illness and Embracing Life as a Healthy Survivor* (New York: Norton, 2005), 34.

(191) "as a chronic disease . . . time": Ibid., 45.

(193) "tells us how": Manning, *Undercurrents*, 119.

(193) "When they told me": Carter and Elit, *Bearing Witness*, 36.

(195) "Sometimes . . . you lose": Ibid., 52.

(196) "To some extent . . . diagnosis": Ramondetta, Fields, and Fisch, "Supportive Care," 185–86.

(197) "peace which comes": Armstrong, *Buddha*, 85.

(198) "Hence": John Milton, "Il Penseroso," in *The Norton Anthology of English Literature*, edited by George M. Logan and Barbara K. Lewalski, vol. 1B, 7th edition (New York: Norton, 2000), 1786–90.

(199) "The eminent conductor": Ralph A. Lewin, *Merde: Excursions in Scientific, Cultural, and Sociohistorical Coprology* (New York: Random House, 1999), 146.

7. REMISSION

(210) "Those with cancer": Marilyn Webb, *The Good Death: The New American Search to Reshape the End of Life* (New York: Bantam, 1997), 125.

(213) "For the first time": Gordon Rustin, "Doubts About Ovarian Cancer Relapse Test," *New York Times* (June 1, 2009), A15.

(213) "recurrent disease": Richard G. Moore and Robert C. Bast, Jr., "Biomarkers for ovarian cancer," in *Ovarian Cancer*, edited by Robert C. Bast, Jr. and Maurie Markman (London: Remedica, 2009), 42.

(213) "the end of chemotherapy": Manning, *Undercurrents*, 20.

(217) "nothing can be sole": Yeats, "Crazy Jane Talks with the Bishop."

(218) "there are many conditions": Van Billiard, *A Feather in My Wig*, 86–87.

(218) "I had a bowel": Carter and Elit, *Bearing Witness*, 74.

(218) "pelvic abscess": Pedro T. Ramirez and David M. Gershenson, "Surgical Management," in *Ovarian Cancer*, edited by Bast and Markman, 74.

(219) "no sight": Larkin, "Aubade," in *Collected Poems*, edited by Anthony Thwaite (New York: Farrar Straus & Giroux and The Marvell Press, 1989), 208.

(219) "Where I am": Epicurus in Warren, *Facing Death*, 19.

(220) "Courage is no good": Larkin, "Aubade," 209.

(220) "the pain of living . . . cataclysm": Solomon, *The Noonday Demon*, 250, 268.

(220) "If that story": Ibid., 44.

(220) "the frequent eruptions . . . door": Rollin, *Last Wish*, 136, 149.

(221) "I am convinced": Van Billiard, *A Feather in My Wig*, xvi.

(221) "Without hope": Chambers, *Hearing the Stream*, 141.

(221) "Never give death": Price, *A Whole New Life*, 186.

(222) "the interdiction": Philippe Ariès, *Western Attitudes Toward Death: From the Middle Ages to the Present*, translated by Patricia M. Ranum (Baltimore: Johns Hopkins University Press, 1974), 94.

(222) "Death . . . bitter end": Atul Gawande, "Letting Go: What Should Modern Medicine Do When It Can't Save Your Life?" *The New Yorker*, August 2, 2010, 49.

(222) "how open we are": Didion, *The Year of Magical Thinking*, 206.

(225) "Soon enough": Powers, *Gain*, 332.

(225) "Thrumming": Godwin, *The Good Husband*, 245.

(225) "her mouth frozen . . . haunt me": Queller, *Pretty Is What Changes*, 78.

(225) "pain was a wild thing": Collier, *Still with Me*, 213.

(225) delirium, hallucinations: Webb, *The Good Death*, 122.

(226) "ease suffering": Ibid., 125.

(226) "Being brave": Larkin, "Aubade," 209.

(227) "Death has dominion": Ronald Dworkin, *Life's Dominion: An Argument About Abortion, Euthanasia, and Individual Freedom* (New York: Knopf, 1993), 199.

(227) "Like birth": Gilbert, *Death's Door*, 200.

(228) "To die 'naturally' ": Webb, *The Good Death*, 4.

(231) "*Once* for each thing": Rainer Maria Rilke, "The Ninth Elegy," *Duino Elegies*, in *Ahead of Parting*, 383.

(231) "death's deep": Doty, *Heaven's Coast*, 157–58.

(231) "We need, in love": Rilke, "Requiem for a Friend," in *Ahead of Parting*, 79–93.

(232) "there is something in us": Browne, *Religio Medici*, 84.

(233) "A crisis": Rose, *Love's Work*, 98.

(233) "everyday use": Alice Walker, "Everyday Use," in *In Love and Trouble* (New York: Harcourt, 2004), 47–50.

(234) "the situation": The film is *One, Two, Three*.

8. LOCONOCOLOGY

(238) "Those truths": Elizabeth Edwards, *Saving Grace: Finding Solace and Strength from Friends and Strangers* (New York: Broadway Books, 2007), 355.

(239) "a contractor": Wadler, *My Breast*, 83.

(240) "ravaged": Creaturo, *Courage*, 153.

(240) "may lead": Cheryl L. Cushine, *The Dust Busting Chronicles: Cleaning My Way Through Ovarian Cancer* (Bloomington, IN: AuthorHouse, 2007), 101.

(240) "risk of uterine cancer": Gail Konop Baker, *Cancer Is a Bitch, or: I'd Rather Be Having a Midlife Crisis* (Cambridge, MA: Da Capo Press, 2008), 99.

(242) "a dress rehearsal": Wadler, *My Breast*, 165.

(246) "someone with very advanced": Byock, *Dying Well*, 143.

(247) "goes into remission": Montz, *A Guide to Survivorship*, 2.

(253) "there's hell": William Shakespeare, *King Lear*, IV, 6.

(255) "If there is no cure": Jason Shinder, *Stupid Hope* (St. Paul: Graywolf Press, 2009), 71.

(256) "the new science": Mukherjee, *The Emperor of All Maladies*, 402.

(259) "Eventually she was told": Alice G. Dewey, private letter, undated, postmarked June 21, 2010.

(259) "We don't want . . . lives": Love, Afterword to Wadler, *My Breast*, 179.

(262) "Is this my protest": Corinne Boyer quoted in Roth, *An Ovarian Cancer Companion*, 102.

WORKS CITED

Améry, Jean. *At the Mind's Limits: Contemplations by a Survivor on Auschwitz and Its Realities*, translated by Sidney Rosenfeld and Stella P. Rosenfeld. Bloomington: Indiana University Press, 1980.

Angier, Natalie. *Woman: An Intimate Geography*. Boston: Houghton Mifflin, 1999.

Ankori, Gannit. *Imagining Her Selves: Frida Kahlo's Poetics of Identity and Fragmentation*. Westwood, CT: Greenwood Press, 2002.

Ariès, Philippe. *Western Attitudes Toward Death: From the Middle Ages to the Present*, translated by Patricia M. Ranum. Baltimore: The Johns Hopkins University Press, 1974.

Armstrong, Karen. *Buddha*. New York: Penguin, 2004.

Atwood, Margaret. "Hairball," *Wilderness Tips*, 31–48. New York: Anchor, 1989.

Auden, W. H. "Miss Gee," *Selected Poems*, edited by Edward Mendelson, 55–58. New York: Vintage Books, 1979.

Auster, Albert, and Leonard Quart. *Thirtysomething: Television, Women, Men, and Work*. Lanham, MD: Lexington Books, 2008.

Bailey, Maxine, and Sharon M. Lewis. *Sistahs*. Toronto: Playwrights Canada Press, 1998.

Baker, Gail Konop. *Cancer Is a Bitch, or: I'd Rather Be Having a Midlife Crisis*. Cambridge, MA: Da Capo Press, 2008.

Balega, Janos, and John H. Shepherd. "Surgical Management of Patients with Epithelial Ovarian Cancer," *Cancer of the Ovary*, edited by Rodney Reznek. Cambridge: Cambridge University Press, 2007.

Barker-Benfield, Ben. "Sexual Surgery in Late-Nineteenth-Century America," *International Journal of Health Services* 5, no. 2 (1975): 279–99.

Beauvoir, Simone de. *The Second Sex*, translated by H. M. Parshley. New York: Vintage Books, 1989.

Beckett, Samuel. *Worstward Ho*. New York: Grove Press, 1983.

Benitez, Sandra. *Bag Lady: A Memoir*. Edina, MN: Benitez Books, 2005.

Blake, William. *Songs of Innocence and Experience*, edited by Robert N. Essick. San Marino, CA: Huntington Library, 2008.

Bledy, Chris. *Beating Ovarian Cancer: How to Overcome the Odds and Reclaim Your Life*. New York: Aviva Publishing, 2008.

Brett, Doris. *Eating the Underworld: A Memoir in Three Voices*. Sydney, Australia: Vintage, 2001.

Browne, Thomas. *Religio Medici*. 1643. Menston, UK: Scholar Press, 1970.

Broyard, Anatole. *Intoxicated by My Illness, and Other Writings on Life and Death*, edited by Alexandra Broyard. New York: Fawcett Columbine, 1992.

Butler, Sandra, and Barbara Rosenblum. *Cancer in Two Voices*. Expanded edition. Duluth, MN: Spinsters Ink, 1991.

Byock, Ira. *Dying Well: Peace and Possibilities at the End of Life*. New York: Riverhead Books, 1998.

———. "Foreword" to Joan Halifax, *Being with Dying: Cultivating Compassion and Fearlessness in the Presence of Death*. Boston: Shambhala, 2008.

Cadden, Joan. *Meanings of Sex Difference in the Middle Ages: Medicine, Science, and Culture*. Cambridge: Cambridge University Press, 1993.

Cameron, Peter. *Someday This Pain Will Be Useful to You*. New York: Farrar, Straus & Giroux, 2007.

Carel, Havi. *Illness: The Art of Living*. Stocksfield, UK: Acumen, 2008.

Carson, Anne. "Putting Her in Her Place: Woman, Dirt, and Desire," *Before Sexuality: The Construction of Erotic Experience in the Ancient Greek World*, edited by David M. Halperin, John J. Winkler, and Froma I. Zeitlin, 135–69. Princeton: Princeton University Press, 1990.

Carter, Kathryn, and Laurie Elit, eds. *Bearing Witness: Living with Ovarian Cancer*. Waterloo, ON: Wilfrid Laurier University Press, 2009.

Chambers, Diane Lane. *Hearing the Stream: A Survivor's Journey into the Sisterhood of Breast Cancer*. Conifer, CO: Ellexa Press LLC, 2009.

Chödrön, Pema. *The Places That Scare You: A Guide to Fearlessness in Difficult Times*. Boston: Shambhala, 2007.

———. *When Things Fall Apart: Heart Advice for Difficult Times*. Boston: Shambhala, 2007.

Clegg, Ellen. *Chemobrain: How Cancer Therapies Can Affect Your Mind*. Amherst, NY: Prometheus Books, 2009.

Cobb, Matthew. *Generation: The Seventeenth-Century Scientists Who Unraveled the Secrets of Sex, Life, and Growth*. New York and London: Bloomsbury Publishing, 2006.

Coixet, Isabel, director. *My Life Without Me*. Producers Esther García and Michel Ruben. 2003.

Collier, Andrea King. *Still with Me: A Daughter's Journey of Love and Loss.* New York: Simon & Schuster, 2003.

Conner, Kristine, and Lauren Langford. *Ovarian Cancer: Your Guide to Taking Control.* Sebastopol, CA: O'Reilly, 2003.

Conway, Kathlyn. *Ordinary Life: A Memoir of Illness.* Ann Arbor: University of Michigan Press, 2007.

Corrigan, Kelly. *Middle Place.* New York: Hyperion, 2008.

Couser, G. Thomas. *Vulnerable Subjects: Ethics and Life Writing.* Ithaca, NY: Cornell University Press, 2004.

Creaturo, Barbara. *Courage: The Testimony of a Cancer Patient.* New York: Pantheon, 1991.

Critchley, Simon. *Very Little . . . Almost Nothing: Death, Philosophy, Literature.* London: Routledge, 1997.

Cumming, Deborah. *Recovering from Mortality: Essays from a Cancer Limbo Time.* Charlotte, NC: Novello Festival Press, 2005.

Cushine, Cheryl L. *The Dust Busting Chronicles: Cleaning My Way Through Ovarian Cancer.* Bloomington, IN: AuthorHouse, 2007.

d'Agincourt-Canning, Lori. "Experiences of Genetic Risk: Disclosure and the Gendering of Responsibility," *Bioethics* 15, no. 3 (2001): 231–47.

Dally, Ann. *Women Under the Knife: A History of Surgery.* New York: Routledge, 1991.

Davis, Kate, director and producer. *Southern Comfort,* 2001.

de Botton, Alain. *The Consolations of Philosophy.* New York: Vintage, 2001.

de Hennezel, Marie. *Intimate Death: How the Dying Teach Us How to Live,* translated by Carol Brown Janeway. New York: Alfred A. Knopf, 1997.

DeShazer, Mary K. *Fractured Borders: Reading Women's Cancer Literature.* Ann Arbor: University of Michigan Press, 2005.

Dewey, Alice G. Private letter, undated, postmarked June 21, 2010.

Dickinson, Emily. *The Poems of Emily Dickinson: Variorum Edition,* edited by R. W. Franklin. Cambridge, MA: Belknap Press, 3 vols., 1998.

Didion, Joan. *The Year of Magical Thinking.* New York: Alfred A. Knopf, 2005.

Disis, Mary L., MD, and Saul Rivkin, MD. "Future Directions in the Management of Ovarian Cancer," *Current Topics in Ovarian Cancer,* Hematology/oncology clinics of North America. Philadelphia: W. B. Saunders, 2003.

Dizon, Don S., MD, and Nadeem R. Abu-Rustum, MD. *100 Questions and Answers About Ovarian Cancer,* 2nd edition. Sudbury, MA: Jones and Bartlett Publishers, 2006.

Doty, Mark. *Heaven's Coast: A Memoir.* New York: HarperCollins, 1996.

Dworkin, Ronald. *Life's Dominion: An Argument About Abortion, Euthanasia, and Individual Freedom.* New York: Alfred A. Knopf, 1993.

Edson, Margaret. *Wit* in *The Norton Anthology of Literature by Women,* edited by Sandra M. Gilbert and Susan Gubar, vol. 2, 1454–87. New York: Norton, 2007.

Edwards, Elizabeth. *Saving Grace: Finding Solace and Strength from Friends and Strangers.* New York: Broadway Books, 2007.

Eliot, T. S. *The Waste Land and Other Poems*. New York: Harvest Books, 1934.

Ellis, Havelock. *Man and Woman: A Study of Human Secondary Sexual Characteristics*. London: Walter Scott, 1894.

Elit, Laurie. "Introduction," *Bearing Witness: Living with Ovarian Cancer*, edited by Kathryn Carter and Laurie Elit. Waterloo, ON: Wilfrid Laurier University Press, 2009.

Epicurus. "Letter to Menoeceus," in James Warren, *Facing Death: Epicurus and His Critics*. Oxford: Clarendon Press, 2004.

Frank, Arthur W. *At the Will of the Body: Reflections on Illness*. Boston: Houghton Mifflin, 1991, reprint 2002.

———. *The Wounded Storyteller: Body, Illness, and Ethics*. Chicago: University of Chicago Press, 1995.

Freedman, Jeri. *Ovarian Cancer: Current and Emerging Trends in Detection and Treatment*. New York: Rosen Publishing, 2009.

French, Marilyn. *A Season in Hell: A Memoir*. New York: Alfred A. Knopf, 1998.

Freud, Sigmund. "Character and Anal Eroticism," 1908, in *The Freud Reader,* edited by Peter Gay, translated by James Strachey. New York: Norton, 1989.

Fuller, Arlan F., Jr. "Introduction," *Warnings, Sighs & Whispers: True Stories That Could Save Lives*, edited by Maureen Ryberg. Bloomington, IN: First Books Library, 2003.

Fuss, Diana. "Corpse Poem," *Critical Inquiry* 30 (Autumn 2003): 1–30.

Gabriel, Sarah. *Eating Pomegranates: A Memoir of Mothers, Daughters and Genes*. London: Jonathan Cape, 2009.

Gawande, Atul. "Letting Go: What Should Modern Medicine Do When It Can't Save Your Life?" *The New Yorker* (August 2, 2010): 36–49.

Gessen, Marsha. *Blood Matters: From Inherited Illness to Designer Babies, How the World and I Found Ourselves in the Future of the Gene*. New York: Harcourt, Inc., 2008.

Gilbert, Sandra M. *Death's Door: Modern Dying and the Ways We Grieve*. New York: Norton, 2006.

Godwin, Gail. *The Good Husband*. New York: Ballantine, 1994.

Goff, Barbara, L. Mandel, H. G. Muntz, and C. H. Melancon. "Ovarian Carcinoma Diagnosis: Results of a National Ovarian Cancer Survey," *Cancer* 29 (2000): 2068–75.

Gonzalez-Crussi, F. *Carrying the Heart: Exploring the Worlds Within Us*. New York: Kaplan, 2009.

Greene, Diane Tropea. *Apron Strings: Inheriting Courage, Wisdom and . . . Breast Cancer*. Highland City, FL: Rainbow Books, 2007.

Grosz, Elizabeth. *Volatile Bodies: Towards a Corporeal Feminism*. Bloomington: Indiana University Press, 1994.

Halifax, Joan. *Being with Dying: Cultivating Compassion and Fearlessness in the Presence of Death*. Boston: Shambhala, 2008.

Happe, Kelly E. "Heredity, Gender and the Discourse of Ovarian Cancer." *New Genetics and Society* 25, no. 2 (August 2006): 171–96.

Harpham, Wendy Schlessel, MD. *Happiness in a Storm: Facing Illness and Embracing Life as a Healthy Survivor.* New York: Norton, 2005.

H.D. "The Master," in *The Norton Anthology of Literature by Women,* edited by Sandra M. Gilbert and Susan Gubar, vol. 2, 291–300. New York: Norton, 2007.

Hennessy, Bryan T., Mark S. Carey, Honami Naora, Roshan Agarwal, Yiling Lu, Katherine Stemke-Hale, and Gordon B. Wills. Introduction to Robert C. Bast, MD, and Maurie Markman, MD, eds., *Ovarian Cancer.* London: Remedica, 2009.

Holmes, Martha Stoddard. "Pink Ribbons and Public Private Parts: On Not Imagining Ovarian Cancer," *Literature and Medicine* 25, no. 2 (Fall 2006): 475–501.

Hopkins, Gerard Manley. "No worst, there is none." In *The Oxford Anthology of English Poetry,* edited by John Wain, vol. 2, 536. Oxford: Oxford University Press, 1990.

Jacobi, Mary Putnam. *The Question of Rest: Women During Menstruation.* New York: Putnam's Sons, 1877.

Jasen, Patricia. "From the 'Silent Killer' to the 'Whispering Disease': Ovarian Cancer and the Uses of Metaphor." *Medical History* 53 (2009): 489–512.

Kahane, Deborah Hobler. *No Less a Woman: Ten Women Shatter the Myths About Breast Cancer.* New York: Prentice Hall, 1990.

Keats, John. Letter to Charles Brown, November 30, 1820, in *Selected Letters of John Keats,* edited by Grant F. Scott, revised edition, 485–86. Cambridge, MA: Harvard University Press, 2002.

Keller, Eve. *Generating Bodies and Gendered Selves: The Rhetoric of Reproduction in Early Modern England.* Seattle: University of Washington Press, 2007.

Kieser, Katharine E., and Helen Steed. "Ovarian Cancer," in *Women and Cancer,* edited by Laurie Elit, 131–46. New York: Nova Biomedical, 2007.

Kingsolver, Barbara. *The Bean Trees.* New York: Harper Perennial, 1991.

Kipnis, Laura. *The Female Thing: Dirt, Sex, Envy, Vulnerability.* New York: Pantheon, 2006.

Kleinman, Arthur. *The Illness Narratives: Suffering, Healing, and the Human Condition.* New York: Basic Books, 1988.

Kubie, Lawrence. "The Fantasy of Dirt." *Psychoanalytic Quarterly* VI (1937): 388–425.

Lansbury, Coral. "Gynaecology, Pornography, and the Antivivisection Movement." *Victorian Studies* 28, no. 3 (Spring 1985): 413–37.

Laporte, Dominique. *History of Shit,* translated by Nadia Benabid and Rodolphe el-Khoury. Cambridge, MA: MIT Press, 2000.

Laqueur, Thomas. *Making Sex: Body and Gender from the Greeks to Freud.* Cambridge, MA: Harvard University Press, 1990.

———. "Orgasm, Generation, and the Politics of Reproductive Biology," in *The Making of the Modern Body: Sexuality and Society in the Nineteenth Century,* edited by Catherine Gallagher and Thomas Laqueur, 1–41. Berkeley: University of California Press, 1987.

Larkin, Philip. *Collected Poems,* edited by Anthony Thwaite. New York: Farrar, Straus & Giroux / Marvell Press, 1989.

Levi, Primo. *Survival in Auschwitz: The New Assault on Humanity*, translated by Stuart Woolf. 1958. New York: Collier, 1961.

Lewin, Ralph A. *Merde: Excursions in Scientific, Cultural, and Sociohistorical Coprology*. New York: Random House, 1999.

Loomer, Lisa. *The Waiting Room*. New York: Dramatists Play Service, 1998.

Lorde, Audre. *The Cancer Journals*. Argyle, NY: Spinsters Ink, 1980.

Love, Susan. Afterword to Joyce Wadler, *My Breast: One Woman's Cancer Story*. Reading, MA: Addison-Wesley, 1992.

Lowe, Sarah M. *Frida Kahlo*. New York: Universe, 1991.

Mahowald, Mary Briody. *Genes, Women, Equality*. New York: Oxford University Press, 2000.

Mann, Thomas. *The Black Swan*, with an introduction by Nina Pelikan Straus. Berkeley: University of California Press, 1990.

Manning, Martha. *Undercurrents: A Life Beneath the Surface*. San Francisco: HarperSanFransisco, 1994.

Martin, Virginia R., and Carol Cherry. "Ovarian Cancer," in *Nursing Care of Women with Cancer*, edited by Karen Hassey Dow, 96–119. St. Louis: Mosby Elsevier, 2006.

McCrae, John. "In Flanders Fields," *In Flanders Fields and Other Poems*. New York: Knickerbocker, 1919.

McCutcheon, Maureen. *Where Have My Eyebrows Gone? One Woman's Personal Experiences with Chemotherapy*. Albany: Delmar/Thomson Learning, 2002.

McGregor, Deborah Kuhn. *From Midwives to Medicine: The Birth of American Gynecology*. New Brunswick, NJ: Rutgers University Press, 1998.

Middlebrook, Christina. *Seeing the Crab: A Memoir of Dying*. New York: Basic Books, 1996.

Miller, Joy Erlichman, and Monica Vest Wheeler with Diane Cullinan Oberhelman. *Cancer: Here's How You Can Help Me Cope and Survive*. Peoria, IL: FB Press, 2005.

Milton, John. "Il Penseroso," in *The Norton Anthology of English Literature*, edited by George M. Logan and Barbara K. Lewalski, vol. 1B, 7th edition, 1786–90. New York: Norton, 2000.

Miron, Agala. *Ovarian Cancer Journeys: Survivors Share Their Stories to Help Others*. New York: iUniverse, 2004.

Montz, F. J., and Robert E. Bristow with Paula J. Anastasia. *A Guide to Survivorship for Women with Ovarian Cancer*. Baltimore: Johns Hopkins University Press, 2005.

Moore, Lorrie. "People Like That Are the Only People Here: Canonical Babbling in Peed Onk," in *The Granta Book of the American Short Story*, vol. 2, edited by Richard Ford. London: Granta, 2007.

Moore, Richard G., and Robert C. Bast, Jr. "Biomarkers for ovarian cancer," in *Ovarian Cancer*, edited by Robert C. Bast, Jr., and Maurie Markman, 35–57. London: Remedica, 2009.

Morris, Joi L., and Ora K. Gordon. *Positive Results: Making the Best Decisions When You're at High Risk for Breast or Ovarian Cancer*. Amherst, NY: Prometheus, 2010.

Moscucci, Ornella. *The Science of Woman: Gynaecology and Gender in England, 1800–1929*. Cambridge: Cambridge University Press, 1990.

Moscucci, Ornella, and Aileen Clarke, "Prophylactic Oophorectomy: A Historical Perspective," *Public Health Past and Present* 61 (2006): 182–84.

Mukherjee, Siddhartha. *The Emperor of All Maladies: A Biography of Cancer*. New York: Scribner, 2010.

Mullen, Barbara Dorr, and Kerry Anne McGinn. *The Ostomy Book*. 3rd edition. Boulder: Bull, 1992.

Nash, Jennie. *The Victoria's Secret Catalog Never Stops Coming, and Other Lessons I Learned from Breast Cancer*. New York: Scribner, 2001.

Norton, Meredith. *Lopsided: How Having Breast Cancer Can Be Really Distracting*. New York: Viking, 2008.

Nuland, Sherwin B. *How We Die: Reflections on Life's Final Chapter*. New York: Vintage, 1995.

O'Dowd, Michael J., and Elliot E. Philipp. *The History of Obstetrics and Gynaecology*. New York: Parthenon, 1994.

Ostriker, Alicia. "Scenes from a Mastectomy." In *Living on the Margins: Women Writers on Breast Cancer*, edited by Hilda Raz, 175–200. New York: Persea Books, 1999.

Park, Katharine. *Secrets of Women: Gender, Generation, and the Origins of Human Dissection*. New York: Zone Books, 2006.

Parker, William H., with Rachel L. Parker. *A Gynecologist's Second Opinion: The Questions and Answers You Need to Take Charge of Your Health*, revised edition. New York: Plume, 2003.

Pinto-Correia, Clara. *The Ovary of Eve: Egg and Sperm and Preformation*. Chicago: University of Chicago Press, 1997.

Port, Dina Roth. *Previvors: Facing the Breast Cancer Gene and Making Life-Changing Decisions*. New York: Avery, 2010.

Powers, Richard. *Gain*. New York: Farrar, Straus & Giroux, 1998.

Price, Reynolds. *A Whole New Life*. New York: Atheneum, 1994.

Prignitz-Poda, Helga. *Frida Kahlo: The Painter and Her Work*. New York: Schirmer/Mosel and D.A.P./Distributed Art Publishers, 2004.

Queller, Jessica. *Pretty Is What Changes: Impossible Choices, the Breast Cancer Gene, and How I Defied My Destiny*. New York: Spiegel and Grau, 2008.

Radner, Gilda. *It's Always Something*. New York: Simon & Schuster, 1989.

Ramirez, Pedro T., and David M. Gershenson. "Surgical Management." In *Ovarian Cancer*, edited by Robert C. Bast, Jr., and Maurie Markman, 59–86. London: Remedica, 2009.

Ramondetta, Lois M., and Deborah Rose Sills. *The Light Within: The Extraordinary Friendship of a Doctor and Patient Brought Together by Cancer*. New York: William Morrow, 2008.

Ramondetta, Lois M., Margaret M. Fields, and Michael J. Fisch. "Supportive Care," in *Ovarian Cancer*, edited by Robert C. Bast, Jr., and Maurie Markman, 185–227. London: Remedica, 2009.

Rich, Katherine Russell. *The Red Devil: To Hell with Cancer—and Back*. New York: Crown, 1999.

Rilke, Rainer Maria. *Ahead of Parting: The Selected Poetry and Prose of Rainer Maria Rilke*, edited and translated by Stephen Mitchell. New York: Modern Library, 1995.

Roger, Jacques. *The Life Sciences in Eighteenth-Century French Thought*, edited by Keith R. Benson, translated by Robert Ellrich. Stanford: Stanford University Press, 1997.

Rollin, Betty. *Last Wish*. New York: Wings Books, 1985, reissued 1996.

Rose, Gillian. *Love's Work*. London: Chatto and Windus, 1995.

Rosenthal, Adam, Usha Menon, and Ian Jacobs. "Ovarian Cancer Screening," in *Cancer of the Ovary*, edited by Rodney Reznek. Cambridge: Cambridge University Press, 2007.

Roth, Diane Sims. *An Ovarian Cancer Companion*. Burnstown, ON: General Store, 2003.

Rothman, Barbara Katz. *Genetic Maps and Human Imaginations: The Limits of Science in Understanding Who We Are*. New York: Norton, 1998.

Rudnick, Joanna, director and producer. *In the Family*. Producers Gordon Quinn and Beth Iams. 2008.

Rushdie, Salman. *Midnight's Children*. New York: Random House, 2006.

Rustin, Gordon. "Doubts About Ovarian Relapse Test," *New York Times* (June 1, 2009), A15.

Ryberg, Maureen, ed. *Warnings, Sighs & Whispers: True Stories That Could Save Lives*. Bloomington, IN: First Books Library, 2003.

Sacks, Oliver. *An Anthropologist on Mars: Seven Paradoxical Tales*. New York: Picador, 1995.

Safran Foer, Jonathan. *Everything Is Illuminated*. 2002. New York: Olive, 2008.

Saks, Elyn R. *The Center Cannot Hold*. New York: Hyperion, 2007.

Salani, Ritu, and Robert E. Bristow. *Johns Hopkins Patients' Guide to Ovarian Cancer*. Sudbury, MA: Jones and Bartlett, 2011.

Scarry, Elaine. *The Body in Pain: The Making and Unmaking of the World*. New York: Oxford University Press, 1985.

Schnipper, Hester Hill. *After Breast Cancer: A Common-Sense Guide to Life After Treatment*. New York: Bantam, 2003.

Schwartz, Peter E. "Current Diagnosis and Treatment Modalities for Ovarian Cancer." In *Ovarian Cancer*, edited by M. Sharon Stack and David A. Fishman, 99–118. Boston: Kluwer Academic, 2002.

Seneca, L. Annaeus. *Minor Dialogues: Together with the Dialogue on Clemency*, translated by Aubrey Stewart. London: George Bell and Sons, 1889.

Sexton, Anne. "The Operation," in *Selected Poems of Anne Sexton*, edited by Diane Wood Middlebrook and Diana Hume George, 52–55. Boston: Houghton Mifflin, 1988.

Shaw, Wilfred. "Ovarian Tumours." In Aleck W. Bourne and Leslie H. Williams, *Recent Advances in Obstetrics and Gynecology*, 6th edition. Philadelphia: Blakiston Company, 1946.

Shelley, Percy Bysshe. "Adonais," in *The Norton Anthology of English Literature*, vol. 2, 718–31. New York: Norton, 1962.

Sherwin, Byron L. *Golems Among Us: How a Legend Can Help Us Navigate the Biotech Century*. Chicago: Ivan R. Dee, 2004.

Shin, Nan (Nancy Amphoux). *Diary of a Zen Nun*, illustrations by Peter Watson. New York: Dutton, 1986.

Shinder, Jason. *Stupid Hope*. St. Paul: Graywolf Press, 2009.

Shrager, Sidney. *Scatology in Modern Drama*. New York: Irvington, 1982.

Skultans, Vieda, ed. *Madness and Morals: Ideas on Insanity in the Nineteenth Century*. London: Routledge and Kegan Paul, 1975.

Slater, Lauren. *Lying*. New York: Penguin, 2000.

Smith, Annie. *Bearing Up with Cancer: Life and Living With . . .* Toronto: Second Story, 2004.

Solomon, Andrew. *The Noonday Demon: An Atlas of Depression*. New York: Scribner, 2001.

Sontag, Susan. *Illness as Metaphor*. New York: Farrar, Straus, & Giroux, 1978.

Stacey, Jackie. *Teratologies: A Cultural Study of Cancer*. London: Routledge, 1997.

Styron, William. *Darkness Visible: A Memoir of Madness*. New York: Random House, 1990.

Surviving Ovarian Cancer (DVD), provided by the Ovarian Cancer Research Fund, 1999.

Swift, Jonathan. *Gulliver's Travels*, edited by Christopher Fox. Boston and New York: Bedford Books of St. Martin's Press, 1995.

Thernstrom, Melanie. "Jason Shinder: The Lure of Death," *New York Times Magazine* (December 28, 2008): 58.

Tilberis, Liz. *No Time to Die: Living with Ovarian Cancer*. New York: Avon, 1998.

Tilt, Edward John. *Diseases of Menstruation and Ovarian Inflammation*. London: John Churchill, 1850.

———. *A Handbook of Uterine Therapeutics and of Diseases of Women*, 3rd edition. London: John Churchill and Sons, 1868.

Van Billiard, Barbara R. *A Feather in My Wig: Ovarian Cancer: Cured*. Portsmouth, NH: Peter E. Randall, 1998.

Vanyo, Ava. *Sarah's Rain*. Lulu Publishing at www.lulu.com, 2005.

Wadler, Joyce. *My Breast: One Woman's Cancer Story*. Reading, MA: Addison-Wesley, 1992.

Walker, Alice. "Everyday Use," 1973. *In Love and Trouble*, 47–50: New York: Harcourt, 2004.

Walker, Lynette. *Mother, Breast Cancer and Selfhood: A Memoir*. Victoria, BC: Trafford Publishing On-demand, 2002.

Webb, Marilyn. *The Good Death: The New American Search to Reshape the End of Life.* New York: Bantam Books, 1997.

Wellman, Kathleen A. "Physicians and Philosophes: Physiology and Sexual Morality in the French Enlightenment," *Eighteenth-Century Studies* 35, no. 2 (Winter 2002): 267–77.

Wells, T. Spencer. *Diseases of the Ovaries: Their Diagnosis and Treatment*, vol. I. London: John Churchill and Sons, 1865.

Wilber, Ken. *Grace and Grit: Spirituality and Healing in the Life and Death of Treya Killam Wilber.* Boston: Shambhala, 1991.

Williams, Terry Tempest. *Refuge: An Unnatural History of Family and Place.* New York: Vintage, 1992.

Wittman, Juliet. *Breast Cancer Journal: A Century of Petals.* Golden, CO: Fulcrum Publishing, 1993.

Woolf, Virginia. "On Being Ill," in *The Moment and Other Essays.* London: Hogarth Press, 1947.

———. "Professions for Women" in the *Norton Anthology of Literature by Women*, edited by Sandra M. Gilbert and Susan Gubar, vol. 2, 244–47. New York: Norton, 2007.

Yeats, William Butler. "Crazy Jane Talks with the Bishop," *The Collected Poems of W.B. Yeats*, 254–55. New York: Macmillan, 1956.

———. "Sailing to Byzantium," *The Collected Poems of W.B. Yeats*, 191-92. New York: Macmillan, 1956.

ACKNOWLEDGMENTS

This book could not have been written without the ingenuity and dedication of my research assistants at Indiana University, first Jamie Horrocks and subsequently Shannon Boyer and Kelly Hanson. In too many ways to enumerate, many people, named and unnamed in the narrative, supported me over the past two years, including Alesha Arnold, Bennett Bertenthal, Judith Brown, Wendy Chun-Hoon, Amanda and Andrea Ciccarelli, Denise Cruz, Shehira Davezac, Ann duCille, John Eakin, Dyan Elliott, Jonathan Elmer, Alice Falk, Mary Favret, Jennifer Fleissner, Shirley Geok-lin Lim, the late Leslie Gould, Ken Gros Louis, Edward Gubar, Justine Gubar, Karen Hanson, Amy Hume, George Hutchinson, Annetta Jenkins, Eileen Julien, Georgette Kagan, Mary Kaye, Yvonne Kieffer, Jon Lawrence, Michael McRobbie, Alyce Miller, Andrew Miller, Richard Nash, Kim Scherer, Ilena Silverman, Jan Sorby, Jayne and Emily Spencer, Mary Jo Weaver, John Woodcock, and Sandy Zagarell. Sandra M. Gilbert urged me on when I had given up hope in this manuscript. The generosity and kindness of my British cousins and of Kieran Setiya stirred and invigorated me.

Drawing upon her interactions with other authors of illness narratives, my agent Ellen Levine suggested readings that enriched my perspective. Her tactful advice was always illuminating. At Norton, Alison Liss has helped me step by step through the arduous process of publication. Supportive and smart, the copyeditor Allegra Huston contributed to the coherence of this book. My editor Jill Bialosky, whose writings have inspired me, has encouraged me through several quite different projects. We who work on women's issues remain greatly indebted to her and her colleagues at Norton, in particular Julia Reidhead.

I am especially grateful for the advice of my daughters, my step-daughters, and my sons-in-law, whose candor and clarity enrich my thinking. I know this book can never do justice to their solicitude or to Don Gray's.

PERMISSIONS